DESIGN AND BRITISH INDUSTRY

Richard Stewart

John Murray

Acknowledgements

I am indebted to Keith Grant, Director of The Design Council, and his staff for their help in the preparation of this book. In particular I would like to thank John Blake, Head of Information and Exhibitions, and Geoffrey Constable, Head of Industrial Division, for their invaluable contributions to the text. The numerous Design Council photographs were obtained with the patient assistance of picture librarians Bridget Kinally and Jane Byrne.

Many individual designers have allowed me to reproduce photographs of work or have supplied information. They include James Gardner, John Makepeace, David Mellor and Robert Welch and I am grateful for their cooperation. In addition a number of organisations and their personnel have offered valuable help, including Wedgwood, the Royal College of Art, West Surrey College of Art, London Transport Executive and the Victoria and Albert Museum. Grateful acknowledgement is made to the following for permission to reproduce photographs on pages as indicated:

Aram Designs, 54, 55, 57; Austin Rover, 213, 215; Belling Fires, 41; BMW, 217; Allan Bowden, 84; Bowman Bros., 68; British Rail, 229; British Telecom, 211; Castle Museum, York, 14; Central School of Art and Design, 236–7; Civic Trust, 178; Colchester Machine Tools, 124, 125; *Country Life*, 15; Robin Day, 115; Entwistle and Kenyon, 21; James Gardner, 143; Honda, 216; Hoover, 41; JCB, 226; Jonas Company/Artek, 52, 53; London Transport Executive, 48; Richard Lord, 122; John McCormick, 239; John Makepeace, 202; David Mellor, 120, 121; Morphy-Richards, 109; Photo Source, 223; Porsche, 212; Pyrex, 58; Race Manufacturers, 190; Wendy Ramshaw, 200; Rolls Royce, 45, 46, 220; Royal College of Art, 117, 122, 239; Dick Russell, 60, 117; Sinclair Radionics, 230, 232; Rotaflex, 193; SME, 230; Leonard Taylor, 133, 136; Herbert Terry, 83; Wedgwood, 32, 202; Robert Welch, 118, 119; West Surrey College of Art, 6, 24, 25; Robin Williams, 203.

The two chairs on pages 12 and 16 are from the collection of Parker Knoll antique chairs. Photographs on the following pages are by courtesy of the Board of Trustees of the Victoria and Albert Museum: 8, 9, 10, 11, 12, 16, 20, 26, 28, 30, 35, 50. The photograph on page 44 is reproduced by permission of the Trustees of the Science Museum, London, and on page 17, of the Geffrye Museum.

To those designers or manufacturers whose work I have reproduced from copyright material, but have been unable to trace, I offer my apologies. I will willingly rectify any error in future impressions.

Finally I would like to thank Noel Carrington for his authoritative help and my colleagues Garth Allan and Colin Fletcher for their constant encouragement.

R.S.

© Richard Stewart 1987

First published 1987
by John Murray (Publishers) Ltd
50 Albemarle Street, London W1X 4BD

All rights reserved
Unauthorised duplication
contravenes applicable laws

Typeset by Fakenham Photosetting Ltd, Fakenham, Norfolk
Printed and bound in Great Britain by The Camelot Press Ltd, Southampton

British Library Cataloguing in Publication Data

Stewart, Richard
   Design and British industry.
   1. Design, Industrial – Great Britain – History
   I. Title
   745.2'0941   TS171
   ISBN 0–7195–4294–4

—CONTENTS—

	Introduction	v
1	**VICTORIAN TASTE**	**7**
	The Great Exhibition	7
	The Society of Arts	17
	Schools of Design and Museums of Art	22
	Design Movements	25
	Engineering and Industrial Design	31
2	**'FITNESS FOR PURPOSE'**	**39**
	Into the Twentieth Century	39
	The Design and Industries Association	42
	The British Institute of Industrial Art	47
	The Council for Art and Industry	52
	Utility	62
	The Council of Industrial Design	64
3	**'BRITAIN CAN MAKE IT'**	**75**
	Swords into Ploughshares	75
	Public Taste	88
	Enterprise Scotland	96
4	**INDUSTRIAL LIAISON**	**101**
	Design Centres for Industry	101
	Gordon Russell	109
	A National Survey of Design	114
	The Training and Employment of Designers	116

5	**FESTIVAL OF BRITAIN**	127
	Centenary Commemoration	127
	The 1951 Stock List	134
	The South Bank and Other Exhibitions	139
	Progress Report	146
6	**PUBLICITY AND PROPAGANDA**	155
	Reaching the Public	155
	Publications and Promotions	161
	The Retail Trade	168
	Official Bodies	174
7	**DESIGN EXHIBITION CENTRES**	181
	Design Centre, Haymarket	181
	Design Centre Awards	191
	Public Opinion	194
	Further Centres	201
8	**ENGINEERING, INNOVATION AND EDUCATION**	207
	Engineering and The Design Council	207
	Evaluation	225
	Innovation and the Graduate Designer	229
	Design in General Education	240
	Postscript	245
	References	248
	Bibliography	251
	Index	254

– INTRODUCTION –

Of the complex interplay of factors contributing to the rise and fall of British industry, variable concern has focused on the element of design. Institutions such as the long-established Royal Society of Arts, the evangelical Design and Industries Association and the ill-fated Council for Art and Industry all have their origins in such concern. A summary of their involvement and interrelationship occupies the opening chapters of this book. However, it is the history of a unique national body, the Council of Industrial Design, which constitutes the principal text. This offers its own perspective on political attitudes, public taste, manufacturing capability and, of course, designer talent.

The Council and its Scottish Committee were set up in December 1944 by the wartime President of the Board of Trade. As a government-financed body its purpose was 'to promote by all practicable means the improvement of design in the products of British industry'. Weaker organisations had previously failed in this task and fundamental problems remained to be solved – problems deeply entrenched in the country's manufacturing, social and educational systems. Under the stoic directorship of Gordon Russell, a two-pronged attack was launched through its Industrial and Information Divisions. The first liaised with complacent manufacturers to promote a supply of well-designed products while the second encouraged a critical public demand by means of publicity and propaganda. Exhibitions complemented these activities, and the London Design Centre, which opened in 1956, became a shop window for innovative design.

Against a backgound of looming industrial and economic crises of the sixties and seventies, Russell's successor, Paul Reilly, extended the scope of activities to encompass failing engineering and capital goods industries. Through diverse strategies involving advisory services, conferences, exhibitions and awards, a renamed Design Council steadfastly pursued its goal. Variously it has seen itself, or been seen by others, as a catalyst, an educator and a stimulant, or as an arbiter, a critic and an irritant. In turn, good design remains problematic, elusive and vital, justifying continued action by this dedicated body under present-day Director Keith Grant.

1.1 A recently discovered photograph of William Morris (1834–96), central figure in the Arts and Crafts Movement revolt against the excesses of Victorian taste. As a young man, Morris reputedly refused to enter the Crystal Palace, declaring everything inside 'wonderfully ugly'.

–1–
VICTORIAN TASTE

INTRODUCTION

The Great Exhibition of 1851 demonstrated to the world Britain's superiority as a manufacturing nation. It also highlighted weaknesses in the design of her products. As early as the 1830s the government, concerned about exports and growing foreign competition, had opened art schools, galleries and museums to train designers and refine public taste. But to its critics these attempts proved largely ineffectual. The Victorian middle classes, creators and consumers of industrialisation, reflected romantic, sentimental values through ornate possessions which were perceived as being unrelated to function or production. No official body existed, or was to exist for many years, to co-ordinate action. However, private concern did prompt formation of the Society of Arts and eventually led to the Arts and Crafts Movement reaction to the excesses of Victorian taste.

THE GREAT EXHIBITION

In the latter years of the eighteenth century the Industrial Revolution gathered momentum, heralding an age of machine-made goods. Subsequently, a voracious consumer market was showered with 'manufactures' emanating from the so-called 'workshop of the world'. Free trade between nations, prophesied Adam Smith, would benefit everyone, particularly Britain, with her new-found productive capacity. Individual enterprise, unrestrained by government regulation, would raise the material well-being of mankind to undreamed-of heights. In 1786, Prime Minister Pitt signed a free trade treaty with France. For the next half century mercantile tariffs were steadily reduced, and trade and industry boomed.

The sheer scale of expansion, exploiting division of labour and primary process machinery, is demonstrated by Smith in *The Wealth of Nations*. One workman could make a handful of pins in a day; ten men could now make 48,000. Similarly, teams of boys were far more productive than time-served craftsmen for a host of manufactures from nails to buttons. Their dexterity in repetitive tasks elicited strong praise: 'The rapidity with which some of the operations of those manufactures are performed

1.2, 1.3 These two rare photographs, taken from the north-west of the Crystal Palace in 1851, together present a more accurate vista than the many artists' impressions of the time. (Halftone illustrations, made directly from photographs for books or magazines, were not possible before the 1880s.) Nevertheless these do not do full justice to the length, from Western to Eastern Nave, of 1848 feet; or the height of the barrel-roofed transept of 108 feet. The *left* view, along the northern length of the building, shows the Transept to the left. This was high

exceeds what the human hand could, by those who had never seen them, be supposed capable of acquiring.'[1] Consequently, apprenticeships and other guild restrictions were dismissed as 'a conspiracy against the public'. By the time Karl Marx wrote *Das Kapital* in 1867, technological progress led him to report – albeit for very different reasons – of one girl operating four machines to produce a staggering 600,000 needles in a day. Ironically, coupled with the demise of craft guilds and traditional skills there arose the practice of professional designer – but not before a troubled and extended period of gestation.

In the eyes of an increasingly competitive world, the zenith of Britain's industrial superiority was reached at the Great Exhibition of 1851. Its patron, Prince Albert, had rallied support at the Lord Mayor's Banquet stating '. . . the great principle of division of labour, which may be called the moving power of civilisation, is being extended to all branches of science, industry and art'. Through his initiative a National Exhibition was transformed into a 'Great Exhibition of the Works of Industry of all Nations' on the premise that 'particular advantage to British Industry might be derived from placing it in fair competition with that of other nations'.

To its organisers the exhibition was an unqualified success. Technologically, Britain outclassed thirteen European, thirteen American and enough to enclose elm trees protected by conservationists, although more trees were allowed to project through the restaurant roofs to either side. The width of the building was 408 feet, extended on the north to a maximum of 456 feet as shown. The end view of the Western Nave (*right*) shows the three tiers and terraces rising to a height of 63 feet. The Western Nave housed exhibits from Britain and the Empire whilst the Eastern Nave was allocated to her foreign competitors.

seven other participating nations, not to mention her colonies. Six million people (the total population of the country was only 27 million) flocked to Hyde Park to enter Paxton's magnificent Crystal Palace. This gigantic structure bore silent testimony to the superiority of British industry. Three times the length of St Paul's, with over a million square feet of glass, it had taken under six months to build. By a convenient exigency its height and proportions had been improved to enclose ten elm trees protected by conservationists. Inside, the public were overawed by 100,000 exhibits worth £2,000,000 which were essentially the amassed products of their own industrial labours.

Queen Victoria, on seeing the magnificent building, wrote, 'It goes to show we are capable of doing almost anything.' And so we were, both good and bad, in architecture and design. To its critics the first industrial nation had, inevitably, achieved another first, namely the embodiment of poor taste and dubious quality in cheap consumer goods. Pins are functional objects, little capable of embellishment. The Crystal Palace itself was proto-functionalist, gigantic and restrained – but not so the majority of products on display. Victorian taste had seemingly precipitated an eclectic plagiarism of styles of all ages and applied them indiscriminately to industrial products and in some cases even to the machines that made them. At the time William Morris, young and puritanical,

1.4 Original photograph taken within the Transept looking north to the elm trees surrounded by sculptures. In the foreground is the Crystal Fountain, centre point of the whole exhibition.

1.5 Original photograph of the Eastern or Foreign Nave (looking west). Many of the foreign exhibits succeeded in being as impressively elaborate as those from Britain herself, but in the right foreground can be seen the entrance to United States exhibits, many of which were simpler, and beyond which lay the German *Zollverein* or Great Customs Union. Both countries were to pose subsequent threats to Britain's industrial superiority.

declared everything 'wonderfully ugly'. A hundred years later Yvonne ffrench, in the spirit of twentieth-century functionalism, proclaimed '... a bastardisation of taste without parallel in the whole recorded history of aesthetics'.[2]

Themes to delight the public but depress the purists spread through every gallery: fanciful carvings, allegorical castings, mechanical absurdities and – overall – decoration. Selected examples of a tasteless nature were a Crusader's altar tomb matchbox, an 110,000-piece marquetry table top and a medicine-cup flower. Bizarre patents included a collapsing alarm bedstead to project the occupant to his feet 'without any jerk or the slightest personal danger' and a pair of trousers which would 'remain as a fixture to the feet without straps, and dispense with braces'. In contrast, much of the engineering bore the elegance of Paxton's architecture. For example, an original photograph of the express locomotive *Folkstone* demonstrates functional form unadulterated by imposed ornamentation. But even machines such as steam engines masqueraded as Egyptian, Gothic or Greek architecture while instruments such as scissors succumbed to painful decoration or performed doubtful multi-functions such as the doctor's walking stick with enema and test tubes.

1.6–1.8 Three pieces of mid- and late-Victorian design exemplifying the application of ornament, new materials and ideas of the period. *Above.* Papier mâché bed with iron sub-frame and brass mounts, decorated with floral designs and elaborate drapes, c. 1851. *Right.* Armchair with deeply buttoned upholstery covered in black American cloth. The back is adjusted by a push-button system of the arms. *Far right.* Cast-iron heating stove with sliding doors and decoration which includes geometrical, floral and neoclassical motifs, c. 1875. The stove is still manufactured today by Classic Garden Furniture.

Understandably, British manufacturers displayed intricate workmanship as a means of advertising, and foreign nations were not without blame. From Spain came an ornamental *Guitarapa* (combined guitar, harp and violin) and from America an elaborate 'air-exhausted coffin to preserve the dead from putrefaction'. But Thonet's Austrian bentwood chair, forerunner of many millions around the world, gained scant recognition compared to an Irish bog-yew carver with wolf-dog arms bearing 'Gentle when stroked' and 'Fierce when provoked'. That such a problem existed perhaps reflected as much on public taste as on designers' and manufacturers' sensibilities. In a lecture at Marlborough House, Owen Jones, architect and critic (whose bright yet subtle colour scheme enhanced the Crystal Palace) retrospectively reviewed the problem:

> Were we to enquire of the artists who designed these melancholy productions suspended on the walls why they had chosen that particular form of fancy; they would undoubtedly tell us, that these were the only style of designs which manufacturers would purchase, and that they had only done as they were told. Were we to enquire of the manufacturers why they had engaged such a vast amount of capital, skill and labour, in production of articles of so little worth; they would undoubtedly tell us that they were the only articles that they could sell, and that it would be useless for them to attempt the production of articles in better taste, for they would infallibly remain unsold upon the shelves. Were we to enquire again of the public how it came to pass that they purchased such vile productions and admitted them to their homes, to enfeeble their own taste and effectually to destroy that of their children; they would infallibly reply, that they had looked everywhere for better things, but could not find them. So ... the vicious circle is complete.

1.9 A representation of a Victorian parlour by the Castle Museum, York, showing the comfort, profusion and confusion of furnishing in middle-class homes.

As 'these melancholy productions' of British industry began to face an increasingly competitive market, the search for solutions to an obdurate problem became more intense. Promotion of 'good design' was to achieve the status of commercial necessity rather than cultural desirability, although solutions were to be more elusive than explanations. Of the latter, Victorian writers themselves traced sources rooted inextricably in the nature of industrialisation and the society which pioneered it. Indeed they were their own most scathing critics, from Augustus Pugin who warned against 'disguising instead of beautifying articles of utility' to Walter Crane who attacked 'the ill-considered bedizenment of meaningless and unrelated ornament'.

Their terminology offered an immediate clue to the problem; the all-embracing concept of design did not exist, only 'ornamental', 'decorative' and 'applied art'. Many categories of design were subsumed under 'art manufactures', a field which ranged erratically from foliage to furniture, from bronzes to bedsteads. All were enhanced for the market, but the designer trifled with additions, not essentials. The British, as an island race, were culturally insular and arrogant, yet equally eclectic and plagiarist in matters of visual taste. Robust vernacular designs had been abandoned in the exodus from rural to urban lifestyles. The newly forming urban middle class, creators and consumers of industrialisation, reflected romantic values in their man-made environment. Equating the

1.10 A room of Saltram House, Devon, contrasts with the Victorian parlour. Designed by Robert Adam *c.* 1768, even the ceiling and carpet are of matching design, while the sideboard moulds to the curve of the wall. Adam was elected to the Society of Arts in 1758.

countryside with happiness, art with nature and ornament with beauty they demanded naturalistic and sentimental decoration in their homes. The interiors they created were comfortable, complex and confused. An Englishman's home was no longer his castle, but rather a miniature Crystal Palace. In order to meet demand and distinguish their ranges from competitors, manufacturers resorted to copying from lavish pattern books. The result was all too often unrelated to function or production.

If terminology offered one clue then technology offered another, for this had armed miscreant manufacturers with an arsenal of materials and machines. Cast iron, wonder material of the revolution, assumed any form from bamboo to Gothic tracery. Electroplating created nickel from brass and gold from silver. Wood-carving machines reproduced intricate craftsmanship and veneer-cutting machines concealed shoddy constructions. Lustre ware pottery imitated metal and painted wood imitated marble. Papier-mâché was the perspex of the age and gutta-percha was the polythene.

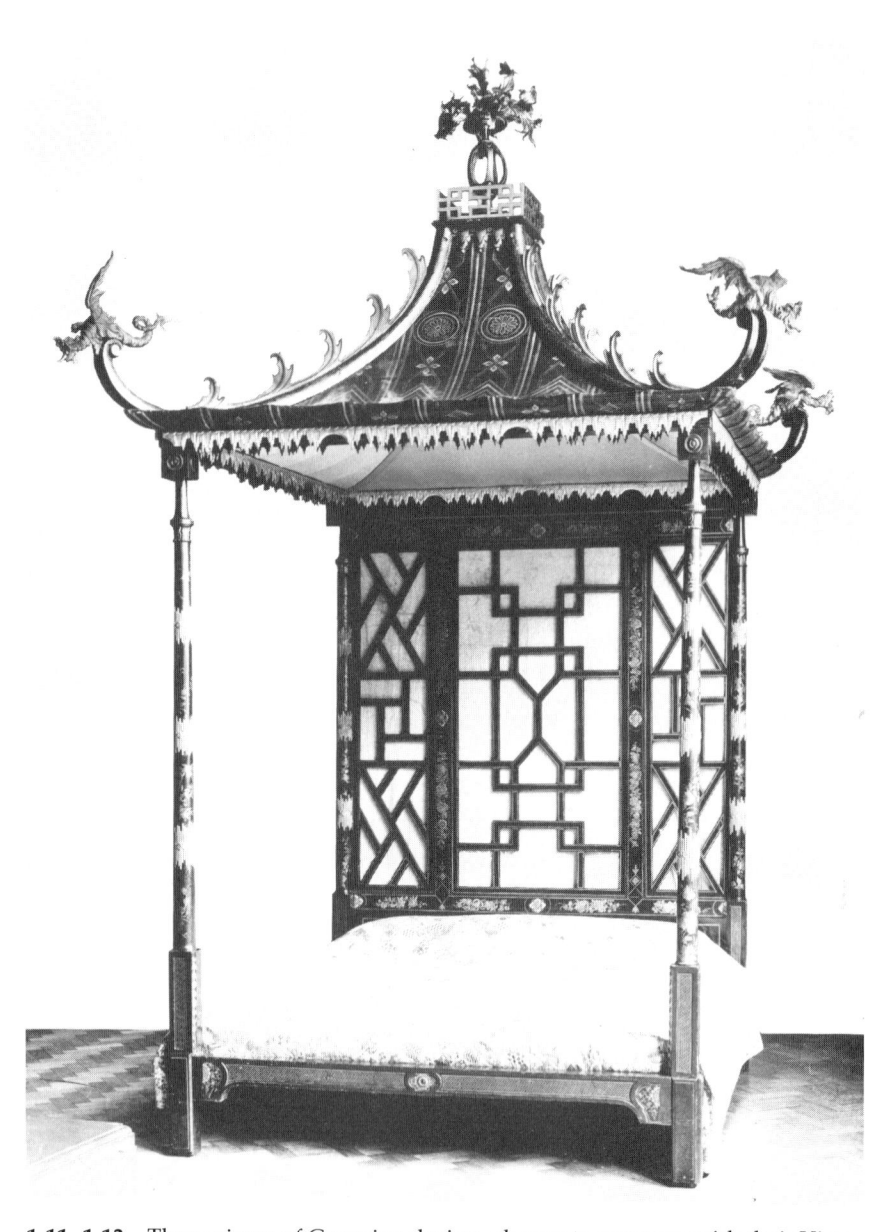

1.11–1.13 Three pieces of Georgian design, chosen to compare with their Victorian counterparts. *Above.* Bed of japanned and gilt wood, c. 1754. Equally elaborate as the papier mâché bed, the decoration was nonetheless exceptionally fanciful for the period. Whereas the Victorian bed might be within the purchasing power of a middle-class family, this bed was designed by John Linnell specifically for the Chinese bedroom at Badminton, Gloucester. Linnell worked for Adam on several occasions. *Right.* Upholstered armchair with restrained carving characteristic of the Regency period. *Far right.* Cast-iron fireplace and fender of graceful fluted design.

Fundamental to the system was a pervasive specialisation at all levels. Just as draughtsman divorced designer from maker so salesman separated manufacturer from customer. No longer could a product be refined in the hands of generations of craftsmen, nor could critical appreciation flow between client and creator. At production level, specialisation generated problems of demarcation, alienation and, inevitably, quality control.

As technological progress accelerated so too did demand for qualified personnel. The historic de-skilling which devastated the crafts guilds was reversed, yet the country remained singularly hamstrung. In particular a divisive social and an elitist education system frustrated attempts at appropriate training. Although deferring to the fine arts it disparaged the applied, leaving much of the population too visually or technically illiterate to function decisively at artisan, consumer or entrepreneurial level.

THE SOCIETY OF ARTS

The Great Exhibition offers an essential perspective upon the problems of industrial design and the search for solutions. Conveniently, the date of 1851 falls almost half-way between the formation of the first voluntary society and the final official, responsible body, the Council of Industrial Design, with an intervening span of nearly two hundred years. The Exhibition was the high point in the activities of the former and, despite subsequent growth of governmental agencies, the latter did not emerge for another century, although there were several abortive attempts, as will be discussed in the next chapter.

If the roots of the problem are to be found in early industrial society, so too are attempts to solve it. Private individuals and organisations made the first significant moves, and only later did the government assume responsibility. One feature of such a society was the capacity to generate voluntary and altruistic movements which were ultimately to inspire official action. The fact that hard-working individuals from different walks of life devoted time, money and effort to the cause of industrial design is an interesting phenomenon which at the very least indicates the depth of concern.

Regrettably outcomes did not necessarily match expectations. As we have seen, behind the problem lay a complex web of factors, not all of which were of an immediate aesthetic or technical nature. Consequently, attempts by a visually sophisticated minority of philanthropists or civil servants often failed to reach the unseeing eyes of the public or fell upon the deaf ears of manufacturers. If design was not the all-embracing term it is today, then neither were the solutions proposed. Too often the attack on ornamentation was the simple answer, yet as public taste dictated so manufacturers responded, and vice versa, in the manner described by Owen Jones. The famous Coalbrookdale Company, centre point of the Industrial Revolution, was only saved from economic collapse by the introduction of ornamental iron castings and today these are still being reproduced in aluminium.

Of the voluntary associations, two, the Royal Society of Arts and the Design and Industries Association, deserve pride of place; the first because its history spans the whole period in question, the second because of its claim to be the godfather, if not the father, of ensuing official bodies. From their inauguration both were to tackle aspects of the problem ultimately posed to officialdom. In doing so they adopted strategies, with varying degrees of success, which have remained remarkably relevant over the years. Additionally they were involved, one way and another, with the major developments in the field and offer convenient perspectives on these.

Thus it was almost a century before the Great Exhibition that the first private attempts to tackle the problem began. A lowly drawing master, William Shipley, in 1754 formed a Society for the Encouragement of the Arts, Manufactures and Commerce. At that time a high standard of design was apparent in the homes of the upper classes. Architects such as Robert Adam co-ordinated buildings and interiors while craftsmen such as Thomas Chippendale demonstrated a crucial understanding of materials and processes when creating often elaborate designs. Adam was elected to the Society in 1758 and Chippendale in 1760. Their influence through commissions and, more significantly, published pattern books like the latter's *Gentlemen and Cabinet Maker's Directory* was considerable. But it was with the future manufacturing industries that Shipley was concerned. In an era before mandatory student grants, as an opening gambit he offered 'Rewards for the Encouragement of Boys and Girls in the Art of Drawing ... Necessary in many Employments, Trades and Manufactures'. (Impressed by the promotional influence of prizes in horse racing, he had applied the same principle to industrial design – although it is doubtful that even Shipley could have anticipated the significance of technical drawing for design and presentation in the following century.) Entry categories for the Society's prizes included drawing for textile, pottery, furniture and metalworking industries. Shipley's move might well have had considerable influence on the flood of future manufactures. Perversely, these categories soon disappeared in a typically English torrent of landscapes and figure studies and a retitled Society of Arts subsequently relegated drawing for manufactures to a peripheral role. Nevertheless, at a time when training otherwise concentrated on classical architecture and life drawing, it had been a necessary step.

Intermittently, the Society did renew the award of prizes to encourage drawing, scholarship and travel. However, a somewhat apposite concern with agriculture, science and mechanics swung the emphasis from appearance to invention. One of industry's most fundamental machines, Hargreaves's spinning jenny, was motivated by a prize of £50, while examples such as Abraham's dust extractor, Davies's fire escape, and Roberts's Respirator illustrate a commendable humanitarianism hand in hand with hard commercialism. Inevitably, the broadening field of concern saw lifeboats and public conveniences take precedence over the styling of manufactures for middle-class homes.

However, most influential, and destined to have long-term repercussion on design, was the Society's exhibitions policy. In 1761 it achieved a notable first with a display of industrial machinery. Here Britain could be justifiably proud, for a line of inventors from Newcomen to Kay had pioneered the resources to project her far ahead of rivals. Their machines not only worked, but had a raw visual appeal which established functionalist tradition long before the twentieth century. And this tradition was to be reflected in a range of domestic machines from the spinning wheel to the wringer. Small annual displays were also held and a 'repository' of prize-winning prototypes gradually accumulated, ranging from turnip slicers to 'instruments to draw spirits and instruments to draw teeth'. But not for many years did the Society exhibit manufactured goods, the raison d'être for the majority of industrial machines.[1]

1.14, 1.15 *Left.* Spinning wheel made by John Planta in a design that combines the simplicity of precision machinery with the elegance of furniture from the age of the cabinet maker. *Right.* The first-known wringer, made by Robert Tasker, a blacksmith of Accrington, in 1850. Though entirely functional, like the spinning wheel, the design betrays the motif of a Grecian urn.

Eventually the Society's concern was revitalised by the choice of the Prince Consort as President: 'To wed mechanical skill with high art is a task worthy of the Society of Arts and directly in its path of duty,' he gently chided. The resultant exhibition, Select Specimens of British Manufactures and Decorative Art, of 1847, gained only lukewarm support from industry at a time when the Society was nearly bankrupt. 'Second founder' Henry Cole and John Scott Russell, who donated his own money for prizes, had to cajole manufacturers into submitting a mere two hundred articles, many out of date – a cautionary message for future policy makers. Fortunately, enthusiastic public attendance led to a reversal of attitude and a second, then a third, exhibition were to be overwhelmed with contemporary specimens. Both illiterate and educated had been provided with a tangible means of arousing their interest and sensibility.

In this period the Society formulated the essential rationale for exhibitions policy. For example, the 1847 Catalogue noted the 'universal complaint' of manufacturers that consumers prefer 'the vulgar, the gaudy, the ugly even, to the beautiful and perfect'. But public taste, the Society felt, could improve by viewing the good and the mediocre:

> We believe that when works of high merit, of British origin, are brought forward they will be fully appreciated and thoroughly enjoyed ... These specimens are not all the best, nor even all good, and the visitor must discriminate for himself. Let him praise in the right place, let him blame in the right place, and the object of our exhibition has been attained.[3]

Sensitivity was, of course, needed when selecting anything less than the best for display; one could hardly inform manufacturers of their dubious honour to represent 'the vulgar, the gaudy, the ugly even'. Cole's one attempt to display a rogues' gallery aroused strong opposition from manufacturers and severely depressed Charles Dickens's Mr Crumpet who discovered the contents of his own Clump Lodge to be in decidedly bad taste!

At a point of financial crisis in the Society's affairs, conviction emerged that government should assume responsibility for exhibitions and matters of art and manufactures. Hitherto this laudable association of philanthropists had maintained responsibility with no official backing. But now visitors to the 1847 exhibition were asked to petition Parliament:

> Systematic Exhibitions of works of art and manufacture are calculated to promote public education, to advance art and to extend commerce ... Your Petitioners therefore pray your Honourable House to take measures for establishing a National Exhibition of Manufacturers to be held periodically.[4]

The following year a deputation urged the Board of Trade to provide a building near Trafalgar Square and hold regular exhibitions. This did secure a lesser offer of Somerset House courtyard, before being overtaken by the repercussions of the Great Exhibition.

Despite the enormity of the latter undertaking no direct responsibility was assumed by the government. Rather, Royal Commissioners, private speculators and independent entrepreneurs carried the burden – happily in the course of events a generous financial legacy was bequeathed to the nation. A total of 6,039,195 orderly visitors paid from a shilling to a guinea entrance fee, leaving a net balance of £186,437 to be lavished on the arts. However, the real success must be measured in social not commercial (and certainly not aesthetic) terms. Fears that so many people converging on the capital would induce civil strife was the government's preoccupation. Charles Sibthorp, Conservative M.P. for Lincoln, predicted riot, rape and robbery, not to mention military and industrial espionage. The ageing Duke of Wellington, commander-in-chief of emergency forces during the Chartist riots, therefore secretly deployed 10,000 troops. In fact, at the end of the day only twenty-five convictions ensued (mainly pickpockets) and the prestige and fortunes of the Society were secured.

SCHOOLS OF DESIGN AND MUSEUMS OF ART

Throughout the nineteenth century any government, as opposed to a private Society of Arts, concern over manufactures sprang from the desire to maintain Britain's superiority in world markets. From the period of the 1830s, a decade or two before the Great Exhibition, there had been therefore some official commitment to the training of designers and education of laymen. Ensuing action, albeit prompted by commercial exigency, ranged from the establishment of directly vocational design schools to broadly cultural art galleries. However, most of these developments were conditioned and, in turn, undermined by Victorian faith that the fine arts, with their superior hierarchical status, would benefit the applied.

For example, as early as 1832 Parliament debated the principal and seemingly invincible export of textiles. Although England had established the world's premier factory system in its northern mills, foreign competition was beginning to cause concern. Sir Robert Peel (whose grandfather had encouraged Hargreaves to build the spinning jenny) attributed the problem to inferior design and advocated raising the discriminatory powers of artisans and consumers. The result was extension of provision for a National Gallery to expose them to works of fine (but not applied) art. Conservative London became the last major European capital to boast a government-sponsored art collection and arguments that artisans would peaceably imbibe beauty instead of beer were all too readily undermined by acts of vandalism. Peel even had to reassure the House that a lame visitor who defaced Jupiter and Leda with a crutch had simply slipped while pointing out such beauties to a friend!

As the century progressed and industrialisation spread across Europe, France, Belgium, Germany and Italy in turn flooded the market with manufactures. In so many fields Britain's lead was challenged and she could no longer claim to be 'cheapest and best'. Government concern increasingly focused on improving the quality of exports and curtailing the quantity of imports. Germany with her *Zollverein*, or Customs Union, and accompanying low, but rising tariff barriers caused sufficient concern for an investigator, John Bowring, to be despatched there in 1840. He reported her superior in the 'arts of design' and in their application to industry, supported by effective technical education. By mid-century, rising politician Benjamin Disraeli was demanding that Britain should introduce her own comprehensive import controls.

On the question of education Parliament took the characteristic action of first appointing a Select Committee on Art and Manufactures in 1836. This was to 'inquire into the best means of extending a knowledge of the arts and the principles of design among the people'. Their 350-page report shocked politicians into granting an unprecedented £1500 towards a School of Design under control of the Board of Trade. Specifically for the training of designers, this evolved into the prestigious Royal College of Art, yet, despite subsequent inquiries, blithely concentrated for reasons of status or resource on fine arts – 'learning to swim in a thousand lessons without water' according to William Richard Lethaby. Provincial schools achieved more variable success but without the equivalent status. The drawing of plant, animal, human and architectural forms for ornament remained the essential syllabi.

In addition the Select Committee recommended open 'Museums of Art' across the country to exhibit 'the most approved modern specimens, foreign as well as domestic', a policy which was to parallel the fate of the schools. Museums were seen as windows upon the past not the present, and a growing national obsession with antiques, compounded by revivalist fashions, conceded modern specimens scant priority.

A reference collection of manufactures was, however, assembled for School of Design students at Somerset House. Like the School this was to evolve into a prestigious and national institution, only to experience a fundamental change of emphasis. The Board of Trade, having expediently availed itself of those exhibits in the Crystal Palace notable 'entirely for excellence of their art or workmanship', created, together with the Somerset House collection, a Museum of Manufactures at Marlborough House. Boosted by annual grants this expanded to encompass the industrial art of all nations and all periods – commendably the first of its kind in Europe. In 1857, as a restyled Museum of Ornamental Art, this moved to the complex of buildings in South Kensington eventually to become the Victoria and Albert Museum. Appropriately the Great Exhibition legacy had provided the funds.

But the intention of retaining both a contemporary and historical collection waned with the passage of time. When the building was at last completed in 1909, the Committee of Rearrangement pronounced:

> The Victoria and Albert Museum is not, and never can be, a Museum of Commercial Products . . . the Committee, after full consideration, are not disposed to make definite recommendation on the acquisition of modern specimens.

Consequently, any commercial potential of such a display, to be viewed by home or foreign consumers, was curtailed. Less acceptable to design students and historians was the cultural forfeit of accumulated modern classics.

Another field of activity to warrant government attention was the wave of international expositions which followed the Crystal Palace. But a

1.16 The showrooms of Morris & Co. which opened at 449 Oxford Street, London, in 1877. The firm had been founded in 1861 to produce articles of fine craftsmanship for the general public.

1.17, 1.18 *Left*. Chair from the Sussex range of 'workaday' furniture based on a traditional cottage style. Probably the most commercially successful product of Morris & Co., the range was in continuous production from 1866 onwards. *Right*. The *Morris* chair with adjustable back and bobbin-turned decoration was adapted from another Sussex style and became popular both in England and America, *c.* 1866. Compare with the adjustable chair on p. 13.

co-ordinated official exhibitions policy for British entries did not emerge until the new century. Before this, to critics such as Owen Jones, the country's industrial weakness, not strength, was exposed 'in fair competition with that of other nations', particularly as younger contestants such as America entered the arena. Undaunted, the mediocrity of British design was flaunted, until a series of mishaps and a period of hasty improvisation precipitated an inquiry. As a result the Exhibitions Branch of the Board of Trade was formed in 1908 and organised one or two effective displays. (The British entry in Ghent, for example, was later transferred to Paris at the request of the Louvre.) It was this experience which laid the foundation for a later permanent institute concerned with industrial art. But the move had been too little and too late before the First World War overtook events.

DESIGN MOVEMENTS

For a period the initiative was to fall back into the hands of voluntary organisations. In the 1880s the dominant design philosophy belonged to a contrasting movement publicised by exhibitions of its own. One of its

1.19 *St George* cabinet designed by Philip Webb and painted by Morris in 1861. Such 'state' pieces were hand produced to satisfy 'the swinish luxury of the rich'.

numerous constituent bodies, the Arts and Crafts Exhibition Society, provided the label for the ensuing Arts and Crafts Movement. With John Ruskin as prophet and William Morris as leading disciple, a powerful crusade to revive the dignity and self-fulfilment of medieval handicrafts set forth. As much a moral stance against factory working conditions as against machinery *per se*, the Intellectual Luddites nevertheless were a painful thorn in the flesh of manufacturers and delayed implementation, if not formulation, of a national machine aesthetic.

Over a century before, in describing his pin factory, Adam Smith had praised the workers' dexterity acquired through repetitive tasks. Ruskin's 'The Nature of Gothic' (for Morris the seminal chapter of *The Stones of Venice*) contrasts sharply with Smith's commendatory tones:

> Glass beads are utterly unnecessary... The men who chop up the rods sit at their work all day, their hands vibrating with a perpetual and exquisitely timed palsy, and the beads dropping beneath the vibration like hail. Neither they, nor the men who draw out the rods or fuse the fragments, have the smallest occasions for the use of any single human faculty; and every young lady, therefore, who buys glass beads is engaged in the slave trade.[5]

Paradoxically, the movement both fostered revivalist handicraft traditions which manufacturers had been criticised for imitating, and yet formulated principles which profoundly influenced twentieth-century industrial design. Many of its leaders, like their philosophies, were remarkably long-lived. Arthur Heygate Mackmurdo, who in 1882 founded the pioneer group the Century Guild, was born in the year of the Great Exhibition and lived until 1942. His aim was to restore crafts 'to their right place beside painting and sculpture'. William Richard Lethaby, founder member of the Art Workers' Guild and later President of the Arts and Crafts Exhibition Society, was born in 1857 and died in 1931. Charles Annesley Voysey, who became Master of the Art Workers' Guild, was born in the same year as Lethaby and lived until 1941. Charles Robert Ashbee, founder member of the Guild of Handicraft and later elected to the Art Workers' Guild lived from 1863 to 1942. It was Ashbee who led the brave attempt to establish a cooperative at Chipping Campden with 150 craftsmen pilgrims from London's East End. But this was eventually to fail when wily manufacturers learnt how to imitate handmade craftsmanship by machine.

Arts and Crafts personnel also had a strong influence on the elementary, technical and art schools, where Handicrafts, in contrast to Industrial Arts in America, were taught. Ashbee, for example, founded the Campden School of Arts and Crafts while Lethaby was one of the first inspectors to the L.C.C. Technical Education Board and became Principal of the new Central School of Arts and Crafts. In practice, many were trained architects who had extended their talents to furniture, fittings and interior design. But while discerning patrons commissioned their work and schools evolved a craft tradition, the general public remained largely unaware. Few were engineers, a fact which, coupled with their Luddite sympathies, regrettably minimised influence in that direction.

Morris's own firm, Morris & Co., exemplifies the quandary of the Arts and Crafts Movement. Subsidised by his own rich inheritance, much of Morris's time and fine craftsmanship was bestowed upon 'State' furniture for himself and wealthy clients. But commercially successful pieces such as the Sussex and Morris chairs were derived from vernacular designs using machinery in manufacture. It was to be in trades such as book printing, textiles and wallpapers that Morris had a profound and permanent influence, for here the roles of both designer and machine were fundamental to success.

With the exception of such examples, the Arts and Crafts Movement by its very nature existed independently of mainstream commercial manufacture. In contrast, the Aesthetic Movement was an attempt by certain companies to employ leading 'artistic designers'. A precedent had been

1.20–1.22   Three pieces of Art Nouveau furniture to contrast with pp. 12–13 and 17–18. *Above.* Bedstead of oak and mahogany with marquetry inlays demonstrating the attenuated elegance of the finest curvilinear styles. Made by Perol Frères for the Paris Exhibition, 1900. *Right.* Oak chair with upholstered seat by Charles Rennie Mackintosh in his characteristic elongated rectilinear style. A similar chair was exhibited at the Sezession Exhibition in Vienna, 1900. *Far right.* Fire screen delicately carved in a rich variety of woods by Emile Gallé for the Paris Exhibition, 1900.

set when Josiah Wedgwood commissioned John Flaxman a century before to design his Staffordshire pottery. In the intervening period the Schools of Design should have produced the necessary designers, but here too architects were to be pre-eminent. Edward Godwin and Charles Eastlake, for example, were both architects employed by Art Furniture Manufacturers. The latter listed themselves as a distinct category in the London Trade Directory, with connotations of discrimination and taste. Characteristic of their style were straight, slender lines in ebonised wood or unpolished oak. Godwin worked for such firms as Gillows, Collins and Lock, and William Watt. When the latter produced in 1877 a comprehensive catalogue of *Art Furniture Designed by Edward W. Godwin, F.S.A.* there was included an introductory letter by the architect himself. Already his designs, particularly a delicate coffee table, had been extensively, if badly, imitated and he warned, 'Little things of this kind to be artistic, imperatively demand no inconsiderable amount of thought and much careful full-sized drawing.'

One former School of Design student who was to be commercially successful was Christopher Dresser, a protégé of Owen Jones. Commissions included cast iron for Coalbrookdale, porcelain for Minton's and silver plate for Elkingtons'. His expertise in Botany at Somerset House did give a scientific, geometric basis to his ornamentation, although it is his strikingly stark metalwork which parallels Godwin's furniture in pre-empting twentieth-century functional form. Another former student employed by Art Manufacturers was Arthur Silver. In the late Victorian period his Silver Studio, working for a number of clients including those from France and America, may be seen as a forerunner of twentieth-century design consultancies.

This commercial employment of the 'artist' was to be a significant step in the establishment of the professional designer. Abroad similar moves were afoot. Even Thonet's furniture company which had exported

1.23 Ebonised wood sideboard with panels of Japanese leather paper and hinges of silver. Designed by Edward Godwin and made by Art Furniture Manufacturers William Watt c. 1867.

millions of bentwood chairs adopted a design by Adolf Loos in 1899. But there remained many fields for which artistic design was deemed irrelevant. In particular, newer industries exploited their engineers or technicians to create prototypes for mass production. If the precedents for self-conscious functional form lay with individuals such as Godwin and Dresser, it was in the latter fields that the roots of twentieth-century industrial design truly lay, particularly in America and to some extent Germany, posing yet further threats to British exports.

Arts and Crafts personnel were also to be the prime movers in the final fashion of the Victorian era. Consequently, Art Nouveau, a new art for a new century, original and non-revivalist, still retained values firmly rooted in the handicraft tradition. The whiplash curves and convoluted forms of its curvilinear style proved to be beyond most sensitive industrial

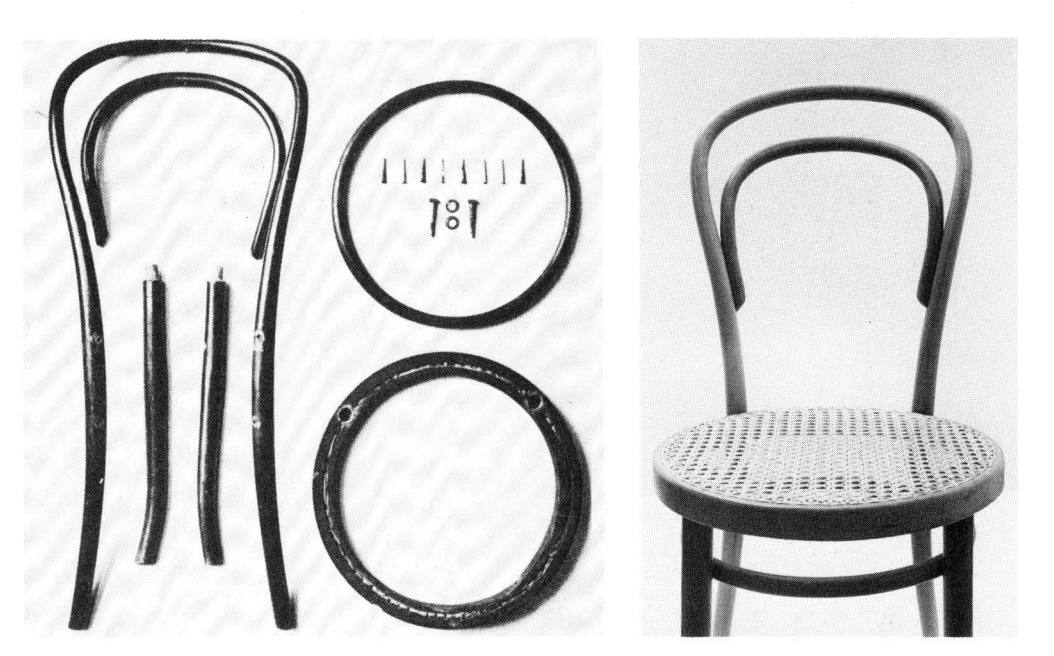

1.24, 1.25 Michael Thonet's bentwood Chair No. 14, designed in 1859 and still in production today. Shown in knock-down (*left*) and assembled form (*right*), the chair can be readily transported and assembled by retailer or purchaser. Millions were sold as cheap, utilitarian furniture in Victorian times, only to be raised to the status of 'classic' in the 20th century.

interpretation. Even the rectilinear style of Charles Rennie Mackintosh required a subtlety of translation from delicate to massive (and expensive) proportions misunderstood by manufacturers. Yet the fashion did create unifying, if unattainable, decorative themes for the designed environment in the transition towards the twentieth century.

However, borne into the new century was a passion for reproduction design amongst the middle classes, plus unquestioned acceptance that the ancestral homes of the upper class were, and would remain, furnished with antiques. Despite the popularity of Ruskin and Morris (who were frequently misinterpreted simply as revivalist) it should be remembered that the most widely read literature, after the Bible, was probably that of Sir Walter Scott, reinforcing a strong vein of romanticism which still persists to the present day.

ENGINEERING AND INDUSTRIAL DESIGN

For many of the six million visitors to the Crystal Palace, Britain's engineering achievements must have aroused the greatest awe and wonderment. Mechanical engineering was majestically displayed, from the Stephensons' locomotive *Folkstone* to James Nasmyth's 30-cwt steam hammer and Joseph Whitworth's 'self-acting' machine tools. The

1.26 Black Basalt fine-grained stoneware teapot developed in 1768 by Josiah Wedgwood. Over 200 years later the teapot was listed in the Design Council's Index of well-designed items in current production. Wedgwood was one of the first manufacturers to employ named 'artists' such as Joseph Flaxman.

triumphs of civil engineering, too, were well represented by a series of elaborate models. Of course, fundamental to the whole grand scheme was the practical application of engineering to industry. Without machines for manufacture and steam engines for power, the majority of exhibits could not have come into being. And without railways and locomotives for transport, neither visitors nor exhibits could have arrived at Hyde Park in such numbers.

To what extent engineering was responsible for the excesses of Victorian taste displayed in the exhibition is more difficult to quantify. Certainly it provided the machines for others to create elaborate carvings, turnings and mouldings. But an analysis of the design of such machines often shows a subtlety of form and finish to delight today's industrial archaeologist. Although the embodiment of architectural features in machinery has been much criticised it cannot be dismissed out of hand. Crankshafts were quite successfully mounted on beautiful entablatures and fluted columns rather than 'A' frames, while 'columnar' steam engines economically contained crankshaft, cylinder and crosshead guides within one elegant column.

However, the cross-fertilisation between architecture, design and engineering was haphazard, being more apparent in civil rather than mechanical engineering. In the words of Bill Mayall:

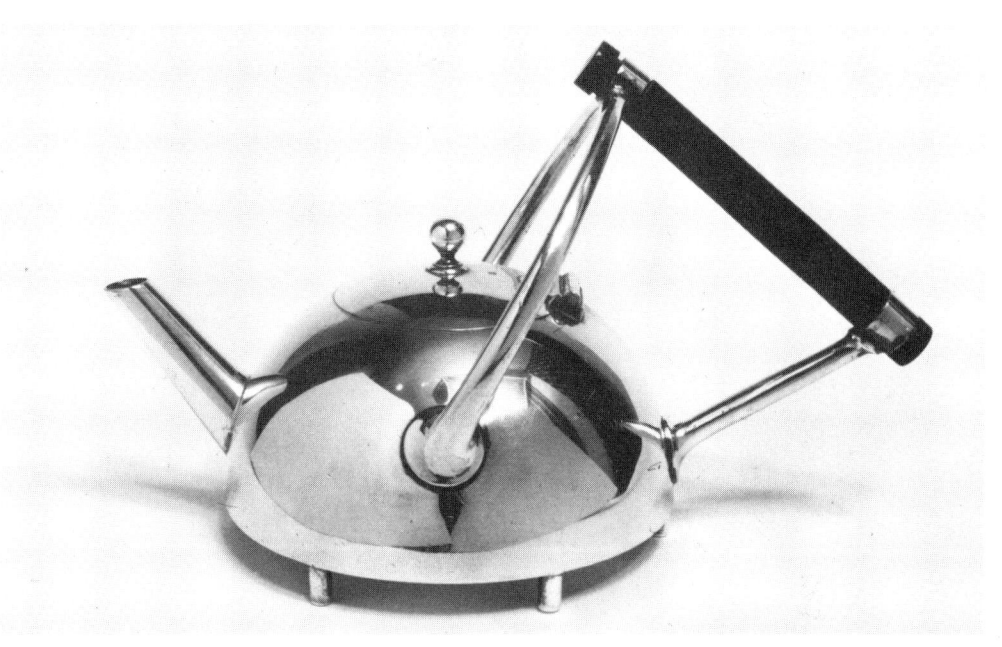

1.27 Silver-plated teapot designed by Christopher Dresser in 1881. Dresser worked for a number of manufacturers including Elkington Bros. for whom he created some starkly simple designs, pre-empting 20th-century functional form.

'Design' for the mechanical engineer in particular, meant almost entirely the creation of new devices coupled with their specification, mainly by 'working drawings', so that they could be made. 'Design' for those who pronounced upon architectural proprieties and upon the forms of products such as furniture, ceramics and textiles ... was a matter of observing what they regarded as proper combinations of forms and colours. Each interpretation was reasonable under the circumstances. And each not only could exist but did in fact exist without upsetting the other for almost a century! The Arts and Crafts movement of the late nineteenth century, Art Nouveau and even so-called Functionalism, which burst through into the twentieth century, mattered little to the engineer...[6]

The first generation of mechanics such as Richard Trevithick and George Stephenson were empiricists, mistrusting theory, even in basic science and mathematics. The origin of their attitude lay in their own social background, education and the then current state of the art. They relied on mechanical aptitude and inventive genius rather than on formal academic training. This is well illustrated in the case of Stephenson who began his career operating colliery pumping and winding engines and first demonstrated his talent in 1811 by setting a new engine to work when all others had failed. A few years later he successfully invented the safety lamp by the hazardous process of trial and error in the gaseous depths of Killingworth Colliery. Simultaneously Sir Humphrey Davy reached the same goal by scientific research in the laboratory of the Royal Institution. As scientific knowledge rapidly advanced the latter approach was to gain prominence and by the end of the century engineers such as Sir Charles Parsons could not have conceived and implemented their designs without rigorous academic training.

But in the early days of transport there was no body of mechanical engineering theory to which engineers could turn. Stephenson's famous *Rocket* was a triumph of inspiration by which all the best practices of the time were heuristically combined and then improved upon. In contrast, his lack of training was evident in civil engineering, resulting in the first Liverpool and Manchester Railway Bill being thrown out. Fortunately, the elder Stephenson relied heavily on his son Robert for whom he ensured a private education supplemented by practical instruction from himself. Thus it was in civil engineering that Robert won fame with such accomplishments as the Menai and Conway bridges and the London and Birmingham railway.

The pioneer civil engineer, canal builder James Brindley, had been, like George Stephenson, a practical man, mistrusting theory to a point where he rarely committed designs to paper and remained virtually illiterate to the end of his life. Yet his most famous successor, Thomas Telford, succeeded in educating himself to an advanced level, becoming in 1818 the first President of the Institution of Civil Engineers. The accumulation of knowledge in the fifty years following Brindley's death had made that profession an exacting science which George Stephenson ignored to his peril. In contrast, Mechanics' Institutes, which opened in industrial centres throughout the country, operated at a humbler level 'to teach the workman those principles of science on which his work began'.

Not until the first engineering professor was appointed at Glasgow in 1840 and the second at London in 1841 did the mechanical engineer gain professional status. Happily in the closing years of his life George Stephenson consented to become first President of the Mechanics' Institute in Birmingham which became in turn the Institution of Mechanical Engineers. By then the Schools of Design had been operating for some years, but no attempt was made to absorb any of their theories. Either they were seen as irrelevant or over-confidence in the invincibility of British engineering did not acknowledge the necessity.

Where there is evidence of links between art and engineering, it is on an individual basis. Nasmyth, whose drawings of the moon observed through his own telescope won a prize medal at the Crystal Palace, was a competent artist who had attended the School of Arts in Edinburgh for five years as well as following chemistry and mathematics courses at the University. However, his father had been a professional artist with many

1.28 The express locomotive *Folkstone* on display within the Crystal Palace, 1851. Designed by T. R. Crampton and manufactured by Stephenson & Co. for the South Eastern Railway, its simplicity of form was a marked contrast to so many other products on display.

contacts from James Watt to Henry Maudslay. It was Maudslay who taught him the importance of lightness and simplicity in design and Joshua Field, Maudslay's partner, who taught him to keep a 'graphic diary' or 'talking notebook'. When Nasmyth himself became an employer he saw little virtue in the training being enforced by the Engineers Mechanics Union, describing it as a 'seven years rut'.

The most celebrated of the Victorian engineers, Isambard Kingdom Brunel, was also a fine artist who spent a period of practical training at the Lambeth works of Maudslay, Sons and Field. His drawings, reflecting his abilities, ranged freely across the whole spectrum of design – from machine parts to station façades. Becase of this, Brunel is best associated with an earlier generation, being a combination of mechanical, civil and marine engineer. Nevertheless, his father, Mark Brunel, famous for installing the block-making machinery at Portsmouth dockyard, had ensured his son the finest theoretical training at the Lycée Henri Quatre in Paris.

Perhaps the first of the great production engineers in the modern sense was Joseph Whitworth, well-known to the layman for his standardised screw-threads. Whitworth won an international reputation at the Crystal Palace with his wide variety of machine tools. By modifying the design of components which these in turn produced, he offered other manufacturers the benefits of standardisation he had achieved in his own factory. *The Engineer* later reported that 'in designing details of machinery, Mr Whitworth contrives to effect a considerable saving of time and labour, by adapting the work to his tools'. A contemporary photograph of the factory illustrates the thoughtful arrangement of machinery, a steam-powered lift and a travelling crane to save unnecessary expenditure of labour.

However, the U.S.A. also gained acclaim with exhibits such as Singer's sewing machine and Colt's revolver. These were designed with standardised and interchangeable parts to suit the 'American System of Manufacture'. The potential threat of the latter led to a Royal Commission investigation with Whitworth himself being appointed to visit the New York World's Fair of the Works of Industry of all Nations in 1853. He subsequently reported that in Britain compared to America 'the working classes have less sympathy with the progress of invention', partly because of the abundance of labour and partly because of the lack of scientific and technical education.

Government concern over education eventually led to the protracted Devonshire Commission Report on Scientific Instruction of 1870–75, followed by the Samuelson Royal Commission on Technical Education of 1882. A further Royal Commission of 1886, concerned with trade, reiterated earlier findings that industrial initiative had moved elsewhere and that education was a significant factor. For example, in Germany, now Britain's most effective European competitor, the state had promoted technical high schools for engineers, managers and industrialists in addition to establishing a national education system.

Whitworth's own prominent role in furthering the cause of practical education illustrates both its strengths and its weaknesses. Although he was one of the founders of the Manchester School of Design in the 1830s, it was not until 1867 that the first chair of engineering was founded at the new university with his generous subscription. The Whitworth Scholarships for young engineers followed a year later with the aim of 'bringing science and industry into closer relation with each other than at present obtains in this country'.

Thus initiatives were often private and mostly independent of schools of design. The views of Redtenbacher, of the Karlsruhe Polytechnic, were unknown in this country:

A school which wishes to give a suitable training for a mechanical–technical career should therefore by no means follow a one-sided scientific course, but must strive to arouse and exercise all the powers which are important for the calling of draughtsman, constructor, engineer and manufacturer.[7]

One of the few lone voices attempting to reconcile art, science and technology in England was Gottfried Semper who planned the Swedish, Danish, Egyptian and Canadian sections of the Great Exhibition. Semper taught at the School of Design at Marlborough House in 1852 but, as we shall see, it was the Deutscher Werkbund in Germany who first widely adopted his principles in the early twentieth century.

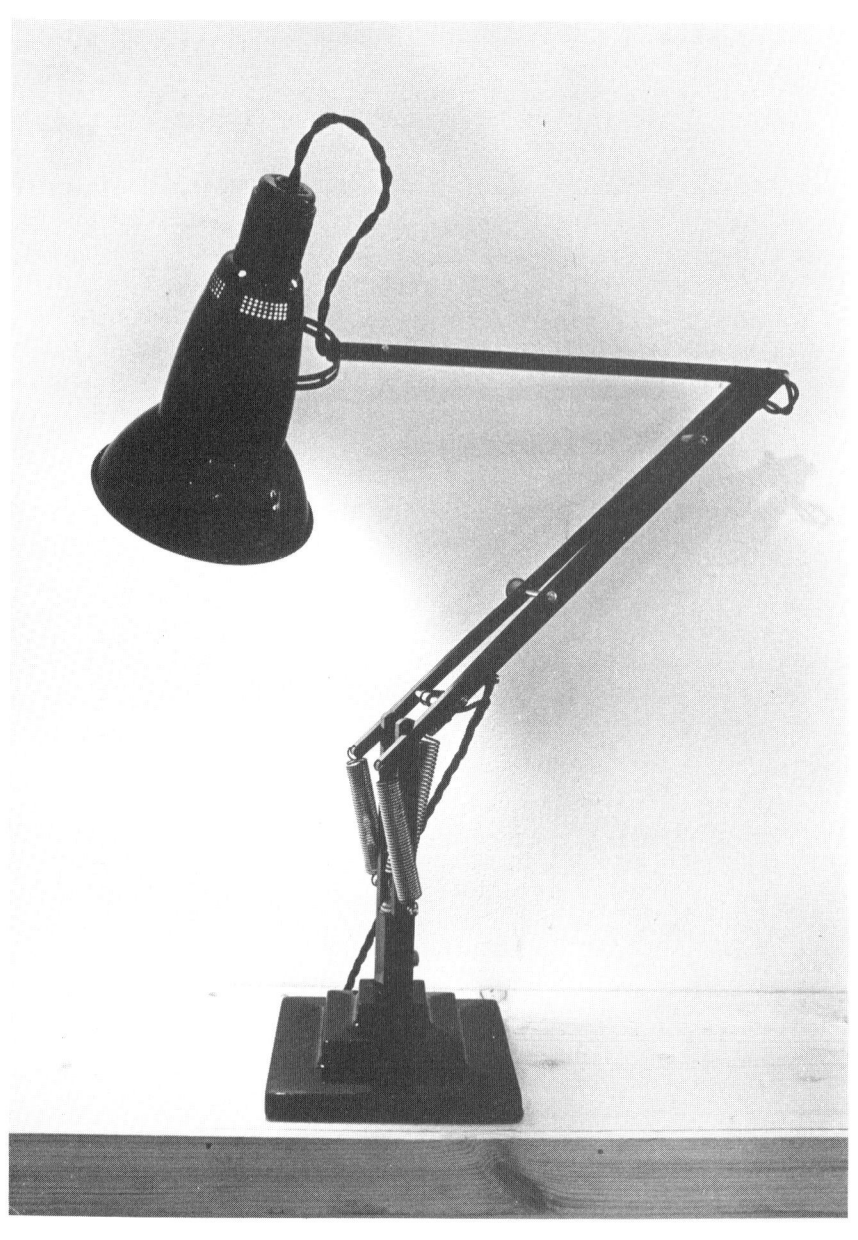

2.1 Adjustable Anglepoise Lamp designed by G. Carwardine for spring manufacturer Herbert Terry in 1932. Based on the mechanism of the human arm, it has become a classic of modern design, remaining in production, little changed, and copied by manufacturers throughout the world.

–2–
'FITNESS FOR PURPOSE'

INTRODUCTION

During the present century, growing concern over Britain's declining industrial performance motivated several concerted attempts to improve the design of her products. In 1915 the privately formed Design and Industries Association (DIA) commenced a determined, though solitary, campaign for 'Fitness for Purpose', the enthusiasm of its members only matched by the indifference of manufacturers and seemingly bad taste of the public at large. Subsequently, members were to witness the optimistic birth and sad demise of two official bodies charged with responsibility to improve design and, by implication, exports. These were The British Institute of Industrial Art, founded in 1920, and the Council for Art and Industry, founded in 1934. However, both failed to gain adequate financial, ministerial or manufacturing support.

Meanwhile, in Germany the mass production of rationalised designs with standardised components had been firmly established, while in America gigantic corporations employed sophisticated private studios to improve their products and images. For a period Britain's wartime Utility schemes gave the Board of Trade central control over design, particularly of furniture. Finally, in December 1944, Churchill's coalition government founded the Council of Industrial Design, 'to promote by all practicable means the improvement of design in the products of British Industry'.

INTO THE TWENTIETH CENTURY

By 1914 the decline of traditional handicrafts as a significant sector of the British economy was more or less complete. Many of the Arts and Crafts societies faced financial bankruptcy, their reprieve only to come later in an age of leisure, itself a by-product of industrialisation. Country crafts all but disappeared, necessitating eventual revival by a government-sponsored Rural Industries Bureau – as much a social as an economic gesture. Even the (by now) Royal College of Art was threatened with closure following reports that its training did not meet the needs of industry. Increasingly, mechanised industries were acknowledged to be fundamental to economic performance, their nurture and growth the key to further prosperity. A Technological Revolution within the Industrial

2.2–2.4 A new generation of mass-produced consumer goods, particularly electrical, evolved during the 20th century. *Above*. The original Hoover vacuum cleaner, Model 0 (*Grandfather*) of 1907. *Centre*. The Belling Sunflower electric fire of

Revolution created assembly lines and conveyor belts to churn out the standardised consumer goods which characterise the twentieth century. Production of domestic appliances and office equipment significantly increased, their designs being suited to mass production and assembly by unskilled labour. Additionally, supplies of military hardware were stepped up in an all too familiar arms race.

A distinctive feature of manufacturing was the way production and demand mutually reinforced one another. Although psychologically work was more stultifying, physically it was less exhausting; as the working day and the working life contracted, so longevity and population increased. Unskilled workers came to enjoy more disposable income and free time than their skilled forbears before the Industrial Revolution. Assembly workers could afford the products which passed through their hands, swelling the ranks formerly reserved for the ostentatious Victorian middle classes. As a bonus, Britain enjoyed the large and uncritical market of an Empire 'on which the sun never set'.

None of these circumstances was destined to dispel manufacturers' complacency or refine consumer discrimination beyond that of the Victorians. Many problems remained, even more firmly entrenched by the Edwardians. Private self-confidence was matched by government reluct-

1920, with a bowl reminiscent of that flower. *Right.* The Genalex electric washing machine and wringer of 1937, before being enclosed by the all-pervasive 'white box' form of today.

ance to intervene. For example, whereas other countries vociferously protected domestic industry with tariff barriers, little was done apart from shoring up 'King Cotton' by crudely banning all imports from India. At the time of Victoria's death, Britain still charged no import duty on manufactures, whereas Germany imposed an average 25% on British goods, France 34%, America 75% and Russia 31%.

Where there emerged evidence of initiative, the country seemed burdened by the material and social consequences of earlier success. Ponderous and clanking steam engines found a parallel in inflexible bureaucratic machinery. This was simply demonstrated by establishment attitudes to two outstanding military innovations: Charles Parsons was forced to race his *Turbinia* through the 1897 Spithead Naval Review to convince the Admiralty of its potential, and Churchill had secretly to by-pass the War Office, the Master General of Ordnance, the Treasury and the Admiralty to build tanks to end the First World War.

Inevitably, despite productivity growth, Britain's annual rate of increase tailed off and her share of world output fell. While the rising tide of industry still remained impressive, it was doubly so in America and Germany. The principle of interchangeability, the very basis of mass production had, after all, been pioneered in America (albeit for muskets with which to fight the British). And one hundred years later, by 1914, Henry Ford had started the production line which was to epitomise modern industry. In Germany, as we have seen, America's energy was matched by efficiency in a range of industries directly challenging Britain.

To what extent design was a contributing factor is difficult to quantify exactly. Nevertheless, if aesthetic appeal defies strict objective assessment, a comparison of creative and technological progress can be gained from patents figures. Between 1750 and 1780 the annual number of patents in this country increased six-fold and Josiah Tucker reported: 'In the metal industries of Birmingham and Sheffield almost every Master Manufacturer hath a new invention of his own, and is daily improving on those of others.' But America's establishment of a Patent Office 'added the fuel of interest to the fire of genius' and soon after the Great Exhibition she was issuing far more certificates than Britain. Germany's progress, quite apart from electrical and engineering, is emphasised by her chemical industry. From the Great Exhibition to the turn of the century German patents for synthetic dyes increased over fifty-fold whereas in Britain they little more than doubled. By 1914 Khaki dye had to be shamefacedly purchased from the enemy, although the initial discovery had been British. Even if Britain did not perceive her performance and her products as inferior, realisation gradually dawned that factors such as appearance, quality and reliability were important in the face of protective tariffs, productive workforces and pressure selling. National pride might accuse foreigners of dumping the cheap and nasty, but the 'British and Best' label would have to be demonstrably more true in future.

THE DESIGN AND INDUSTRIES ASSOCIATION
In contrast to the British aesthetic movements of the late Victorian period, in Germany, where Art Nouveau had been subdued into stylised geometric forms, an altogether different movement had evolved. This was, in 1914, to have important repercussions in Britain. Founded in 1907, the Deutscher Werkbund, like other continental craft movements, respected Morris and Mackintosh, but brought rustic principles such as 'truth to materials' and 'sound workmanship' firmly into line with those of industrial production. Dissident voices were overruled by realities which faced Germany (and, even more so, Britain): firstly, the need to supply goods cheaply in quantity without resort to sweated labour; secondly, the need to ensure consistency of quality; and thirdly, the need to create a new generation of consumer goods, particularly electrical, which had no craft precedent and which necessitated the use of new materials, machines and technologies. The Werkbund's founder members included Peter Behrens, design consultant to AEG, Germany's massive General Electri-

cal Company. Behrens represented a group of designers, more in evidence on the continent and in America than Britain, who combined a sculptor's eye with technical understanding to create pure forms for industry.

But Germany, like Britain, was equally capable of producing mediocre, albeit cheaper, goods for export – the penny penknife being an example where Birmingham's lead in the 'toy trade' (i.e. small metal products) had long been usurped. This problem, in the peculiar circumstances of world war, was to precipitate at last the foundation of both voluntary and official British organisations concerned exclusively with industrial design.

Through exhibitions, booklets and *Die Form* magazine, the Werkbund's influence had spread across the Channel and reached at least a select group of enthusiasts. In 1914 several returned home from the seventh Deutscher Werkbund exhibition in Cologne, determined to found an equivalent organisation. The advanced display in Walter Gropius's specially commissioned model factory had convinced them of the need to act immediately. The resultant Design and Industries Association took up cudgels abandoned by the now diversified Royal Society of Arts, adopting an uncompromising functionalist motto 'Fitness for Purpose'.

Before many weeks had passed the opportunity for decisive action was to occur. War with Germany and Austria abruptly stopped crucial import of consumer goods and, free to act against the enemy, the Board of Trade planned exhibitions of designs for manufacturers to plagiarise. But the DIA, horrified by the trashiness of selections, persuaded Permanent Secretary Sir Hugh Llewellyn Smith to represent the best not the worst. The subsequent display at Goldsmiths Hall contained many members' own possessions brought home from Germany. In addition to propagating good design, the exhibition acted as a rallying point for the Association itself.

The bulk of the membership was actively engaged in manufacturing or selling, but about one third were craft workers, architects or teachers. Of these, many had Arts and Crafts backgrounds but unlike their predecessors had accepted industrialisation as inevitable and irreversible. Among founder members were Ambrose Heal, Frank Pick, Harry Peach, William Richard Lethaby and, joining in 1920, a young Gordon Russell. Although lacking the inspiring literary skills of a Ruskin or Morris, such men nevertheless combined considerable talents of charisma, business acumen and design awareness. Only the paucity of such talents in the country at large was to frustrate their efforts. Heal designed the entirely appropriate, if severe, DIA insignia and, as manufacturer and retailer, ran his own store as a prototype 'Design Centre'. Pick promoted, as Commercial Manager of London Underground Railways, a corporate image ranging from advanced rolling stock to poster design. Lethaby, by now having

2.5 For the Design and Industries Association transport was one field to achieve the 'functional beauty of good design and workmanship'. The Norton motorcycle of 1909 still retained the refined skeletal structure of a bicycle, yet its lettering delightfully succumbed to Art Nouveau styling.

become first Principal of the Central School and Royal College Professor of Design, grappled with conflicting ideologies of the Arts and Crafts and Modern Movements. Russell spanned the two in practice, from village furniture to his brother's mass-produced radio cabinets. Peach, as founder of Dryad Cane Furniture and Dryad Handicrafts, offered a fusion of craft and manufacturing which perhaps most nearly reflected the hybrid nature of the Association.

Through pamphlets, year books, exhibitions and eventually radio broadcasts the DIA strove to combat lack of interest in the nation. Something of its early philosophy, not to mention evangelical spirit, is captured in A. Clutton Brock's 1916 pamphlet *A Modern Creed of Work*:

> We shall do nothing if we make up our minds that machinery is a device of the Devil, which must destroy all beauty and joy of life. Machinery is a device of man, and one which he cannot now do without. There is no reason why an object of use made by machinery should not be well made, or should not have the functional beauty of good design and workmanship. That is proved by motor cars, battleships, sporting guns, and a hundred other things. It may not be universally true, but one may lay it down, as a practical rule, that an object made by machinery is better without ornament.

2.6 The Rolls Royce earned a reputation as the best-engineered and most beautiful of cars. Yet, like the finest pieces of Georgian furniture, it was beyond the reach of the masses, emphasising the problem of equating cost with quality. Shown is a chauffeur-driven New Phantom of 1926.

> And in our own time, at any rate when all taste has been so much demoralised by excess of ornament, we need to make a strict rule with ourselves about ornament, as a drunkard, if he would cure himself, needs to take the pledge. If only they (the public) could be persuaded that plain things are the most beautiful, they would soon see for themselves that they are far more beautiful than most of the ornamental things, from fire-irons up to grand hotels, with which their taste has been depraved.[1]

Other early pamphlets reflect this puritanical abhorrence of ornament. The term 'beautiful' was, in fact, rarely used in the conventional sense, honesty and respect of materials being far more of a commendation, and, of course, 'Fitness for Purpose' when it came to function.

The breadth of field covered was enormous: simple product design in an early 'Sensible Presents for Christmas Guide'; systems design with Pick's Underground included as 'the outstanding example of Fitness for Purpose on a vast scale'; and environment design covering 'The Face of the Land' in different year books. The lack of tactical support from manufacturers made the task even more difficult. An early textile exhibition elicited only three replies from sixty companies, so members had to collect the exhibits personally.

2.7 The Rolls Royce radiator bears the car's only excess ornamentation – the Spirit of Ecstacy by Charles Sykes – perhaps the most famous piece of British sculpture.

One of the most effective methods of promoting interest was arranging for a regional store to display living rooms or kitchens, planned by a small committee. Goods were loaned by compliant manufacturers who, like the store, gained local publicity and increased sales. This did involve a great deal of work for the team involved, but invariably fertilised a seed of interest in the area. It is interesting that exactly the same method of propaganda was adopted by the Council of Industrial Design some twenty years later, when it was able to offer the service on a larger and more efficient scale.

In London a number of stores similarly commissioned large-scale exhibitions of new furnishings with the intention of testing public taste. Amongst the architects to use the opportunity to good purpose was Serge Chermayeff at Waring and Gillow in Oxford Street in 1927. At this time the effect of the great Paris Exhibition of 1925 was becoming apparent. But this was by no means all to the taste of the DIA, particularly the Cubist and Jazz influence in textiles and the gaudy interiors of each new Odeon, Lido or Palais de Danse. More to the preference of members was the sober functionalism of the emerging German Bauhaus.

Membership of the DIA was always to remain small, usually never more than a few hundred scattered across the country. Described as 'a body of enthusiasts pursuing divergent aims together' its appeal swung erratically between Arts and Crafts socialism and trade commercialism.

As the country collapsed from war into massive social and economic unrest, then eventually fought another war against the old protagonist, public and industry were insufficiently aware of its existence. In turn, visually sophisticated members were bemused by the crudity of public taste, the indifference of manufacturers and the cold shoulder from many artists. The over-literal interpretation of 'Fitness for Purpose' which had earned the DIA the nickname of 'Pots and Pans Brigade' was only slowly overcome. It was to be Frank Pick, commissioning leading artists to design his London Underground posters, who healed the breach with the artists. Yet, in general, lacking permanent facilities and full-time staff, the task for a voluntary body such as the DIA was daunting – intrinsically and operationally.

Against this background, the (usually) gentlemanly persuasion and support for government action persevered. Over the years it was to experience the birth and demise of two official bodies before the eventual foundation of the Council of Industrial Design. Following the first, so soon after its own formation, the DIA possibly felt 'to some extent out-smarted by the Government of the day'. But the Council it definitely perceived as its own brainchild. Lord Pakenham (now Longford) justifiably addressed members in 1946: 'The Council of Industrial Design would never have come into existence had it not been for the hard self-sacrificing work of the Design and Industries Association.'

THE BRITISH INSTITUTE OF INDUSTRIAL ART

Until 1919, preoccupation with total war distorted official concern with the products of manufacturing industry. Nevertheless, as we have seen, the Design and Industries Association interacted with the Board of Trade and already in the air was the notion of a permanent government body. Its chief purpose would be to stimulate exports by improving their design. As Noel Carrington was to recall:

> 'Exports' is always a sure password in Parliament and the press, but I think it very likely that the mandarins at the Board had come to view the DIA as lacking in tact and manners. An organisation under its own wing and with its own officers would be more trustworthy.[2]

The origins, in fact, do go back to 1914 when the Board of Trade and the Board of Education proposed a joint organ through which they both could act. Exhibitions would be central to strategy, in close liaison with the Victoria and Albert Museum. However, it was to be 1920 before the idea actually materialised as the British Institute of Industrial Art, incorporated under the Chairmanship of Sir Hubert Llewellyn Smith.

2.8–2.10 Under the inspired leadership of Frank Pick, London Transport evolved a corporate identity in the formative years of modern design. Architect Charles Holden, who was on the Committee of the DIA with Pick, designed the distinctive new-generation stations from 1930 on. *Above.* Arnos Grove Station, designed 1932. *Below left.* Hampstead poster, designed by S. T. C. Weekes in 1912. *Below right.* London Underground Map, first designed by Harry Beck in 1931. This classic example of graphic design reduces route directions to verticals, horizontals and diagonals.

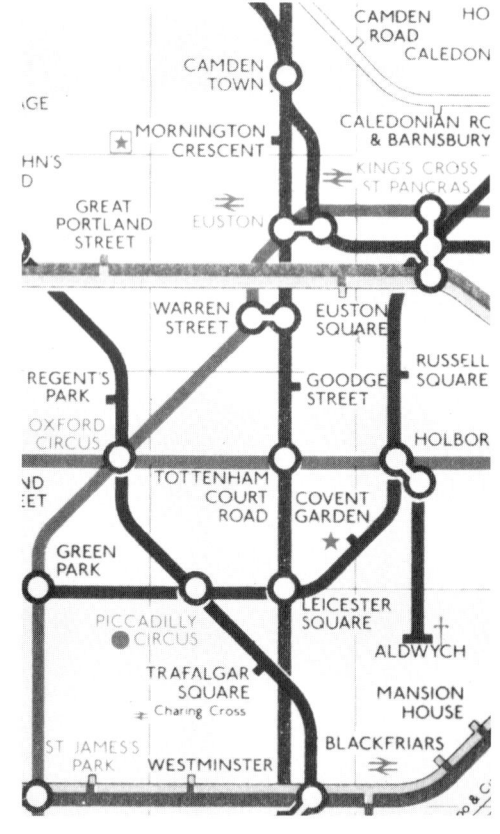

The new body seemingly had most of the features of the later Council of Industrial Design, but on a much smaller scale. Firstly, it received an annual treasury grant which injected life-blood and vigour from the outset. At the same time it remained free of government interference, combining independence with security. And, coming immediately after a world war, a new mood of optimism pervaded its efforts. Strategies and activities were also similar. There was a centre in the West End for the exhibition of designers' work, and a small permanent, if restricted, collection retained at the Victoria and Albert Museum along the lines originally intended. Exhibitions were organised for the Museum which were then sent around the country. By displaying craftwork, something of the spirit of the present-day Crafts Council was also embraced. But its main purpose was the promotion of industrial goods and their exhibition overseas in the interests of exports. This the Institute did, holding exhibitions in Paris, Brussels and other centres. The DIA, which could not have afforded such activity, was content to leave it to the official body. However, there was inevitably some friction between the two when enthusiasts felt the Institute was over solicitous not to offend important companies in the selection of exhibits.

Regrettably, soon after the optimistic birth of this embryonic body, economic crisis hit the country and the Institute's grant of £10,000 was abruptly withdrawn. Dedicated to serving industry, ironically its work had been curtailed by industrial slump. Bravely, though, it survived through the twenties on a minimum budget of private subscriptions, providing small exhibitions and slim publications which prophetically included 'Industrial Art for the Slender Purse' and 'Public Departments and Industrial Art'.

Eventually the Institute petered out, leaving matters back in the hands of the DIA with a budget of only hundreds, not thousands, of pounds. But useful themes for the future had been explored including low-cost goods, retailing, craft training and university education. Crucially its own demise highlighted the need to specify clearly defined aims and functions, the danger of dissipating energies across too broad a front, and the necessity for official status and finance. As the Meynell–Hoskin Report noted when later recommending a Central Design Council:

> . . . Its functions were never clearly defined and it failed for lack of support; and, when the Treasury grant was withdrawn, it died of starvation.[3]

For a decade the government remained distant from the struggles of industrial art. As something of a half-way house, the Federation of British Industries set up its own Industrial Art Committee to represent manufacturers' views. True to form, this sent representatives to other committees

2.11 The Omega Workshops, founded in 1913, produced radically new designs by employing part-time artists and sculptors. Some attractive pieces were created, such as this dressing table in holly, inlaid with ebony. However, the realities of 20th-century industry led to closure.

or produced detailed reports. Usefully, in a period of high unemployment, it commenced a Register and Employment Bureau for designers and a card-index of sympathetic companies – ideas which were to be seized upon by others later. Meanwhile, the policy of *Typisierung* (mass production of rationalised designs and standardised components) was firmly established in Germany, initiated by state-owned industries. Equally important, America's gigantic corporations were utilising sophisticated private studios, such as that of Norman bel Geddes, to improve their products and images. Despair over the relative lethargy of Britain is evident in an article by Phillip Morton Shand, one of a select group of contemporary writers:

> It is a melancholy and humiliating confession for an Englishman to make that the great movement towards standardisation of design in terms of functional fitness, to which the genius of the German people is now applying itself, should find no echo in the country which initiated the

2.12 De Stijl artefacts such as Gerrit Rietveld's red/blue chair of 1918, although not meant as functional objects themselves, profoundly affected 20th-century design philosophy, in particular through their influence on Bauhaus students including van der Rohe and Breuer.

> Industrial Age ... The depressed state of British Industry and the progressive decline of our foreign markets are the direct result of innate conservatism, and a refusal to live and work in the spirit of the present age.[4]

An elegant exhibition of Swedish design at Dorland Hall in 1930 finally brought home the point that craftsmanship and tradition were no longer the prerogative of the British. Clearly another nation had skilfully integrated craft with industry to the decided advantage of the latter. Furthermore, to those enthusiasts who led the campaign for better design the truly inspiring designs were to be increasingly of continental origin. In Finland Alvar Aalto's laminated birch chairs were an innovation to equal Thonet's bentwood furniture, while in Germany Bauhaus designers were creating their own classics in metal and chrome. Not only were their designs suitable for mass production and use in public building, they were to achieve the status of *objets de luxe*.

2.13 The Finnish architect Alvar Aalto's laminated birch furniture has been as significant an innovation this century as Thonet's bent beechwood of Victorian times. This cantilever design dates back to 1935 and is still manufactured by Artek (Finland) and distributed by Jonas in this country.

THE COUNCIL FOR ART AND INDUSTRY

By 1931, growing consciousness of the international design movement and the impending economic slump, convinced the government of a need for reappraisal. Subsequently, a Committee on Art and Industry was appointed by the Board of Trade to report on 'The Production and Exhibition of Articles of Good Design and Every-Day Use'. Under the Chairmanship of Lord Gorrell, the membership was a large one and carried considerable aesthetic, intellectual and establishment weight. Included were Sir Eric Maclagan, Director of the Victoria and Albert Museum; Roger Fry, art critic and founder of the Omega workshops; Clough Williams-Ellis, architect and critic; and Sir Hubert Llewellyn Smith, Chairman of the aforementioned British Institute of Industrial Art. Clearly some big guns had been returned to the fray, as well as those of the DIA.

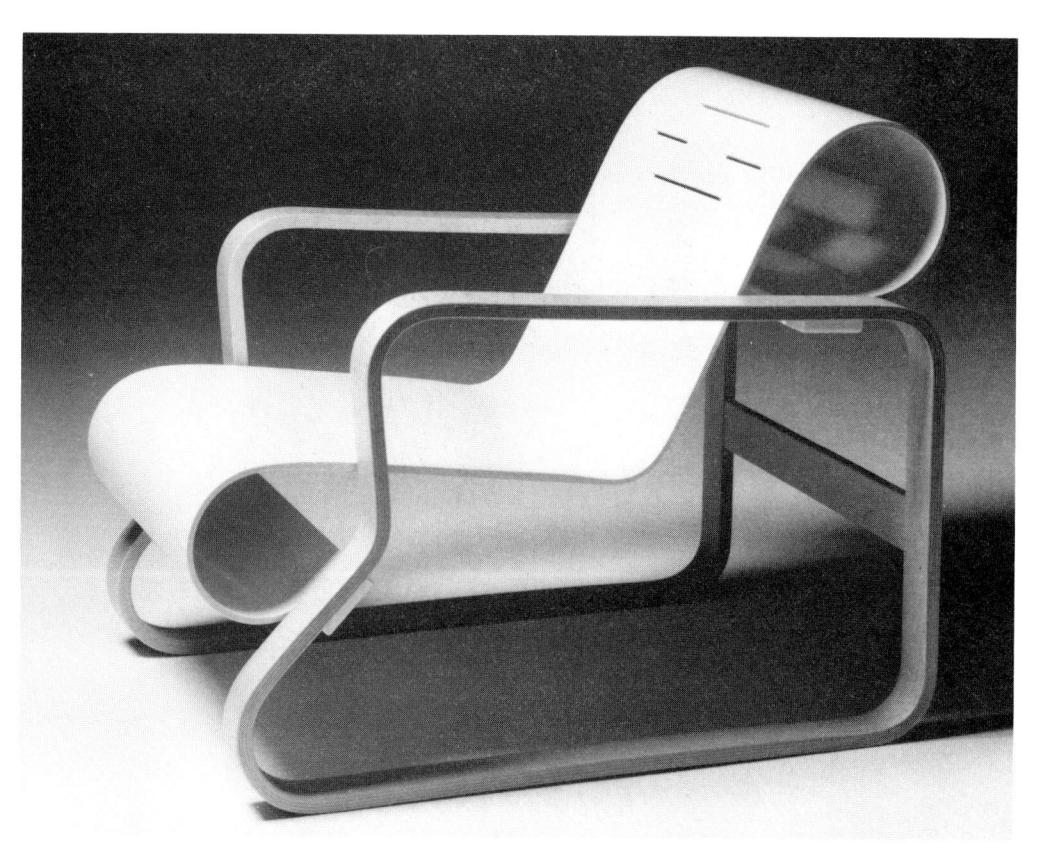

2.14 Aalto's Armchair 41 was developed for the interior of the Paimio Sanatorium by 1932 and first shown abroad in Fortnum and Mason in 1933. Laminated birch slats compose side frames for the moulded plywood seat.

Even for such an august body, to inquire into the whole question of 'production and exhibition' was a daunting task. Sensibly they restricted their investigation to: formation in London of a standing and temporary exhibition; organisation of local and travelling exhibitions; constitution of a central co-ordinating body; and sources of finance. The emphasis, therefore, was on exhibitions, but more significant was the central co-ordinating body. Exhibitions come and go, as they had been doing since 1761, while central bodies, hopefully, stay. The economic crisis had already 'starved' one such body. If this was to be avoided in the future the question of adequate finance had to be settled.

In preparing its Report the Committee received evidence from diverse official sources and, most importantly, the DIA, whose memorandum was closely followed in their final draft. This commenced with an historical and contemporary survey, noting in a mildly critical manner the lack of support from manufacturers such that the good intention of concentrating on exhibitions had to be broken: 'the mere organisation of exhibitions

2.15 Marcel Breuer's Wassily chair of 1925 makes an interesting comparison to Aalto's Armchair 41. Aalto was influenced by Breuer's work, although he found chrome too cold. Breuer's chair is still manufactured today, distributed by Aram Designs. The coach hide adds an element of warmth.

of this type is incapable, by itself, of solving the vital problem.' Subsequently, woven around its theme the Report tackled, in measured if occasionally sweeping terms, a broad range of issues from education to piracy of designs.

Eventually the important recommendation was made that an all-powerful, all-embracing central body should be formed to control exhibitions, and that the resources of other organisations should be placed at its disposal for this purpose:

> In order to differentiate sharply between the new scheme and the piecemeal efforts that have been made in the past, there must be something essentially and unequivocally national which will strike the imagination of the public and command national support. In other words, there should be a central body controlling Exhibitions of Industrial Art, whether in this country or abroad.[5]

2.16 Breuer's Cesca A side chair of 1928 contrasts with Aalto's cantilever chair 406. Made in chromium-plated tubular steel, ebonised bentwood and cane, it is claimed to be the most popular chair of its kind in the world today.

Indeed, the exhibition activities of others were expected to cease in their present form in order that this 'newer, stronger and more efficient body may function without competition'. But their specialist knowledge might entail requests to act as 'agents'.

A necessary provision would be an exhibitions building, preferably with outdoor space and situated in the West End. (A short but significant shift from the Society of Arts' request for Trafalgar Square a century before.) While this was being purpose-built, the Committee expected, presumptuously in the event, that temporary premises would 'act as a barometer of possible support and serve as a field of experiments'.

The exhibitions would be 'periodic' of about six weeks' duration, being convenient for organisation, maintenance, novelty, and social or trade visits. Only 'beautiful modern manufactured goods' would be chosen, but with due regard to 'modest means'. The question of a standing exhibition as 'propaganda for excellence' was postponed on the excuse that even generous updating might not 'combat public lassitude'.

However, acquisition of specimens was recommended for 'absorption into the National Collections'. In particular, a permanent collection in the Victoria and Albert or adjacent building should accrue for students, manufacturers and public to study the 'best examples of modern design'.

Regarding the constitution of the central body, the Report recommended executive rather than advisory powers, answerable to Parliament. The President of the Board of Trade would appoint between six and twelve members representing education, manufacturing and retailing, with the proviso that taste, cultural standards and an 'international outlook on Art' were the important criteria. To secure the 'best men available' a small honorarium should be attached and periodic retirement encouraged to obtain 'new blood'. A chairman of 'energy, knowledge and taste' would be required plus a full-time director to implement policy.

Finally there was the thorny question of finance. Clearly the most expensive item was the West End building, but because of the economic crisis, the Committee prudently deferred this matter. Instead, by confining itself to salaries, honoraria, hire of halls, lease of office, cleaning, lighting and heating, a figure of £10,000 per annum was arrived at. Offset against this might be revenue from rents, subscriptions, levies, admissions, commissions and catalogues. In detailing such sources, members were probably aware of undermining their case for an officially financed body as distinct from the DIA and consequently ended with something of a long shot; in the event of 'public monies not being available' the 'best hope' would lie in the 'generosity of some far-seeing reformer with great public spirit'. No doubt they suspected that for the government of the day even £10,000 was too much. But there is little evidence to suggest that Industrial Art had either the personal appeal or the cultural status for wealthy benefactors that it had for themselves.

Additionally the Gorrell Committee made several further recommendations as part of a 'general co-ordinated plan' to achieve 'improved status for the best industrial artists, increased use of first-rate artists by manufacturers, better art education, and research into the needs of particular industries'. Additionally, almost contradicting the idea of a central body and problems of finance, they recommended that the Board of Trade be made specifically responsible for the advancement of Industrial Art in this country.

This 50-page report charging the state to accept such responsibilities at first came to nothing: Parliament refused to vote the minimum £10,000 seed money. Impetus for action came one year later from an exhibition, initiated by a voluntary body, financed by private enterprise and patronised by a prince – an interesting parallel to the Great Exhibition, if on a much smaller scale.

2.17, 2.18 Steel furniture came to be acknowledged in this country during the thirties. However, designs by internationally famous architects have all too often been perceived as *objets de luxe* rather than prototypes for mass production. Eileen Gray (1878–1976) witnessed her own revival in recent times, with designs being manufactured in England, France and Italy. *Above.* The adjustable table dates back to 1927 and is today marketed by Aram Designs. *Below.* Despite the influence of Hollywood, the excesses of Art Deco were criticised by fervent Modernists. The comment on this sideboard was 'What is the purpose of all the chromium plate?'

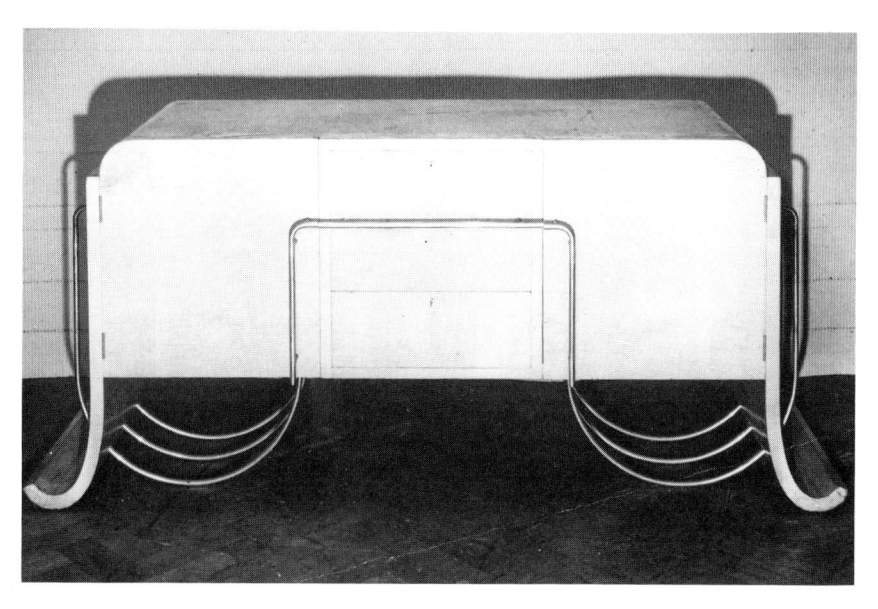

2.19, 2.20 *Left.* The technology to mass produce Gerrit Rietveld's hanging lamp was not readily available in 1920. Wood block, laboratory-glass tubes and electrical strip filament lamps were used for his elegant prototype. *Right.* Pyrex glass, c. 1908, was first developed for lamp covers resistant to extremes of heat, snow and rain on the American Railroad. Pyrex casseroles of 1931 have changed little in form over the years.

Demise of the official Institute of Industrial Art had left the DIA free to attempt its own major exhibition. Lectures and pamphlets were all very well, but the prestige and impact of the Crystal Palace always haunted DIA and RSA imaginations. The idea of an exhibition in London to rival the Great Exhibition had been under discussion for several years. The more ambitious talked of Hyde Park itself, but it was soon made clear by the government that it would find no funds for such a scheme. Realistically, members knew that sufficient good design was hardly available to fill a large hall, quite apart from cash to finance it. In the event Christopher Hussey of *Country Life* magazine (which was to update its image from antiques and country houses) and architect Oliver Hill mustered sufficient support to guarantee a sum of £2000 to rent two floors of the new Dorland Hall in Lower Regent Street. Would the DIA collaborate in finding exhibitors and help with the selection? While purists disliked any involvement when they did not have complete control, Frank Pick, who was then President, threw his weight behind the proposals and undertook to serve. Lord Gorrell became Chairman of the Exhibition Committee, Frank Pick became Vice-Chairman, and the DIA formed a substantial part of its membership. As something of a coup, the Duke of York became Patron-in-Chief. Unfortunately, because the DIA did not assume overall responsibility, its name never appeared on any publicity. London's need for an appropriate exhibitions building was reflected in the choice of Dorland Hall. In practice, despite its limitations, it proved advantageous for creating domestic interiors such as kitchens and dining rooms realistically displayed with goods. Such was the curious origin of what came to be known as the Dorland Hall Exhibition of 1933.

The trade exhibits, selected by the DIA, filled about half the space, but some six specially designed rooms by a team of architects were the more important feature. Amongst them was a Weekend Home by Chermeyeff, a Study by R. D. Russell and a Minimum Flat by Welles Coates, the latter being a replica from a block of flats in Hampstead he had designed. These and Oliver Hill's dramatic entrance hall proved the main draw for the public who came in increasing numbers such that an extension of showing was necessary.

Although the Dorland Hall Exhibition has been criticised as 'a microcosm of all the false hopes and misconceptions which have bothered British Industrial design ever since', concentrating on 'soft furnishings and glassware at the expense of real industrial designs',[6] considerable growth of public interest, design publications and ultimately government support did follow. The title was, after all, 'Exhibition of British Industrial Art in Relation to the Home' and manufacturers such as Heal and Russell and architect/interior designers such as Oliver Hill and Richard Dudley Ryder were able to demonstrate their potential. (Ryder, who had been lent by the Architectural Press, in particular discovered a new métier which he was later to exploit with the Council of Industrial Design.) A more immediate criticism was that 'good' usually meant 'expensive' and 'modern' meant 'austere'.

A further problem, well known to the DIA (and the RSA), was manufacturers' reluctance to exhibit. Nevertheless, once success (including financial success due to Ryder) had been assured they were keen for more. Next year a second exhibition was held, but without involving the DIA who felt there could be little new to show. As a result, contributors resorted to novelty and showmanship, invoking the criticism of an aesthetic elite reminiscent of 1851. Yet this was nothing compared to a third attempt by the Royal Society of Arts and the Royal Academy of Arts at Burlington House. Critics led by Herbert Read dismissed the exhibits as ornamental, expensive and unsuited to industrial production. Raymond

2.21, 2.22 *Left.* New materials such as Bakelite, patented in 1909, freed the forms of new products such as radios. Ecko and Philco cabinets received considerable designer attention during the thirties. *Right.* The machine-made walnut-finish cases of Murphy Radios, designed by R. D. Russell and manufactured by Gordon Russell Ltd throughout the thirties, were attractive, economical and functional.

Mortimer wrote in the *New Statesman* of 'an opulent bourgeoisie, emerald necklaces and revolving beds for expensive tarts':

> But for that vast section of the population which is rather helplessly looking for better objects at a possible price, the exhibition of Art in Industry is worse than no exhibition at all. For the standards it sets are both costly and depraved.[7]

Read himself made the important administrative point that the selection committees consisted chiefly of manufacturers, the very people it was the object to advise and educate. The DIA had been particularly careful at the first exhibition, but to its chagrin was never consulted over Burlington House. More surprisingly a brand new Council of Art and Industry now actually existed to avoid these very problems. For the government had indeed relented, following Dorland Hall, and implemented Gorrell's recommendations.

The Council for Art and Industry or the Pick Council, as it became known, began work in 1934 with minimal funds but with high aims including education of consumers, training of designers, and a general raising of standards of industrial design. Exhibitions were fundamental to all three, yet, lacking an authoritative pronouncement of its powers, the Council was unable to co-ordinate national exhibitions, offering instead specialist displays – silversmithing, pottery, domestic metalwork and educational materials – but never achieving a centre of its own. Potentially important were international exhibitions at Brussels in 1935 and Paris in 1937 but, with lukewarm support, the Council received 'more kicks than half pence',[8] and criticism came from press and public alike. Their creditable display of quality goods emphasising British craftsmanship failed to realise Gorrell's hope that 'a genuine representative exhibition organised by an experienced body will enhance considerably national prestige'. Britain's attempts were completely overshadowed by the gigantic German and Russian pavilions making strident claims for the proofs of fascism and communism.

This is unfortunate because, despite the Depression or in some cases because of it, examples of effective industrial design were apparent and the work of identifiable designers was becoming known. By 1937 the Board of Trade, on the suggestion of the Pick Council, had indeed established a National Register of Industrial Art Designers. Furthermore companies such as PEL (Practical Equipment Ltd) and Isokon were challenging continental sales of steel furniture. Actually, Isokon, founded by engineer-economist Jack Pritchard and architect Wells Coates, employed both Marcel Breuer and Walter Gropius at this time. (One positive result of fascism had been the influx of refugee architects and designers from Nazi Germany, including Gropius and Breuer. Until 1939 they were able to work on important projects with British colleagues. It was to be Britain's loss and America's gain when so many internationally known names moved to America at the outbreak of war.) Responding to the declining market for expensive handmade furniture, Gordon Russell in turn orientated his own firm's designs towards mass production. Particularly significant is the range of radio cabinets designed by Dick Russell for Murphy. Dick Russell had in fact, spent some time at the Architectural Association, studying design for mass production.

A necessary condition for operation of the Council was to have a well-planned scheme of research and this proved to be a more successful, if less glamorous role, than exhibitions. Recognising that the problem was immense, Gorrell had proposed detailed inquiry, industry by industry, into 'economic, educational and technical, as well as aesthetic factors'. Subsequent Council reports reflected this and included 'Design in the Jewellery, Silversmithing and Allied Trades', 'The Working Class Home: its Furnishing and Equipment' and 'Education of the Consumer'. By far the most influential was 'Design and the Designer in Industry' of 1937, which demonstrates the strengths and weaknesses of design philosophy at that time. Emphasis was placed on design for 'large-scale production of goods by machinery' but continually referred to traditional values and craftsmanship. However, the call for closer cooperation between industry and colleges to train high status designers was to be crucial. In turn, it became the basis of the later Weir Report leading to the Council of Industrial Design. More central to its own work was the 'Proposal for an Industrial Art Centre' to fulfil the Victoria and Albert Museum's long neglected function of encouraging 'a sanely critical attitude towards things of everyday use and service'.

Having completed the most thorough research to date into industrial design, this second official body suspended work at the outbreak of war. Its membership of thirty now realised that only a smaller, richer, more authoritative organisation, with a permanent home and exhibition centre could survive the future. They themselves had suffered the same weaknesses and fate as the Institute of Art and Industry before them.

UTILITY

The one and only opportunity for total government control over manufactured goods came with wartime Utility schemes, in particular the design of furniture. Requiring as it did considerable amounts of timber, otherwise needed for the war effort including aeroplane construction, it soon became necessary strictly to control supply. Although the Utility label CC41 initially had connotations of second-best, it was furniture which came to reverse this into a guarantee of quality. So successful was the venture that it operated well after the war until pressure from manufacturers led to control reverting back to individual companies.

A Board of Trade Advisory Committee on Utility Furniture was appointed in early 1942 with manufacturers' representatives, trades unionists, one clergyman and one housewife. From a selection of drawings by various designers the work of two men was chosen as a starting point – Horace Cutler and Edwin Clinch, both of High Wycombe. As a tribute to them the first range was named Chiltern. One member of the Committee was Gordon Russell who feared that in a period when reproduction Jacobean was more prominent than Modern, trade hostility would be forthcoming. But there was neither the timber nor labour for bulbous carvings. For DIA stalwart Russell, 'contemporary design ... should prove its mettle in a national emergency':

> Just think for a moment what we were proposing to do. In a trade which was always pretty chaotic, with hundreds of small firms all fairly competitive and literally thousands of patterns existing, we were planning to reduce the total number of pieces to perhaps thirty with at the most three designs to each piece of a type that was unfamiliar to many members of

2.23, 2.24 *Left.* The 1942 Utility Furniture Scheme strictly controlled the design and manufacture of furniture at a time when skilled labour and materials were in short supply. This type of easy-chair continues to adorn many school staffrooms, hotels and even homes. *Right.* Three well-known designers on the Utility Furniture Design Panel: (*left to right*) Robert Gooden, Dick Russell and Gordon Russell.

> the trade, and to prohibit any other furniture whatsoever from being made. Come, come! That's pretty drastic, if you like. But needs must when the devil drives.[9]

Regarding the public, Russell felt the reduction in choice was not so serious as it first appeared: 'After all, there wasn't much freedom of choice before the war. Then you could have almost anything you liked except good design.' Chiltern was characterised by no-nonsense lines and panelled doors on carcase constructions. Hardwood was used throughout, although as plywood became unobtainable, experiments were made with such materials as hardboard veneered on each side. A strict control on prices operated: for example, a fireside chair in oak cost £2.9s.0d., a dining table in mahogany £5.15s.3d. Prior to the Chiltern range, as more and more homes were bombed and with marriages running at half a million per year, shoddy plywood furniture with cardboard sides and bottoms had been selling at three times pre-war prices.

Russell now recommended that a small panel of designers continue to modify the range, working to maximise variety according to ongoing materials supply. Somewhat to his surprise he was appointed chairman of the panel and the Cotswold Range evolved. Clinch perceived his own designs as 'common sense – nothing more', but some subtle styling became involved within the apparently austere variations to follow. The designs also had to suit manufacture by quite small firms, many larger ones having been given over to aircraft production. Consequently detailed and specific plans were drawn up. Even so Russell recalls seeing pieces in an East End shop, decorated with 'appalling carvings' to extract an extra few pounds from purchasers. Another shock for Russell was to be informed just before D-Day that softwood might have to be used. One wonders at the effect on the present-day vogue for stripped pine if this had happened.

Of other Utility products, pottery is worth noting, for although no strict specifications were laid down (other than prohibition of decoration!), Wedgwood responded with 'Victory Ware'. From Autumn 1942 the whole of production was turned over to art director Victor Skellern's white earthenware designs. These were ingeniously simple, allowing for ease of manufacture, durability, storage and cleaning. The DIA enthused:

> Good design – or the lack of it – has never been so apparent as it is under the new restrictions, and Wedgwood have come unscathed through the Utility acid test...

Yet once war was over the British public were to demonstrate their penchant for frills and frivolities. A major exhibition to celebrate the return to peacetime production elicited some telling opinions in a survey of visitors' preferences (see Chapter 3). Timber, however, was in short supply and Utility furniture continued in production until the early fifties. Further modification of design took place, exploiting manufacturing capacity and labour released from the war effort. By now Russell's team included Dick Russell, Eden Minns and Robert Gooden. But in September 1947, Gordon Russell left the Directorate of Utility Furniture Production to become Director of the Council of Industrial Design and to begin a new battle to raise standards of design.

THE COUNCIL OF INDUSTRIAL DESIGN

By 1943, it was becoming clear that Germany would lose the war, confronted with the massive resources of the world's two superpowers. Britain, although virtually exhausted, demonstrated that indomitable spirit which had carried her through the previous three years. The Board of Trade envisaged not only that industry would quickly transform from military to civilian production, but also that it would regain a leading international position. A sub-committee of the Department of Overseas

2.25 Utility designs continued to be manufactured for a few years in the post-war period. The *Diversified* range of 1948 followed earlier *Chiltern* designs, remaining essentially unchanged but with more subtle shaping and proportions in an attempt to retain public appeal. However, it never went into production, as pressure grew to free manufacturers from government controls.

Trade was now appointed to consider 'Industrial Design and Art in Industry', a title which reflected a transition in name and some still unresolved dichotomies. With Sir Cecil Weir as chairman, the twelve-man team included Kenneth Clark, Ernest Goodale, Francis Meynell and Josiah Wedgwood. They had the task 'to consider the place of design in post-war planning for industry with particular reference to export trade, and to recommend measures to ensure that the United Kingdom shall reach and maintain a leading position in the field of industrial art'.[10]

The resultant Weir Report implicitly acknowledged America as the world's leading manufacturer, and explicitly emphasised design as a major cause. Her rise in a twenty-year period was explained in terms of a five-fold increase in designers, critical consumers, and newer machinery. In contrast, British manufacturers, traders and consumers were felt to doubt the importance of design, necessitating a 'means of setting up and maintaining standards'. After endorsing the reports of the Pick Council, the sub-committee noted that 'we are adding to a long series of recommendations which so far have had no decisive influence'. In war, they could be more forcefully critical of peacetime neglect of their cause.

2.26, 2.27 Upholstered Utility furniture like this settee (*left*) inevitably did not stand the test of time as well as all-wood constructions such as wardrobes, chairs and tables. It makes an interesting comparison with the non-Utility chair (*right*), favoured by the public and frowned on by the CoID, although the subtlety of the difference was probably lost on the layman.

In view of this 'discouraging past history' they felt it their duty to suggest sufficient means of authority and financial backing, namely:

(a) the institution of a central body which shall act as an authority on design to be named the Central Design Council;

(b) the simultaneous action of the various industries, through cooperative action, in the formation of Industrial Design Centres.[11]

The first of these recommendations was to have a far-reaching effect, not only in this country but also abroad, where several industrial nations followed Britain's lead. For the time was fast approaching, argued Weir, that such an organisation was inevitable if the State accepted 'its responsibility towards design in itself, as an amenity for the consumer and an essential tool in our economic life'. If critics interpreted the Council as a censor of taste, so be it – the principle of discrimination already operated in museums, galleries and exhibitions anyway.

Having provided its rationale, the Report detailed constitution, composition, powers, finance and function. Bearing in mind the fate of previous attempts, these were of considerable importance and remained essentially unchanged, if inevitably curtailed, in the eventual Council.

First, the constitution: this would be an independent body of appropriately qualified individuals, appointed by the Lord President of the Board of Trade and resourced with a Secretary and secretarial staff of civil servants. Although relating to a number of government departments there might be 'considerable objections' to its being placed under control of one of these. Instead, executive powers were proposed, comparable to the Medical Research Council, the University Grants Committee or the Department of Scientific and Industrial Research. Finance would be a grant-in-aid, found to be most practicable in 'matters connected with the arts'. A sum of £20,000 was suggested plus a few additions – rather a derisory amount compared with manufactured exports of £400,000,000 before the war, but this was still 1943.

Composition would include leading designers, artists, manufacturers and 'large users of goods'. Government departments should be represented, but not as *ex officio* members. Appropriate sub-committees would perform functions such as reviewing articles of furniture purchased by the state. A man of talent was needed as chairman with a salary equal to that of a permanent secretary. He and members should resign at stated periods in order 'to keep a continual public confidence and contemporary attitude'. Clearly, Weir was proposing a team to contend with, working under strong leadership. If no more eminent than their forerunners, they were certainly less likely to be brushed aside.

Functions were clearly spelt out, in contrast to the Institute and Pick Council – criticised for being 'never clearly defined' and 'left vague'. The first was the need 'to establish and finance a Pavilion of British Industrial

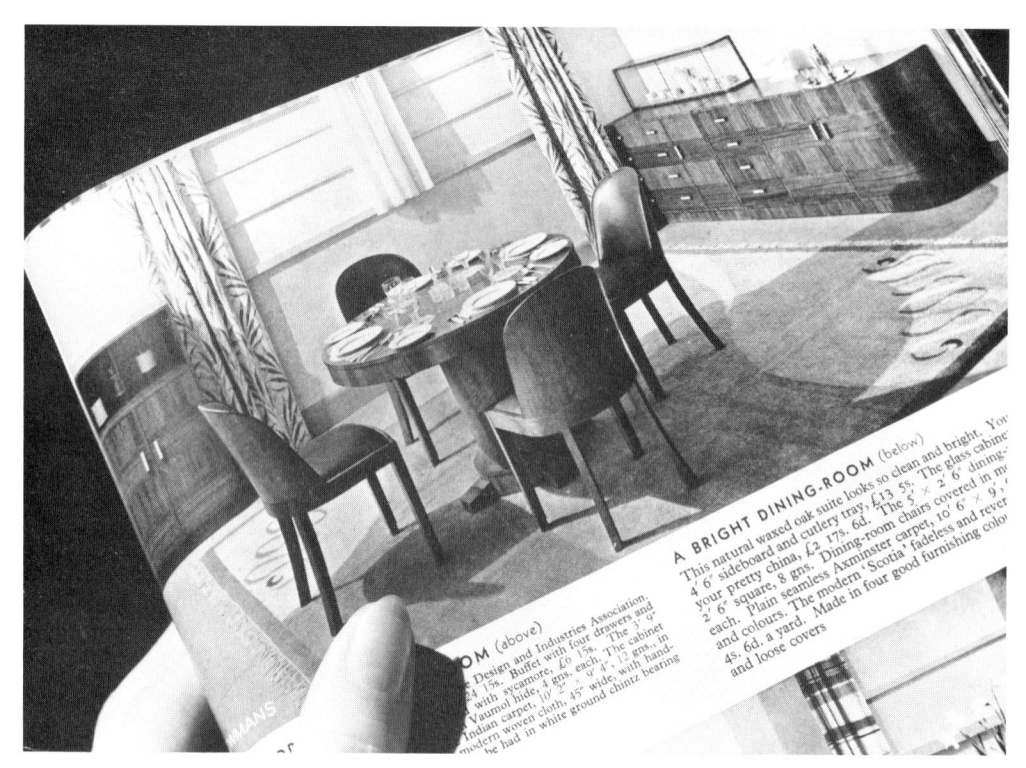

2.28 Between the extremes of chromed steel and Jacobean oak there evolved during the mid-war period what might be termed a 'popular plywood' style. This dining room range by Bowman Bros. was approved of by the DIA for its use of the new material. Plywood was, however, denied the Utility designers, being required for aeroplane production. Following the war, it was to be seen which of the earlier styles, if any, would come to dominate design and which the newly formed CoID would come to endorse.

Art as a permanent building with changing exhibitions'. A strong nationalistic attitude is reflected in the statement:

> If it is important to show the foreigner on his own territory the best in British industrial art, it is surely equally or even more important to be able to show him on our own territory, in one centre on a prominent site, a selection of the best that British can produce; side by side, possibly, with the best examples of the industrial art of other countries.[12]

Secondly, the Council would strictly select items for international exhibitions and for the 'Hall of Honour' at the British Industries Fair. More sweeping, all articles of furniture and decoration for the state would be vetted – to include embassies, legations and consulates where 'modern' styles would replace 'conventional'. Despite the experience with Utility furniture, these were ambitious functions for the Council to perform.

After considering powers which might overcome any problems the Report turned to Industrial Design Centres. Specialist centres were to assist industries to improve the design of goods at home and abroad, including furniture, jewellery, silverware, pottery, glassware, carpets, cotton and wool. Services would provide technical advice, market research and select displays. In addition, close links would be established with art schools for training designers. The Council would act as catalyst, but industry would finance and organise itself in the post-war 'push'. Both the Weir Report and subsequently the Council of Industrial Design devoted a substantial amount of attention to the centres.

Although the Report was concerned with industry and exports, before concluding it considered the vexed question of the Royal College of Art. An earlier Board of Education Report, Hambledon 1936, had suggested a substantial change of emphasis:

> The Royal College of Art should be reconstituted, and while continuing to provide for the teaching of fine art should take for its primary purpose the teaching of applied art in all its forms, with particular reference to the requirements of industry and commerce.[13]

Weir fully endorsed this recommendation but felt doubtful that the College could gain the confidence of industry without building status and prestige around the concepts of 'design' and 'designer' rather than 'art' and 'artist' (a problem which, of course, bedevilled the Institute and the Pick Council). Therefore, it proposed a change of name to 'The Royal College of Art and Design' with the Board of Trade itself involved with new training, staffing and curricula. Specifically, the Chairman of the Central Design Council was recommended to be Vice-Chairman of the governors.

The immediate result of the Report was, once again, nothing. But, as it neared completion the Boards of Education and Trade appointed yet another committee to inquire into 'ways and means of making art training more effective for practical purposes'. On the four-man team was Francis Meynell, and its terms of reference managed to include exports, as Weir had included education. Indeed, the Meynell–Hoskins Report confessed: 'While we do not disparage culture and educational reform, we wish here to emphasise the new, urgent and still largely unsuspected exigencies of commerce – plain and coloured.'

Subsequently, after praising America's discovery of 'eye appeal' for a vast array of goods, Meynell–Hoskins in turn endorsed Weir, adding valuable riders such as the need to consult the Scottish Office, supervision of the National Register and further rationalisation of the maligned Royal College to 'The Royal College of Design'. As an envoi it suggested 'the whole subject be discussed with the Minister of Reconstruction'. Francis Meynell describes the ensuing discussion with the Minister and his request for a 'strong Design Council':

> I waited on him in his charming but fragile office in Richmond Terrace, Whitehall. He was at his most Lordly and assured, I at my most diffident. My mission was of great future importance for British industry, but a difficult one to justify while the war still dominated the scene. I was in the middle of my first 'ers' and 'ums' when a 'doodle' [flying bomb] alert sounded. We instantly obeyed the official instructions – and our own instincts – to take the nearest available cover. Down we went under Wootton's table, he still the Lordly Minister, I his suppliant. Then came an 'imminent' followed by the crash of a nearby bomb. When the 'all-clear' sounded we arose from our head-to-head posture on an equality, two frightened men. All was easy after that. Wootton promised a recommendation of our plan to the Cabinet. It was accepted.[14]

Parliament debated the matter on 19 December 1944. 'Industrial Design (Appointment of Council)' fell between such pressing concerns as 'British Prisoners of War (Conditions, Far East)' and 'Arms Surrender, Belgium (British Military Action)'. Consequently questions were brief and to the point:

> Mr John Dugdale: Has the President of the Board of Trade, having regard to the importance of design in post-war planning for industry, taken steps to encourage good design in British industry?
>
> Dr Hugh Dalton: Yes, Sir. I have appointed a Council of Industrial Design to promote by all practicable means the improvement of design in the products of British Industry. I have also appointed, after consultation with my Right Hon. Friend the Secretary of State for Scotland, a Scottish Committee of the Council. I am glad to say that Sir Thomas Barlow has consented to become Chairman of the Council and Sir Steven Bisland, Chairman of the Scottish Committee. Industries will be invited to set up Design Centres to study and encourage the improvements of design of their own products. The Government propose to make financial grants to these Centres on the recommendation of the new Council. Provision will be made for the expenses of the Council and for the grants to the Design Centres in the Estimates to be introduced this Session. I am circulating in the Official Report a list of the members of the Council and of the Scottish Committee, and a copy of a letter which I have addressed to the Chairman defining the functions of the Council.
>
> Mr Tom Driberg: Can the Right Hon. Gentleman say whether practising designers will be represented on that Council – for instance, the Society of Industrial Artists?

2.29 Superficially similar to the Anglepoise, but technically and aesthetically at the opposite end of the design spectrum, this electric table lamp with imitation drips of candlegrease epitomised the popular taste which 20th-century design organisations campaigned against.

> Dr Dalton: Nobody is represented in the strict sense, but I have, in fact, put several practising designers on the Council.

Finally, a Council had been appointed, its functions defined and finance provided. Design Centres, designers and Scotland were also included. And one of the practising designers was Gordon Russell who soon, as Director, was to take the helm and steer the Council on its future course.

*Letter from the Rt Hon. Hugh Dalton, P.C., M.P.
To Sir Thomas Barlow, K.B.E.*[15]

Board of Trade,
Millbank, S.W.1.
19th December, 1944

My dear Sir Thomas,

I am very glad that you have felt able to accept my invitation to become the first Chairman of the Council of Industrial Design. Now that the Council has been appointed and is ready to start work I think it will be useful to you if I set out, in some detail, the tasks which I propose that it should undertake.

The purpose of the Council is to promote by all practicable means the improvement of design in the products of British industry. Its main functions will be

(a) to encourage and assist the establishment and conduct of Design Centres by industries, and to advise the Board of Trade on the grant of financial assistance to these Centres;

(b) to provide a national display of well-designed goods by holding, or participating in, exhibitions and to conduct publicity for good design in other appropriate forms;

(c) to co-operate with the Education Authorities and other bodies in matters affecting the training of designers;

(d) to advise, at the request of Government Departments and other public bodies, on the design of articles to be purchased by them, and to approve the selection of articles to be shown in United Kingdom Pavilions in international exhibitions and in official displays in other exhibitions; and

(e) to be a centre of information and advice, both for industry and for Government Departments, on all matters of industrial art and design.

The functions of the Design Centres, whose activities the Council will co-ordinate, will be:

(a) to study the problem of design in relation to the products of the particular industry;

(b) to collect and make available to the industry information relating to changes in public taste and trade practice in home and overseas markets and to hold exhibitions both at home and overseas;

(c) to conduct and encourage research and experiment in the design of the products of the industry;

(d) to co-operate with the Education Authorities and other bodies for the training of designers and in the provision of special equipment, prizes and grants, and to arrange factory visits and training in factories for art students.

Grants to Design Centres will be made by the Board of Trade, after consulting the Council, on a similar basis to that adopted by the Department of Scientific and Industrial Research for Research Associations.

The Council will make an Annual Report on its activities, which will be presented by the President of the Board of Trade to Parliament.

I am confident that under your leadership the Council will become firmly established and, by promoting in British industry a real appreciation of the importance of design, will play a vital part after the war in stimulating the sale, at home and overseas, of a wide range of goods of which we can all be justly proud.

Yours sincerely,

(Sgd.) HUGH DALTON,

Sir Thomas D. Barlow, K.B.E.,
    1 Wimpole Street, W.1.

DESIGN 46

**A SURVEY OF BRITISH INDUSTRIAL DESIGN
AS DISPLAYED IN THE 'BRITAIN CAN MAKE IT' EXHIBITION
ORGANISED BY THE BRITISH COUNCIL OF INDUSTRIAL DESIGN**

3.1 Souvenir catalogue of the 1946 'Britain Can Make It' exhibition. A white dove signifies the return to peacetime conditions. Twenty-seven informative articles discuss design in a variety of fields, with a witty conclusion by George Bernard Shaw.

−3−
BRITAIN CAN MAKE IT

INTRODUCTION

Following the Second World War, the new Labour Government immediately decided to hold a major exhibition of consumer goods and asked the fledgling Council of Industrial Design to take charge. The purpose was to demonstrate to the world the quality of British design and to raise public morale. It also provided a unique opportunity to arouse general interest in design and, through a Mass Observation survey, evaluate public taste. The Council's Scottish Committee, too, was to have its own exhibition. Despite a shortage of manufactured goods, particularly for home markets (leading to jibes of 'Britain Can't Have It'), both exhibitions were a commendable start to the Council's activities.

SWORDS INTO PLOUGHSHARES

In the dark days of war, the heavy and indiscriminate bombing of Britain's industrial centres resulted in serious loss of civilian lives, homes and possessions. Industry, additionally starved of materials by U-boat blockade, had little opportunity to satisfy domestic needs. Silk, plywood, timber and steel were all requisitioned for parachutes, planes, bunkbeds and Bailey bridges, plus the thousand and one priorities of modern warfare. Even the official Utility scheme suffered severe restrictions imposed on materials, design and production.

A slogan popular at the time, which captured the nation's dogged determination to win through, was 'Britain Can Take It'. Appropriately, the first post-war exhibition to celebrate the return to peacetime production was 'Britain Can Make It' – and the newly formed Council of Industrial Design found itself charged with responsibility for its organisation. Although something of a surprise this was, of course, in keeping with the second of its five specific functions, 'to provide a national display of well designed goods by holding, or participating in, exhibitions'.

As the first major venture of the Council the exhibition was an overwhelming success. Indeed, in retrospect, it is hard to imagine any display of 5000 assorted goods in immediate post-war Britain being a failure. Hugh Casson recalled that the public had 'an appetite so

3.2 The old makes way for the new. 90,000 square feet of the Victoria and Albert Museum are temporarily given over to post-war design.

soured and starved and sharpened by coupons and utility goods, building licences, bomb damage, tension and fatigue, it was almost manic, frightening the wits out of that year-old baby, The Council of Industrial Design'.[1]

The 'year-old baby' had moved to its new home at Tilbury House, Petty France, in May 1945 with a full-time staff of ten, and by the following March this had grown to over a hundred. Included were secretarial, clerical and junior civil service grades, but more significantly, over a third were temporary exhibition administrators who in turn controlled approximately 200 shift workers. In addition there were the Council Members themselves, eighteen in England, twelve in Scotland, many being eminent designers and industrialists with relevant knowledge and contacts to promote the exhibition.

Hugh Dalton had done a characteristically thorough job in setting up the CoID under a wartime government. Indeed, both his letter to Sir Thomas Barlow, the Council's Chairman, spelling out its functions, and his speech to the inaugural meeting were proudly printed in the 1945 Annual Report. But on 26 July Britain's first majority Labour Government took office with Clement Attlee, Churchill's wartime coalition deputy, as Prime Minister and Hugh Dalton as Chancellor. In the latter's

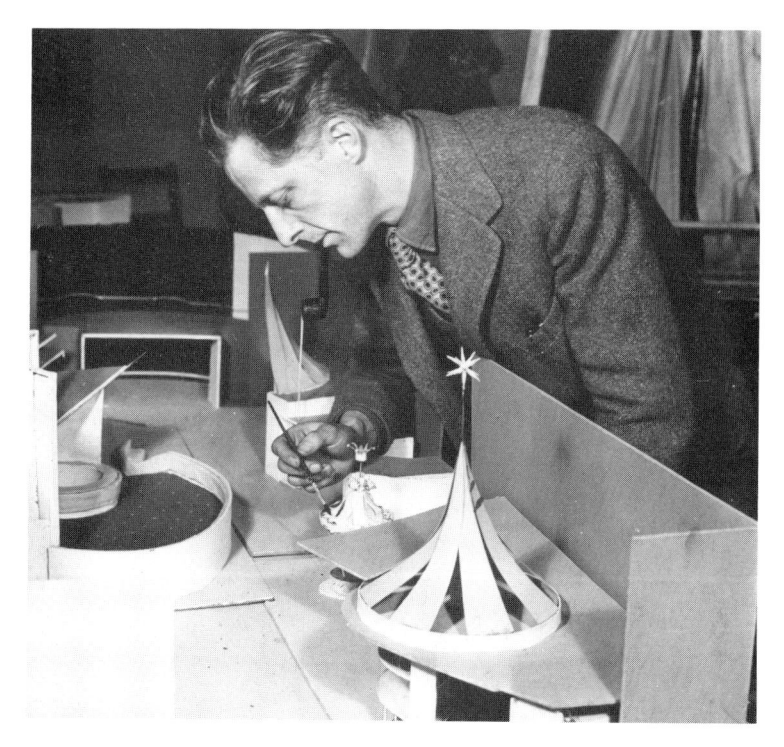

3.3 Chief Exhibition Designer James Gardner putting the finishing touches to a model of 'Britain Can Make It'.

place, to the Board of Trade, went Sir Stafford Cripps – happily an enthusiastic amateur woodworker. Within hours he had promoted the exhibition, delegated responsibility to the CoID, and granted an extra £200,000 plus to their budget.

The primary purpose was to demonstrate the quality of post-war British industrial design and stake a claim to world leadership in the field. For the government the propaganda emphasis was on production, for the Council on design, but the two were wholly compatible and one enhanced the other. A dramatic title 'Swords into Ploughshares: British Goods for the New Age' was quickly abbreviated to a more manageable 'Britain Can Make It', following the first meeting of the Exhibition Policy Committee. This suggestion came from S. C. Leslie, Director of the Council, who credited the idea to Miss Goodwin, their librarian. Permutations on the title theme were to be endless. *Architectural Review*,[2] characteristically a stern and informed critic, asked the question, 'Is it really worth making?' More relevant to the commodity-deprived public was 'Britain Can't Have It', in effect reversing the morale-boosting intent when they discovered that many goods were not yet available.

It was to be through the unstinting efforts of Leslie and his team in the face of innumerable obstacles that success was achieved. Even a suitable

3.4 King George VI declares 'Britain Can Make It' open on 24 September 1946. Prime Minister Clement Attlee, whose Labour Government had sponsored the exhibition, is seated in the left foreground. Behind the Queen can be seen James Gardner with Exhibition Manager Dudley Ryder on his left. In the background the Quiz booth awaits the public to test their tastes against those of eminent designers.

site was initially unobtainable, the possibility of Earl's Court having been abandoned. Eventually, part of the Victoria and Albert Museum was restored to its pre-war glory, absorbing London's entire supply of new glass in the process – an interesting parallel to 1851 when the Crystal Palace accounted for a quarter of the whole of Britain's output.

The twin themes of war and restoration were skilfully exploited for the exhibition, with wartime industrial achievement offering the context for the contemporary display. From 1939 to 1945 the factory floor had been a forcing bed for day-to-day research into new materials and techniques to match the ingenuity of Germany. Opportunity was now taken to rally the country to a further, if all too familiar, problem:

> The threat of national extinction provided the impetus for our war achievements. In the face of yet another threat – the threat to our overseas trade – industry is maintaining this impetus, freed from aerial attack, reinforced in spirit and body by the men and women returning from the forces.[3]

3.5 Massive crowds gather outside the Victoria and Albert Museum to welcome their Majesties and enter the exhibition. Until the final hour of the final day lengthy queues were to stretch along the Cromwell Road to see the displays of post-war goods.

A fixed circulation route, about one third of a mile in length, led the public 'from war to peace' and the full range of consumer goods planned for post-war production. These had been painstakingly selected from 20,000 articles, submitted by 3385 manufacturers. Some seventy to eighty designers, working under the supervision of Chief Exhibition Designer, James Gardner, and Consultant Architect, Basil Spence, were responsible for arranging them into sub-sections and groupings. Together this team represented Britain's leading display talent, including many younger men direct from related wartime experience such as utility design and camouflage. Many had been employed by the Ministry of Information†, both to design posters and to form an Exhibitions Unit publicising campaigns such as 'Dig for Victory' and 'Make Do and Mend'.

---

† Variously called 'The Ministry of Malformation' and 'The Mystery of Information' this nevertheless had proved to be a powerful foil to Dr Goebbels' Ministry of Propaganda, with some technically quite brilliant and subtle work.

3.6, 3.7 *Above.* One of the many novel display techniques in 'Shop Window Street'. Millinery emerges from a giant hatbox designed by D. Stuart-Bell. *Below.* Dress fabrics draped effectively from 'bird in flight' and 'tree women' whose fingers stretch like branches. Designed by Raoh Schorr.

3.8, 3.9 *Above.* Robert Gooden's elegant Sports Display achieves gaiety without the vulgarity associated with the British at play. *Below.* A corner from 'Things for Children' showing groups of toys assembled by Peter Bicknell to delight young visitors.

3.10 The continuing shortage of timber led to post-war experiments with Utility aluminium furniture. In general this did not meet with public approval, although the Ernest Race chair was a notable exception. Shown above are his chair and metal cabinet. The lamp is the famous Best Lite designed in 1930.

As an introduction, twenty domestic articles were shown against a vivid background of bomb-shattered London, picked out by beams of light, reminiscent of the Blitz. Each had evolved from wartime technology and was shown side-by-side with its origin. For example, a saucepan appeared next to the exhaust stub of a wrecked Spitfire, with an explanation of how a new refractory process had extended its life from ten to 2000 hours – incidentally striking a chord for those housewives who had formerly sacrificed their pots and pans to provide metals for Spitfires.

The route then led along 'Shop Window Street' which seemingly stretched away beneath a dark-blue sky, charged with a faint afterglow of sunset. The many novel display techniques employed in this section were under the personal control of Gardner himself. Small toys, for example, were displayed on a fourteen-foot-high revolving spiral roundabout and a miniature theatre was peopled with soft toys and dolls.

The path continued through room settings reminiscent of Dorland Hall. For additional interest, the designers had been given imaginary families around whom to focus attention. Nicolas Bentley provided the cartoon illustrations and John Betjeman the commentary. With an element of class consciousness, the settings included such attention to detail as bedrooms labelled 'Working class with double bed' or 'Middle

3.11 The Radio Section display. Designed by Clive Entwistle, it included one of the coveted products of the exhibition, namely a television receiver showing marked styling similarities to radios and gramophones of the time, with their richly veneered cabinets.

class with twin beds'. In keeping with the Council's function of advising official bodies on design, several fully equipped offices and a schoolroom were also included. The emphasis throughout was on new materials and designs, and so, apart from the 'working class kitchen', Utility design was relegated, whenever possible, to another area of the exhibition. Passing such attractions as dress fabrics draped from winged horses in flight, the wonders of television and a tea lounge imaginatively if incongruously disguised as a gypsy encampment, the route led to the central feature, that of women's fashions, occupying nearly a quarter of the floor space. Here the autumn and winter collections of London's leading couturiers stood on a complex revolving stage 25 feet high.

Other sections to follow, competently and often no less spectacularly displayed, included men's clothing, travel goods, sports equipment and gardening tools – designs for which Britain deservedly retained an international reputation for excellence. Robert Gooden's sports display was acknowledged to be the most sophisticated of the whole exhibition, managing to achieve gaiety without the vulgarity which so often characterises the British at play. Finally there was a display of Utility furniture as this was still planned for production for several more years and was inextricably linked with the Council through Gordon Russell.

3.12–3.16 Examples from 'The Designer Looks Ahead': *Above.* 'The super streamlined cycle' by Allen Bowden. *Below.* 'The future taxicab' by Milner Gray. *Above centre.* Portable electric sewing machine by F. H. K. Henrion and J. W.

In addition, the Council lost no opportunity to publicise its own work and that of the designer. The concept of 'design', as opposed to 'industrial art', as a unifying theme hardly then existed in the public consciousness. No fewer than four specialist displays were provided: 'Great British Designers', 'The Council of Industrial Design', 'What Industrial Design Means' and 'The Designer Looks Ahead'.

Woods. *Above right.* 'The Wingsail Catamaran' by Wells Coates. *Below.* 'The air conditioned bed', by F. C. Ashford.

The first offered an historical perspective on individuals such as Chippendale, Adam and Mackintosh who in their own times would have been described as architects or craftsmen. Due acknowledgement was also made to other institutions ranging from the City Livery Companies of the twelfth century to the Design and Industries Association of the twentieth. For itself, this being the starting point, little more than a

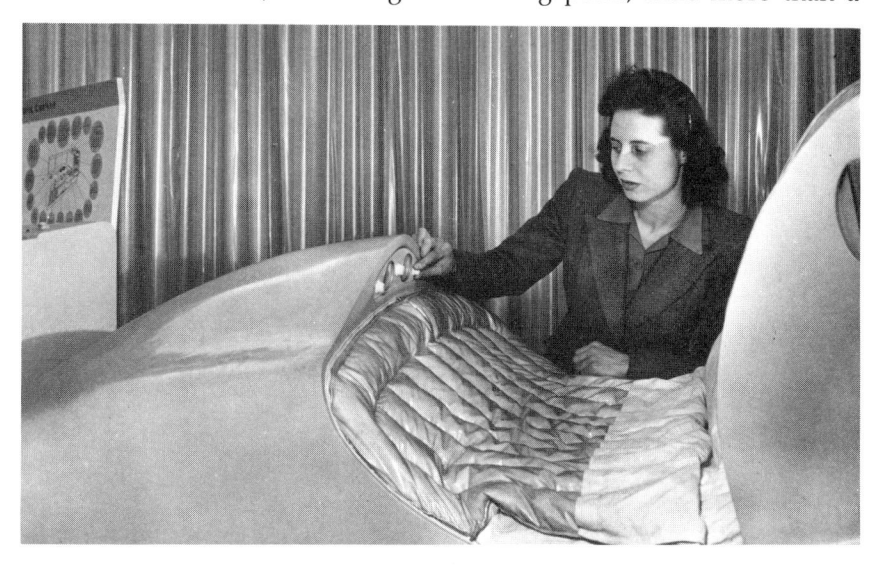

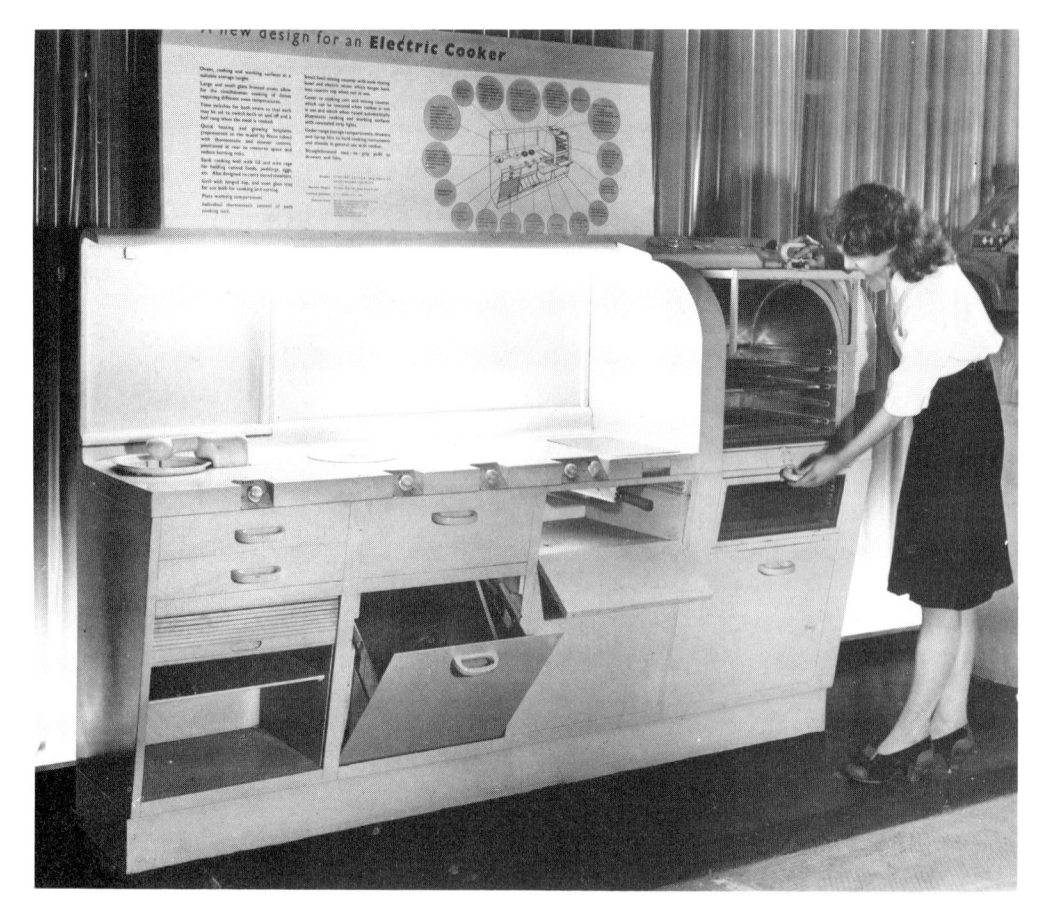

3.17 Kitchens and equipment which are today taken for granted aroused considerable interest. Milner Gray and William Vaughan's prototype cooker has units for grilling, boiling, simmering, toasting and 'heating canned goods'. Automatic timers and a food-mixer are added attractions.

manifesto and future programme of services to industry, albeit an optimistic one, could be offered. But for 'the meaning of design' a vivid demonstration was conceived under the direction of Misha Black and his associates from the newly formed Design Research Unit. With the theme 'Birth of an Egg Cup', the total process of industrial design was enacted only to be weakened perhaps by the peculiarly mundane choice of object. A witty poem concluded the display with:

> So you see designing me
>
> Is as tricky as can be:
>
> A thousand other problems lie
>
> In every object you may buy.

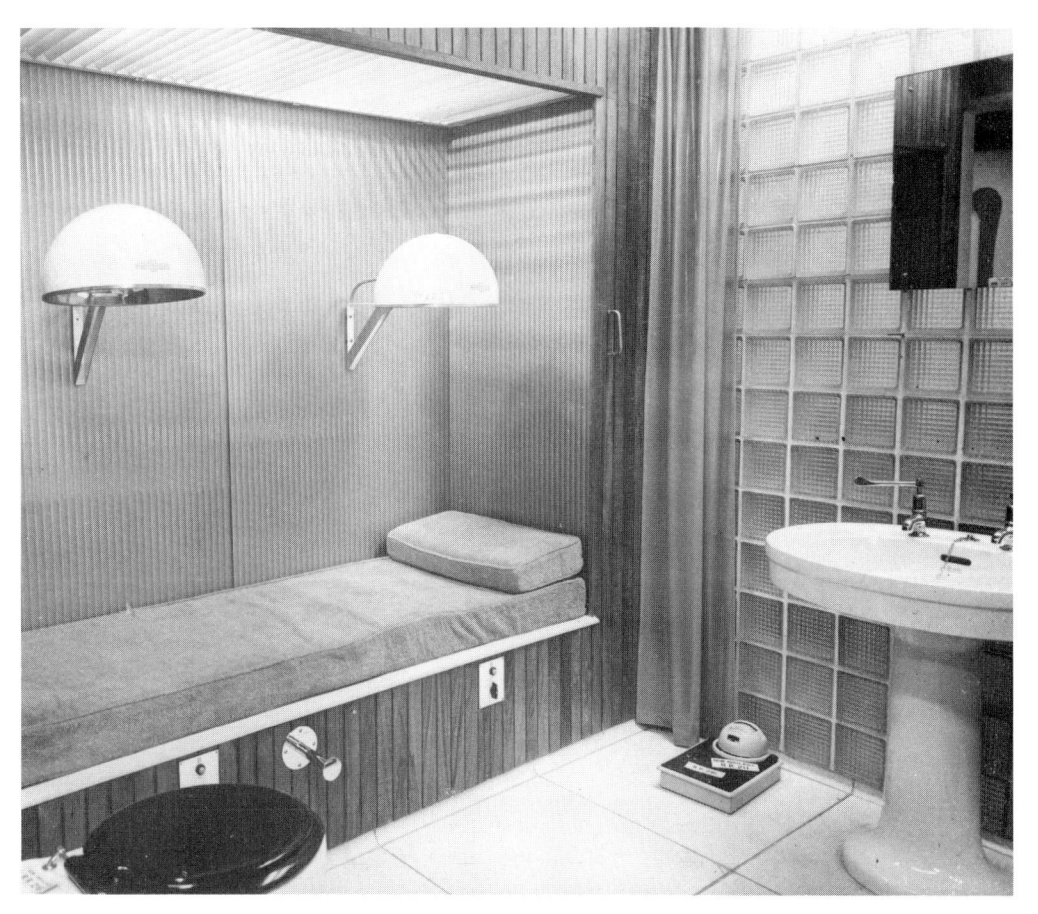

3.18 This luxury bathroom designed by Clive Entwistle was a Hollywood dream for most visitors. One recess is for the bath, the other as shown is for the 'artificial sunbathing couch'. The low-level W.C. had a matching bidet, thought by most people to be a badly designed lavatory!

On completing the set route the public were treated to an imaginative display of futuristic projects whereby commissioned designers projected technical trends five to twenty years ahead. In retrospect, their lightweight portable sewing machine and interplanetary space ship seemed well on target. Indeed the only feature which now dates these products is 'streamlining'. The taxicab had many details to be seen on modern cabs, while the bicycle had a pressed metal frame similar to today's mopeds. However, Wells Coates's catamaran still seems innovatory nearly forty years later and air-conditioned beds exist only in the dreams of inventors! Such projects could be contrasted with the more advanced features of the furnished rooms, including sunbeds, television sets, food mixers, automatic cookers, bidets and bathroom scales.

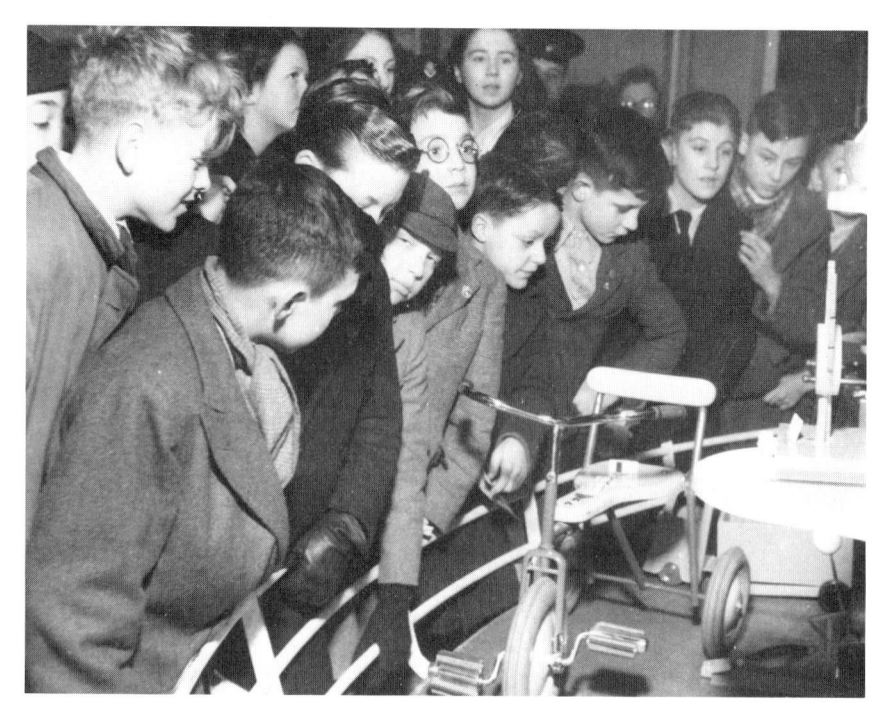

3.19 A generation of children, raised in wartime, gaze in wonder at the lavish display of toys.

PUBLIC TASTE

That the exhibition would be a complete success was never in doubt. It was opened by the King and Queen and attended by the Prime Minister and 1,432,546 visitors. The Council quickly had to extend the closing date from October to November and eventually to the end of December. Unofficial estimates of orders were up to £50,000,000 from British and foreign trade visitors. If this colossal figure could not be proved, many others could – for the Council had commissioned Mass Observation, the excellent forerunner of today's market research organisations. Not only did this provide specific information on 'Britain Can Make It', it offered a fascinating insight into public taste and habits in the mid-forties†.

Any exhibition of design should itself be well designed. But in this case, so outstanding were the Council's settings that they put many goods to shame. Despite this overall success, it came as something of a shock to discover two out of three visitors did not know who had organised the

---

† Fifteen field investigators were employed and carried out 2523 valid interviews, both formal and informal. Of yet more interest they made records of about 1000 overheard comments and casual conversations.

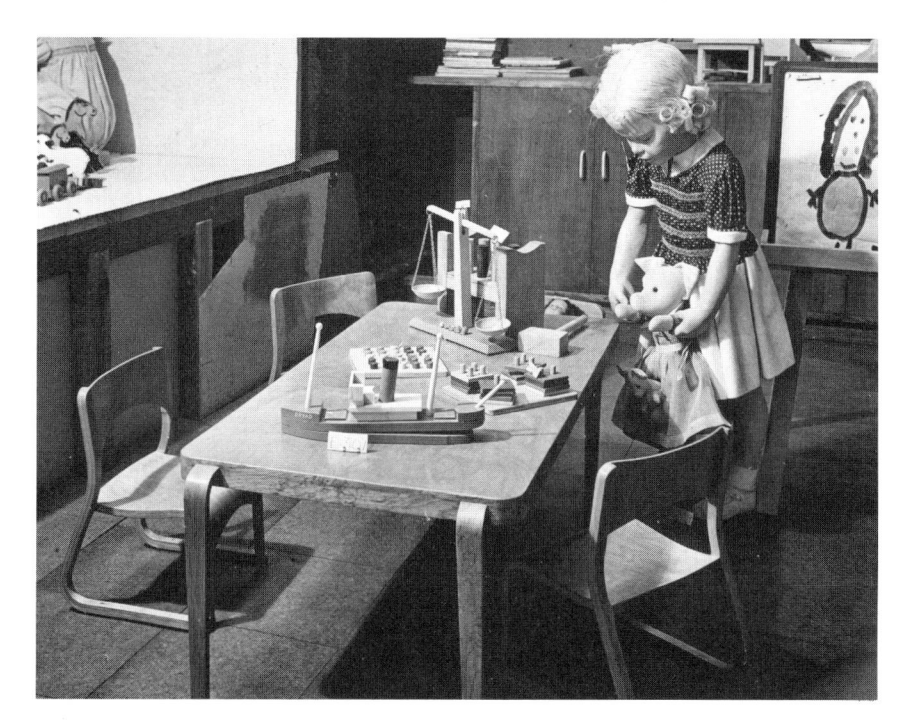

3.20 Ralph Tubbs's well-resourced nursery school reflects the ideals of the new Labour Government. But not all furniture was as sturdy as these designs by Educational Supply Association. One boy commented of another display, 'We'd soon smash those desks up.'

exhibition, and of those who said they did know, only two in seven were correct! The majority of criticisms, in fact, were directed not at the displays, nor the designs, but at the facilities – or lack of them. In its enthusiasm, the Council had overlooked the point that the British public are seemingly more concerned with toilets and tea bars than with design. To be fair, many had travelled long distances and queued several hours, and so justifiably spent 16% of their time meeting basic human requirements. One family from Manchester became faint half-way through and wrote to complain 'those who can last out can truthfully say, "Britain can TAKE it"'.

The queue itself was a typical British phenomenon, stretching far down the Cromwell Road until the final hours of the final day. Rather than taken to be a deterrent, this was seen as part of the entertainment, something to be enjoyed, complete with street musicians. Many Londoners did actually go only as an alternative to the cinema, but, on leaving, the majority said they would recommend their friends to follow.

Overwhelmingly, the main centre of interest was the furnished rooms, followed by women's fashions and then fabrics and furniture. Correspondingly, women's dresses and furniture were two aspects most disliked by

3.21 Rear view of the Race chair BA/3, showing its careful design and construction. Having gained experience in the wartime aircraft industry, Race skilfully combined die-cast aluminium, bonded plywood, latex foam and a variety of coverings to overcome public prejudice against metal furniture.

people questioned on leaving. In particular, exception was taken to a spindly-legged sideboard – a reaction unfortunately unheeded by designers, for this became an unsatisfactory characteristic of the New English style to be propagated in years to come. Another surprise for the

CoID was the lack of interest in Utility furniture; few people looked at the display and fewer still commented favourably. Unreasonably, it had acquired a reputation for flimsiness and poor quality. A typical comment was: 'It's a damn shame that these young people setting up home have to deal with this sort of furniture. Because in ten years' time it won't be worth a farthing.' The trend, it seemed, was as much away from wartime austerity as towards a specific style. The only design feature which was universally condemned, was the use of aluminium which was regarded as cold and unnatural: 'I do not like the steel stuff. I wouldn't have known that was a sideboard – looks more like a 'fridge to me'.† And yet, one of the most successful designs of the whole exhibition was to be the Race cast-aluminium chair. Not surprisingly television sets in their lavishly veneered wooden cabinets were coveted items, although their screens were relatively small by today's standards.

Within the furnished rooms the kitchens were the most popular, particularly amongst unskilled workers for whom the miner's kitchen was the most desirable of all. In retrospect, these were the only designs which might conceivably be transferred into today's catalogues and a fortune might have awaited any Council official who correctly interpreted Mass Observation's findings two decades before Hygena! Sadly, although the majority of visitors wished to own items, only a minority believed they would ever do so: 'Wish we'd a sink like that – a blinkin' dream.' Reminiscent of Dickens's Mr Crumpet, many confessed they now realised how shabby their own homes were. Ironically, of only two 'crank letters' received, one accused the Council of using the display to mislead 'Froningers' that the British were living in comparative comfort:

> Saw what you declare is a miner's home. In our opinion you are a lot of f...... liars. We had to walk half a mile to get water!
> Signed Pratt of Monte Cristo

Some of the reactions no doubt did baffle upper-middle-class civil servants, company directors and army colonels prominent on the Council. For example, bidets were mistaken for lavatories and universally criticised as such, abstract paintings were roundly abused in contrast

---

† Because of the large amount of scrap left from the war, aluminium was increasingly considered as a substitute for wood. For several years it was used in such furniture as chairs, kitchen cabinets and beds, and often for utility designs.

3.22 Packaging design was a major feature of 'Britain Can Make It', although less so of 'Enterprise Scotland'. The introduction to the former showed how great-grandmother went shopping to contrast with the contemporary displays. The Scots were accused by a critic of still preferring 'a good piece of plain brown paper and a bit of string'.

to figurative ones, and a docker's wife approved the design of plastic kitchen cabinets because 'they do keep the mice out'. A commendable educative move adopted by the Council was 'Design Quiz' in which the public had to place three designs in rank order, compared to a panel of experts. But in the case of an upright chair, 94% disagreed (with some justification) with the experts!

At the same time there was clearly an increased consciousness of design among the public. Although the term was not otherwise in general use in the forties, it appeared in one third of the comments in the exhibition, the simplest reaction being of the kind, 'I liked the china. We loved the design.' In this sense it was a term of general commendation, referring to an overall visual impression.

A few people, however, used it almost as a term of criticism: 'I rather thought the whole exhibition was over-designed' and 'some of the stuff's too arty – as if the designers wanted to show off how clever they were'. A reassuring number of people felt their taste had been altered, possibly not radically, but rather through the planting of new ideas. There was a trend towards some degree of ornamentation in all sections – in the words of Mass Observation: 'It is the simple delight of being able to get again twopenny coloured as well as the onepenny plain.' Possibly this was not quite what the Council had in mind, but London retailers were already

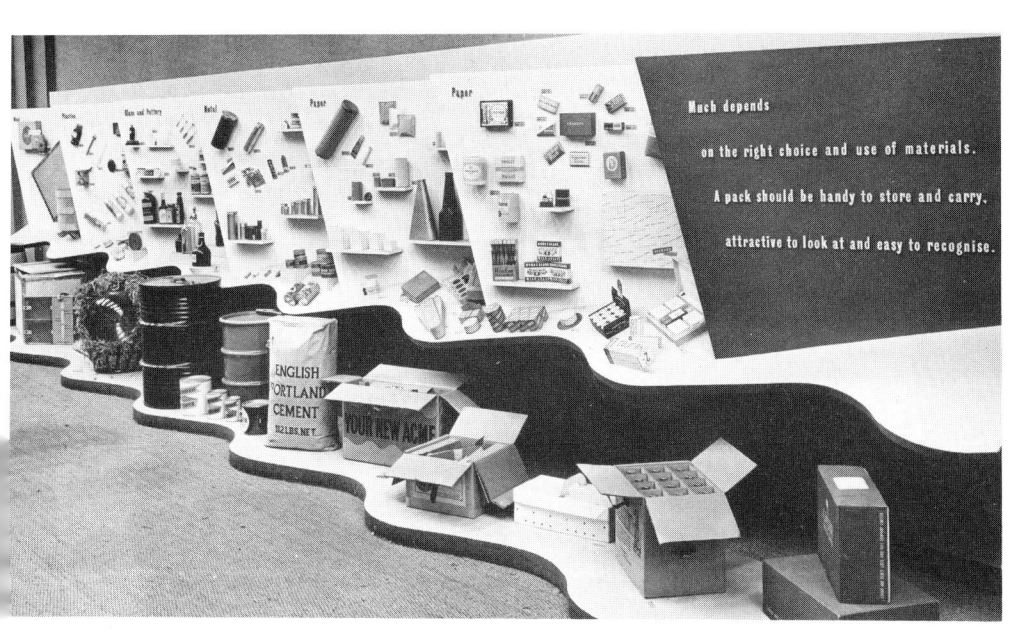

3.23 Many of the modern packages on display, particularly for protection, resulted from wartime experience gained 'in the field'. The above caption adds that 'A pack should be handy to store and carry, attractive to look at and easy to recognise.'

confirming public demand for newer and more exciting designs as a result of the exhibition. A reciprocal process of enlightenment–improvement was now under way.

Pockets of resistance, of course, did still exist. For many people 'pre-war' was evidently a Golden Age, equal to the Georgian or Victorian periods, whose products were not to be rivalled by those of the present. Even the children felt the bright, cheerful post-1944 Education Act school furniture was not up to Victorian cast iron and oak. In the words of one fourteen-year-old boy: 'We'd soon smash those desks up. They're like tissue paper.'

Yet everyone associated with the Council was justifiably delighted and John Gloag, already well known for his books on industrial design, was moved to write:

> ... it is without exception the finest exhibition that has ever been put on in this country or ever put on by British interests in any foreign country. With this we finally get rid of the Victorian hang-over in design.

Sir Francis Meynell, by then at the Cement and Concrete Association, wrote:

> Praise, praise, practically nothing but praise for the Exhibition; and from me nothing but delighted congratulations.

3.24 Instruments and sports equipment featured in both London and Edinburgh exhibitions. The Sumlock Adding Calculator of 1946 was described as 'the only all British key driven full key-board adding calculating machine'.

Mass Observation's rather extended reports were later returned to Gordon Russell with a secretary's note: 'Sir Francis's comment is: they are as bad as MO reports always are and are returned glanced at – certainly not read!'

To a degree, Mass Observation's insights into public reaction may have been overlooked. Behind one seemingly innocuous conclusion lay indications of frustrations to come. This concerned Design Research Unit's attempt to explain the industrial design process. Public attention was riveted to a plastic moulding machine producing 3000 egg cups per day. But apparently this was the only *moving* feature in the whole exhibition and 'they watched it as they would a man drilling a hole in a road'. What the public failed to grasp was that this was only a single stage in the total process being demonstrated. The Council's statement that industrial design was 'a unity, a governing idea that owes something to creative design, something to the machine, something to the consumer and links them all together',[4] was still a long way from being achieved in 1946.

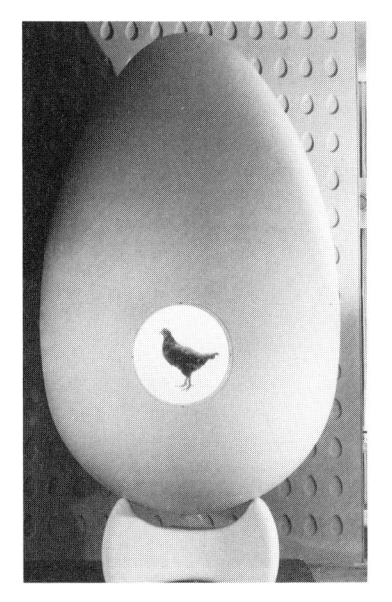

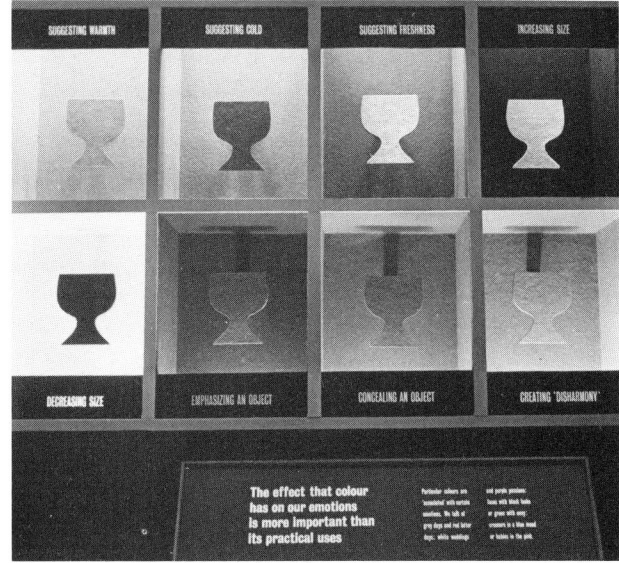

3.25–3.27 'Birth of an Egg Cup' by Misha Black introduces the layman to the process of design. A giant egg marks the display while captions explain such concepts as texture and colour: 'The texture of an object appeals to our sense of touch – our eyes anticipate how it will feel,' and 'The effect that colour has on our emotions is more important than its practical uses. Particular colours are associated with certain emotions. We talk of grey days and red-letter days: white weddings and purple passions: faces with black looks or green with envy: crooners in a blue mood or babies in the pink.'

3.28 The Ross Ensign was claimed to be a unique 'full view' camera offering a 'pre-view of the picture almost as large as the finished photograph'.

ENTERPRISE SCOTLAND

North of the border, the Council's Scottish Committee had been formed with a dozen members under the Chairmanship of Sir Stephen Bisland. However, suitable premises were not found until June 1945 when full-time staff were finally appointed and duties commenced. Initially, they worked in close cooperation with London, contributing in no small measure to the success of 'Britain Can Make It'. The decision not to take the exhibition to Edinburgh was therefore greeted with disappointment.

Happily, the committee was given the opportunity to stage its own 'Enterprise Scotland' in 1947 – a more practicable alternative enabling it to boast a diversity of products from forty industries. In total, 1000 manufacturers submitted 7000 goods; from these 3000 were selected by a weeding-out process, of necessity less drastic than London's.

If Scotland seemed relatively remote for an exhibition, publicity was suitably aggressive. Fiery Crosses†, for example, were despatched to all

---

† Traditionally a charred cross dipped in blood and carried around the Highlands as a call to arms.

3.29 Despite dramatic changes in camera and calculator design this pair of 1946 binoculars by Barr & Stroud of Glasgow would seem little dated forty years on.

quarters of the globe, travelling more than 80,000 miles, visiting twenty-six countries and crossing four continents. The timing was planned to coincide with the Edinburgh Music and Drama Festival when the city is flooded with visitors. Additionally, 'Shop Window Street' was quite literally so, with fourteen shops along well-trodden Princes Street holding complementary displays in their windows.

The main exhibition was held in the Royal Scottish Museum, in an area one third of that allocated in the Victoria and Albert. It was opened by the Duke of Gloucester and visited by the Queen, Princess Margaret, the Princess Royal and 456,000 subjects. Although not intended to be a trade exhibition, the emphasis was very much on 'Scotland Can Make It Too' and an estimated 1000 buyers from twenty-eight countries placed orders. Many availed themselves of the special Buyers' Service for contacting manufacturers, although figures were inevitably well down on 'Britain Can Make It'.

Four sections comprised the exhibition: 'Scotland Yesterday', 'The Country', 'Scotland Today' and 'Scotland Tomorrow' – themes which were to be developed later in the Festival of Britain. 'The Country' conveniently provided the setting for sports goods, travel goods, hotel equipment, tartans and souvenirs while 'Scotland Today' presented the products of industry in commodity groups or composite groups in Domestic Interiors. Additionally, 'Scotland Today' included a Textile Hall, Shipbuilding, Printing, Scientific Instruments and Tool displays.

Once again the imaginations of Basil Spence and James Gardner as Chief Planner and Chief Designer ensured a feeling of elation for the public emerging, none too quickly in Scotland, from an age of austerity. This was achieved by a sumptuous 'big top' effect within the lofty halls of the museum, using lavish quantities of woven material and all the bright lights of a fair. Again, so good were the settings, that the exhibits were in danger of being humbled by their surroundings. This was particularly so with some of the souvenirs, despite having being selected via a prize-winning competition.

Fortunately there were many products in which Scotland excelled, obvious examples being sports equipment such as golf clubs and fishing rods. Authentic Scottish tweeds and tartans naturally attracted attention, although the opportunity to create new designs in the manner of the French had not been taken – an indictment of her traditional industry's attitude to innovation. As in London, the major feature of Domestic Interiors attracted considerable interest, although reproduction Persian rugs in the first room raised the further problem of traditional designs plagiarised from other countries.

The excellent printing display was quite genuinely Scottish and included examples from Nonesuch Press, Sir Francis Meynell's own company which had so successfully bridged the gap from hand to machine production, rarely achieved in other industries. Commendably, the work of Schools of Art was in strong evidence and, indeed, the symbol for the Scottish Committee was designed by A. Imrie of Edinburgh College of Art, practising what so many reports to date had preached. In contrast the packaging display reflected a Scottish conservatism to the extent that one critic accused them of preferring 'a good piece of plain brown paper and a bit of string'. (This was unlike the London exhibition where modern packaging was imaginatively displayed. The need to transport supplies and munitions safely to theatres of war was yet another example of wartime experience influencing peacetime design.)

For a nation whose economy was inextricably linked with shipbuilding, even an exhibition emphasising consumer goods could not ignore some appropriate reference to a central feature of her industrial base which included many ancillary trades. In 1946 the United Kingdom launched more than half the world's shipping, with Scotland contributing 41%. Consequently, a display of skilfully executed models featured such export attractions as the world's largest tug. The illustrated exhibition handbook also included a photograph of the liner *Queen Elizabeth* in contrast to its frontispiece of a toy drum – both products at two extremes of the spectrum and highly vulnerable to foreign competition.

Walter Elliott M.P. was so impressed by the overall quality of Scotland's goods that he confidently stated that her people needed no further stimulus:

> Enterprise Scotland, therefore, in pressing upon the Scots the motive of design, may have the same sort of effect as that of recommending to a morphinomaniac the virtues of some new deliriant.[5]

However, there was always the lurking danger of complacency. Together the two exhibitions had demonstrated that 'Britain Can Make It' and 'Scotland Can Make It Too'. Whether they could redesign it was still open to question. For the time being full order books were reassuring. But farsighted Council officials knew a mammoth task lay ahead in convincing manufacturers of the importance of design, research and development. The burden of this responsibility was to fall in future on the Council's Industrial Division. Of 'Britain Can Make It', Noel Carrington claimed:

> Apart from the lift it gave to national morale, it had two important effects. It established once and for all the status of the industrial designer in modern civilisation; and it gave the Design Council a professional pride and confidence in its future.[6]

In the ensuing years both of these assumptions would be critically put to the test by reticent manufacturers.

4.1 Gordon Russell, furniture designer and manufacturer, DIA member and Chairman of the Utility Furniture Design Panel, became Director of the CoID in 1947 and evolved its future policy and structure.

−4−
INDUSTRIAL LIAISON

INTRODUCTION

During the post-war period, government agencies assumed increasing responsibility for industry and the economy. Consequently, the Council of Industrial Design became the principal organisation for promoting good design. For immediate progress to be achieved its most direct route was via manufacturers and designers. With the former, attitudes would have to be changed; with the latter, aptitudes developed. But in a period of austerity the Council, being what would later be termed a quango (quasi-autonomous non-governmental organisation) had to pursue a careful course.

In 1947, under the skilful Directorship of Gordon Russell, the CoID was reorganised into two principal divisions – Industrial and Information. The energies of the former were concerned with setting up industrial Design Centres according to Hugh Dalton's original brief. But being dependent upon the cooperation of manufacturers, little progress was achieved. However, the Council's national Survey and Stock List of good design, prepared for the Festival of Britain, became a valuable means of liaising with industry. In addition, new emphasis was laid on the professional training and employment of designers, particularly through the much maligned Royal College of Art whose students came to achieve noticeable successes. Gradually certain manufacturers began to accept that a conscious design content achieved by named designers could actually sell products.

DESIGN CENTRES FOR INDUSTRY

Despite having fought a second protracted and debilitating war, Britain in 1945 held a relatively superior industrial position to that of most other countries. She retained a reputation as provider of quality exports, boasted technological superiority over friends (excepting the United States) and foes alike, and held strong cultural links with many expanding export areas. In contrast to her principal competitors she had suffered no widespread destruction of industrial plant and no loss of territory. Britain's first majority Labour Government led a disciplined law-abiding

4.2 Panels of experts laid the foundations of industrial liaison when selecting exhibits for 'Britain Can Make It'. Shown is the panel for hand and garden tools: (*from left to right*) Noel Carrington, author on industrial design; P. S. Harding of George Harding & Sons; W. M. C. Campbell of The Royal Botanical Gardens; W. Allsworth of W. Allsworth and Sons; W. J. Bassett Lowke, toy manufacturer; J. L. Beddington of Coleman, Prentis and Varley; C. Bunyard of the CoID.

population who had inherited a powerful work ethic. But gradually the balance changed and the old enemies of antiquated equipment, lack of investment and technological complacency became a burden. Divisive class attitudes reinforced workers in blaming incompetent management, civil servants and politicians, and the latter in blaming irresponsible and destructive unions.

At the beginning of this period the Council of Industrial Design commenced activities. The planning of the 'Britain Can Make It' exhibition had, of course, occupied the Council's industrial liaison officers from autumn 1945 until spring 1947. However, unlike previous official bodies, 'to hold and participate in exhibitions' was only a secondary function. The first and foremost purpose was 'to encourage and assist the establishment and conduct of Design Centres'. Whilst other statements were general, this was specific. Consequently, the Council of necessity nailed its banner to this mast and gave pride of place to publicising all such progress in official reports.

At the time there existed but one example to justify such wholesale commitment: the Colour, Design and Style Centre. Founded in 1940 by Cotton Board Chairman, Sir Raymond Street, its function was to improve

4.3 Part of the CoID stand at the British Industries Fair, 1947, attempting to persuade industry that 'Design will conquer our export markets' and to 'Help us to build Design Centres'. Within the wall display are figures in national dress representing the many countries of the world to which British products might be exported in the post-war period.

design for both dress and furnishings. Appropriately, this was the industry which had so concerned Sir Robert Peel over a century before. As always the prime motive was to increase sales, particularly exports. But because costs were met by a levy imposed upon raw material, at first there was considerable opposition from the trade. In particular, big companies felt that smaller ones received disproportionate benefits for their contributions. Nevertheless, by 1946 all the essential ingredients of a Design Centre for textiles were in existence, including imaginative displays, co-ordination with other industries, a register of designers, a stock of foreign designs and a library of specialist books. Despite such a full programme, Michael Farr subsequently reported in his national survey:

> And yet, with all this activity in the centre of the industry, manufacturers are still producing hundreds of furnishing fabrics of poor, enfeebled designs. One wonders indeed just how much propaganda is needed before a general improvement in the design of cheap and expensive fabrics can be noted.[1]

The CoID's newly formed Design Centres Committee, under the chairmanship of Ernest Goodale, now proceeded to contact thirty different

4.4 Furniture typical of the post-Utility period, in production in 1949. The pre-war vogue for reproduction furniture had been resuscitated by manufacturers, to satisfy middle-class aspirations not entirely to the approval of the CoID or DIA. The Council's dry comment was, 'Whether or not the simpler lines of the Utility range have given the public a taste for something more in keeping with contemporary life remains to be seen.'

industries. Confidence came from the understanding that the Board of Trade would, on their recommendation, make 'substantial' financial contributions for the formation of any centre. In practice, under the Industrial Organisation and Development Act of 1947, grants were only to be made equal to the amount subscribed by that industry, for a trial period of three years. Consequently, for several years the Council found itself in lengthy discussions with Board of Trade industrial working parties which had been formed 'to strengthen the industry and render it more stable and more capable of meeting competition in home and foreign markets'.

As a result of the Committee's endeavours the *First Annual Report* optimistically listed: firm proposals for three centres (Rayon, Silk and Jewellery), active discussion on four more (Linen, Leather – including Boots and Shoes, Printing and Cast Iron), preliminary discussions on a further five (Aluminium, Pottery, Electrical Goods, Glass and Plastics) and finally a recommendation that one industry (Corsets) concentrate instead on setting up a school for the training of designers.[2] Of the firm proposals, two ironically were in competition with the centre already in existence and the final negative decision offered no more details.

Following numerous further meetings ranging from wallpapers to watches, only two centres had actually been established. Against this

4.5–4.7 Of Utility designs, ironically, it was the simplified Windsor chair that stood the test of time. The furniture industry, although the focus of considerable attention, was one of the last to be mechanised. *Above left*, the bending of yew bows for Windsor chair backs, and *right*, the machine at Plumridge Saw Mills, High Wycombe, which enabled twelve to be bent at once. Finished chairs continued to be assembled and packed by hand.

4.8 'Background to Design' exhibition, 1949, at the Rayon Design Centre, Upper Grosvenor Street. The furniture was chosen to show how a room in the house would have looked in the late eighteenth century and, indeed, still matched the interiors of many wealthy homes which retained original pieces. Regrettably they were often badly reproduced by post-war manufacturers.

limited progress, the Council bravely maintained 'we are led to believe, many individual firms are much more intensely concerned with the problem of design than formerly'.[3] But already the weakness of any official body, that of perceiving meetings as a precursor for action, was discernible.

The first of the two new centres had a lengthy title of 'The Design and Research Centre for the Gold, Silver, and Jewellery Industries'. This resulted from pressure by the Department of Scientific and Industrial Research for 'research' as well as 'design' – rather undermining the all-embracing concept of design which the Council wished to propagate. Despite the speed of establishment, not a great deal of credit could be apportioned to the trade. The Worshipful Company of Goldsmiths provided the premises but, because much of the funding came from the Jewellery and Silverware Council, which was to close down in 1952, activities were soon severely curtailed. Additionally, the centre found itself orientated towards handcrafts rather than industrial techniques, sometimes thinly excused as creating prototypes for mass production. It was to be some years yet before the dramatic revival and then the resurgence of these industries came about through influence from the Goldsmith's Company and the colleges.

The second and, strictly speaking, only other centre organised with CoID help was for the Rayon industry. This received joint support from the British Rayon Federation but, in contrast, carried out no research. However, it was initially housed in attractive premises near Grosvenor Square, offering an up-to-date collection of British fabrics for foreign buyers and a reference collection of foreign fabrics for British designers. More importantly it held small but exciting displays, including the work of students, in a convenient location for overseas visitors. Disappointingly, in 1952 this centre too closed down, only a limited function remaining at the Federation's own premises. A successful three-year trial period had proved no guarantee of continuation.

A third centre, the Crafts Centre of Great Britain, did commence in 1948, although, by definition, this was not an industrial Design Centre as originally conceived. Also the Scottish Committee was instrumental in setting up the Crafts Centre in Edinburgh where, because of the rise of tourism and decline of heavy industry, the emphasis was perhaps more justified.

By now it was becoming clear that all was not well on the industrial front. The Council's *Second Annual Report* had admitted that a position only 'a little along the road' had been reached and 'we cannot say that we are unconcerned by the fact that the programme has not yet developed

4.9, 4.10 A Design Centre for cast iron was proposed in 1946 but never opened. However, specialist bodies such as the British Coal Utilisation Research Association promoted developments in their own fields. Shown are two of the simpler fire surrounds from the Victorian and post-war periods. Eventually nostalgia and the energy crisis led to renewed demand for the former, which today are being reproduced in aluminium.

4.11, 4.12 The Design and Research Centre for the Gold, Silver and Jewellery Industries encouraged research and development. Above are the modest, though carefully conceived changes to a coffee percolator by F. H. K. Henrion for F. & F. Electrical Fittings, 1948. CoID comments of approval were, 'Note the flat lid for easy cleaning and storage, and the new type of handle. This handle fits every size hand and protects it against contact with the hot metal. It is fixed to the percolator in one place and is therefore easier to clean at the joint of the plastic grip and the metal bracket.' For manufacturers it was noted that now only four, instead of six rivets were required!

very far'.[4] Nevertheless, reference to Design Centres occupied more column-inches than any other subject, notwithstanding 'Britain Can Make It'. But the following year, any mention of Design Centres had been seriously curtailed. There was little to note beyond tentative references to 'hand-blown domestic glass-ware, carpets, and rubber-proofed clothing'. Finally, by the *Sixth Annual Report* no mention was made of Design Centres at all. More significant, the work of the Council's Information Division now took precedence over the Industrial Division. Publicity and propaganda were seemingly proving more productive than industrial liaison. Possibly the major industries were too amorphous for single centres to cope with, while specialist organisations and major companies felt they could adequately cope with research and development work themselves.

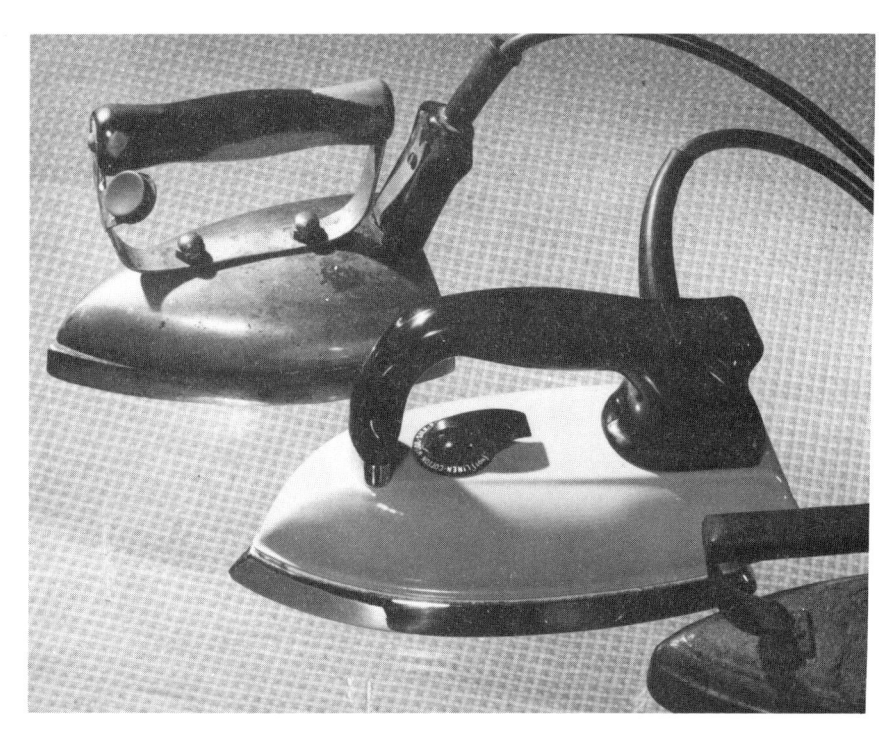

4.13 Another proposed Design Centre that never opened was for Electrical Goods. However, improvements and regulations were inevitable in such an important field. Illustrated is the evolution of the thirties electric iron to the post-war Morphy-Richards model. Acceptance of such designs on the CoID Stock List gradually became a means of influencing manufacturers.

GORDON RUSSELL

Born of long DIA experience, the Council from the start was well aware of the difficulties of liaising with industry. An early reference to 'Co-operation: the Fundamental Problems' expounded the impossibility of proving that 'improved design invariably means improved sales'. Having achieved official status, the Council had to face the 'lingering suspicions' of many industries:

> When a body – especially one with the Government crest on its notepaper – approaches them with a programme for the improvement of design, they assume that it comes on an assumption of superior knowledge, which the manufacturer has no reason to concede.[5]

Far from it, the Council argued. To provide expert knowledge on sixty different industries would be totally impractical and implausible. What it aimed to do was create goodwill, combat prejudice and convince manu-

4.14, 4.15 America pioneered many post-war furniture innovations, exploiting new technologies. Harry Bertoia's wire-mesh chairs mounted on steel rod frames and Charles Eames's moulded plywood seats are two examples. However, Eames's commercial use of moulded fibre glass (*below*) in 1948 laid the foundation for a significant British success by Robin Day.

facturers that the two halves of its own working motto 'Good design and good business' truly belonged together.

The Director responsible for implementing this policy was Gordon Russell. His predecessor, S. C. Leslie, had directed public relations at the wartime Ministry of Home Security and had been an ideal choice for liaising with both government and industry. Russell was one of the few individuals capable of replacing him, being most things to most men, at least in the field of design. He was a former infantry officer who had survived the First World War with honour and returned home to become a successful furniture manufacturer, gaining an international reputation. He was highly articulate on design matters and, as an active member of the DIA, had broadcast several talks and written many articles. Above all, he had considerable experience of liaising with industry as Chairman of the Utility Furniture Design Panel at the Board of Trade. Despite the sentiments of some visitors to 'Britain Can Make It', Utility furniture, as we have seen, offered a simple, well-constructed range at modest prices, and was one of the most successful domestic ventures of the war.

Initially, Russell found the Council facing criticism from several quarters. When his chairman, Sir Thomas Barlow, resigned, on grounds of ill-health, only to take up chairmanship of the District Bank, he felt even more vulnerable. Treasury critics in particular worried him because ultimately they held the purse strings. It was all very well, they argued, to subsidise or control industry in wartime, but it was unnecessary in peacetime. Should industry require a Council, then industry should pay for it. Unwillingness to do so meant industry did not need one:

> There was only a small group who thought a Council of Industrial Design a good idea, the majority regarding it as a waste of money. It is useful today to remember at the time no country in the world had set up such a body and backed it with an adequate government grant. There were people in the Treasury and the Board of Trade who argued that public money ought not to be spent on such a project.[6]

Russell, of course, realised that full order books were creating a false sense of security. But the post-war consumer boom would pass. The long, hard battle for improved design to stimulate home demand and exports would commence too late.

In characteristic style Russell prepared a policy report, as he had for the wartime Utility Furniture Panel. The first and foremost role must still be 'to offer a service to industry'. Paradoxically he had to acknowledge that 'Design Centres could not be set up without more preparatory work in the industries to be served'. Hopefully, the Treasury would not in

4.16, 4.17 *Left*. Mark Hartland Thomas, Head of CoID's Industrial Division, who conceived and implemented the Stock List (later called *Design Index*) of approved designs. *Right*. American designer Henry Dreyfuss, scanning *Design Index* during a visit to London.

future judge the Council too severely in this context. Russell then reorganised his main staff groupings into two divisions – Industrial and Information – to reflect his treatment of the problem as one of supply and demand. The former would stimulate supply of good design, the latter would create demand for it.

Two years later Russell prepared a further policy report reiterating the need to influence industry. The sellers' market, as predicted, was now passing and the export drive was more urgent than ever before. At the same time, pressure to reduce government expenditure threatened the Council's own future. It must be clearly seen supporting exports and 'showing the flag abroad'. Almost as an afterthought Russell added 'we must work towards the setting up of Design Centres, which was written into our original commission'.

The Head of the Industrial Division in this period was Mark Hartland Thomas, a talented architect and designer who was to be awarded the OBE for his work on the Festival of Britain Exhibition. Like Russell, he was a clear thinker on design matters and was attempting to come to terms with the Council's founding brief. In response to the Director's report he observed:

> ... the time has come for us to be frank with ourselves and realise that our original commission is no longer sufficient reason for doing something about Design Centres. It was a piece of bad constitution making to set up a Council like ours with such very wide terms of reference but with one specific preconceived commission, namely to set up Design Centres.[7]

Hartland Thomas felt that, apart from information and publicity (which, by definition, did not get close to the heart of industrial matters) the functions of Design Centres were unrealistic. The principal task of maintaining contact with Research Associations, interpreting their results to designers and in turn presenting designers' problems back to researchers, was impossible for 'a little man in a Design Centre'. Indeed, the centres had not been conceived with the real needs of industry in mind, but belonged instead to public relations, the consumer and the retailer:

> I submit that before we are called to task for not setting up any more Design Centres than the first two, we come out into the open and say that we have only set up two because we have found that it is not a good idea.[8]

Regarding future policy, Hartland Thomas felt that total absorption with, in turn, Design Centres, 'Britain Can Make It' and the ensuing Festival of Britain had diverted attention away from the Industrial Division itself. Post 1951, the Council had to consider if there was a meaningful role to play. Perhaps the answer was for 'all of us to go back into industry and carry on the good work at the point of manufacture'. Mark Hartland Thomas, Chief Industrial Liaison Officer, professed some sympathy with the General who immediately dismissed anyone termed a Liaison Officer!

As a former army officer himself, Gordon Russell took the philosophical view of his hero Marlborough, perceiving a command as more political than military. He was well aware of the need to steer a careful course wherever industry was concerned. To impose further Design Centres under the aegis of Development Councils would be unpopular because of the financial levies involved. In turn, this might undermine Board of Trade confidence in the Council's diplomatic ability. In keeping with his occasional tactic of L.S.D.L. – 'Let Sleeping Dogs Lie' – he quietly dropped the mention of Design Centres from Annual Reports.

> In such a situation little boats keep close to the shore and I repeated to my staff my determination to make friends wherever we could – or at the very least, not to make enemies.[9]

A NATIONAL SURVEY OF DESIGN

Following the proposed Festival of Britain a new industrial role would have to evolve. The problem was, how best to reach manufacturers without unduly rocking the boat. The answer came to Hartland Thomas while co-ordinating the choice of exhibits for the Festival itself. Earlier overtures had been made to manufacturers for 'Britain Can Make It' displays. Now an extensive national survey was taking place to discover new designs for the 1951 display teams to select from. Hartland Thomas realised the survey would be of little value without a systematic means of recording its findings. Consequently the Stock List, a pictorial reference library of annotated photographs and samples, was born. This was to develop over the years into the principal tool, both for the Industrial Division and for the Council itself, to maintain meaningful contact with industry.

The concept of such a list, like so many design innovations, can be traced to the Deutsche Werkbund of 1914. By 1921 this had become an illustrated record, the Deutsche Warenkinde, of German quality products. During the war it was exploited by the Nazis for their own political ends, but returned to the Werkbund afterwards. Coincidentally with the CoID, the Swiss Werkbund also compiled its own Schweizer Warenkatalog.

Not only did the Stock List offer a valid excuse to place a foot in manufacturers' doors, it provided the personnel to do so. In April 1948 a derisory number of three officers was engaged in maintaining regular contact, but by the end of the year this had increased sixfold. The new Survey Team had the dual function of combing the country for designs and of stimulating an adequate supply. By April 1949 it had selected 1400 products and a year later almost 3800. With a further influx of temporary staff, the team consisted of thirty-three officers who by the opening date had selected a staggering 20,000 designs.

Initially, viewing access was granted freely only to exhibition staff. But once their task was over the Stock List itself became part of the exhibition with the title of 'Design Review'. This was a wise move for it offered a consolation to those firms whose products could not be included physically in the Festival. More importantly it provided a ready reference point for home and foreign trade buyers as well as a curious public. To avoid further jibes of 'Britain Can't Have It', only finished products in current production qualified for a place – mock-ups, scale models and one-off craft products were omitted, along with component parts, except those which bore a special design interest.

Tentatively, in 1949 it was noted, 'the Stock List may well become a permanent feature of the Council's work'.[10] By 1952 it most certainly

4.18, 4.19 Robin Day carrying out development work on his polypropylene stacking chair for Hille International, 1961. Millions of these chairs have now been produced – together with many more derivatives of the design, which epitomises the best of *Design Index* ethics.

had – but in that year a reduction was announced in the grant-in-aid, and Design Review had to suffer cuts along with all other services. Consequently, a modest 5000 entries were retained, being consumer rather than capital goods. This narrower horizon was only slowly opened up in later years, with a renewed emphasis on engineering – perhaps too little and too late, following the virtual collapse of that major industry.

Selection committees met weekly to weed out obsolete products and admit new ones. Initially only one in five submissions was rejected, but this soon grew to one in every two. In this way the Council achieved a simple and, within limits, effective means of influencing design. When a product failed to make the grade, a carefully phrased letter of explanation was despatched, accompanied by an offer of help. The Council's industrial officers or the firm's staff designers would then restyle and resubmit, usually with success. Of course, rejection could also lead to a shrug of the shoulder or, worse, a lingering resentment. But criticisms from the trade for being too elitist were balanced by those from the purists for being too lax – a condition which Gordon Russell judged to be about right. Earlier in his appointment he had evolved a sensible attitude to such situations: 'I took some consolation from the fact that the sniping came from all sides. My army experience stood me in good stead and I hope I managed to appear imperturbable.'[11] The fact that Council members had as many Military Crosses (including Russell's) as civilian qualifications was probably no bad thing.

THE TRAINING AND EMPLOYMENT OF DESIGNERS

Other than direct involvement in industrial design, the training and employment of designers would now seem to offer the most fruitful and least problematic course of positive action. Influence could be exerted in three ways: by improving art school training, by maintaining a professional register and by obtaining actual commissions for designers.

Of the art schools, the Royal College rated foremost as a training ground for industrial designers. By coincidence or calculation, College and CoID became intricately linked. Robin Darwin, Principal, had worked for the Council, Robert Gooden, Professor of Silversmithing, had worked for Gordon Russell and Dick Russell, Professor of Furniture, had of course, worked in partnership with his brother.

During its long history the College had suffered repeated criticism for ignoring industrial design. Yet, lacking encouragement from manufacturers, it had blithely continued a fine art focus. Only in 1889 when Walter Crane became Principal was a conscious change discernible. Even this was handcraft-orientated and eventually petered out. After all, the cost of a lathe could finance many yards of canvas or pots of paint. Nor were Ministry attitudes particularly supportive. Just as two world wars had delayed plans for the Council, so the College similarly suffered. In 1946 many facilities still remained inadequately housed in a series of huts.

Several reports, including Meynell–Hoskins and Weir, had highlighted the deficiencies. Now the Council's Training Committee produced its own report. Written by Robin Darwin, this sophisticated document balanced 'depth versus breadth' arguments in training:

> It is the same with art and design as it is with general education. Only in a fairly narrow and concentrated field will a student's interests be sufficiently aroused to evoke his deeper creative instincts and only then . . . will he come up against the essential difficulties which must be faced. It is far better to learn through one's subject the values which will be found later on to apply to many others.[12]

As the one post-graduate institution creaming talent from all other schools, the Royal College was critically examined. In particular, Darwin stressed that appointment of a new principal would be a factor of 'pivotal importance'.

The following year the Minister of Education asked Russell to assist in the selection, little realising the latter felt 'time was ripe for a strong Principal who would goad the Ministry into action'.[13] Russell persuaded

4.20–4.22 *Above left.* Robin Darwin, a former CoID Education Officer, was appointed Principal of the Royal College of Art in 1948 and succeeded in achieving substantial reorientation towards industrial design. *Above right.* Dick Russell, designer of furniture and radio cabinets for mass production, was one of the RCA's first post-war professors. *Below.* Students at work in the well-equipped drawing office of the RCA's School of Industrial Design (Engineering), 1964.

4.23–4.25 *Above left.* Robert Welch graduated from the RCA in 1955 to become both a successful silversmith and industrial designer. In the foreground is one of a pair of hand-made candelabra commissioned by the Worshipful Company of Goldsmiths. Many of his designs feature in *Design Index* and have won awards. *Above right.* Interestingly, Robert Welch has his studio in the 18th-century Silk Mill, Chipping Campden, formerly the home of Charles Ashbee's Guild of Handicraft. *Opposite, above.* From the mid-fifties Robert Welch began a long and productive association with Old Hall, initially with designs for a stainless steel toast rack and this three-piece coffee set which successfully adapts a traditional form to new material and processes.

Darwin, by then Professor of Fine Art at Durham University, to apply. Subsequently his appointment was announced in *The Times* alongside Russell's own promotion to Director of the Council. The two allies could now do battle together:

> We were able to forge a close link between the two bodies, to the great advantage of both, for it was the Council's job to persuade industry to employ the more highly trained designers which the reorganisation of the College would provide.[14]

Darwin succeeded in reorganising the College with conspicuous success. At the time Professors of Fine Art were not unknown, whereas Professors of Design most certainly were. One of the first acts, after lobbying ministers for industrial facilities, was to appoint professors to each practical specialism including ceramics, fashion, glass, graphics, silversmithing and furniture. Qualifications equivalent to higher degrees were to be awarded. In 1951 the first graduates gained their DesRCA's, later to become 'Masters of Design'. Over two thirds of these initially obtained posts in industry, although many became freelance designers.

4.26 *Below.* Sales of Robert Welch's stainless steel cutlery have run into several million pieces, challenging strong competition from abroad. By 1980 he was being asked to produce designs for cutlery and holloware for Japanese manufacturers Yamazaki.

4.27–4.29 *Above.* David Mellor, contemporary of Robert Welch, has his cutlery factory in this splendid Georgian house, equating the ideals of William Morris with 20th-century industry. *Below.* Production and assembly work is carried out by a closely knit team who are able to vary their tasks in the conducive environment of the factory. *Opposite.* David Mellor at a Design Council display to celebrate 25 years of cutlery design after graduating from the RCA. Mellor is unique in that every range he has ever designed is still in production, winning five Design Council awards.

To obtain employment as a professional designer, let alone realise the aspiration of being a nationally or internationally famous name, was no easy task. One former RCA student already to achieve this was Robin Day, working in a field – furniture design – where American and Continental designers held a strong lead. But of the new graduates the example of the silversmiths is particularly interesting for they were at the heart of the revival of their craft. Robert Welch makes a useful case-study. In his final year at Birmingham School of Art there were only two silversmiths and, apart from teaching, employment prospects were remote. At the Royal College he was the only silversmith in his year but between 1952 and 1955 he met others, most notably Gerald Benny and David Mellor. Following a travelling scholarship to Sweden, Welch specialised in stainless steel in his final year and submitted a thesis entitled 'The Design and Production of Stainless Steel Tableware'. The only British manufacturers of such products were then J. & J. Wiggin of Bloxwich, near Birmingham, who marketed under the now famous name of 'Old Hall'. So impressed were they by his final project, an entrée dish, that they bought the design and offered him a post as design consultant.

Thus, in the summer of 1955 Welch came to look for a studio-workshop in the Midlands. Gordon Russell consequently received an inquiry from Robert Gooden for premises for the newly qualified student. The old Guild of Handicraft workshops in Chipping Campden, well known to Russell, happened to have a vacant top floor and subsequently the lease was arranged. Robert Welch proceeded to combine the roles of craftsman

4.30, 4.31 An example of the major industrial design projects tackled by RCA students. Richard Lord and Peter Parkinson developed this coach interior for the new Victoria Line in collaboration with London Transport Executive, 1964.

and industrial designer. These encompassed consultancy for Old Hall, silverware commissions for institutions and individuals, work in cast iron, ceramics and glass, and product design for British, German, American and finally Japanese companies. He has received various awards for his work and the MBE for his contribution to industry. Similar stories of enterprise and innovation could be told of his colleagues Gerald Benny and David Mellor.

The Industrial Division of the CoID endeavoured to obtain commissions for other students and designers which might lead to permanent appointments. In turn, here was a means of influencing industry without having to employ a permanent team of specialists. Of course, not all designers had enjoyed the luxury of postgraduate training and it would take some years to accumulate sufficient DesRCA's. However, soon after its formation the Council conveniently inherited a complete list known as the National Register of Industrial Art Designers.

This Register had been an attempt in pre-war years to offer manufacturers a reservoir of talent, boasting a minimum level of practical efficiency. The idea had, in fact, come from the Pick Council and been taken up by the Board of Trade in 1936. Membership was approved by selection committees and carried the qualifying initials of NRD (National Registered Designer). By the time the CoID absorbed the Register, membership had reached almost 800, including full-time staff designers, architects and hundreds of freelances. Unfortunately, industry was not over-impressed. Lacking any coherent national system of training, professional organisation or selection criteria it proved extraordinarily difficult to monitor standards. Consequently the initials NRD hardly carried the status of CEng or MIMechE. Additionally, many manufacturers feared their staff designers on the list might be tempted away by more lucrative offers from others.

Instead, the Council decided to maintain the Register as a List of Designers and itself suggest names to industry. No further NRD's would be granted as blanket stamps of approval. The Council felt that to run a designer index of people was fundamentally more complex than a design index of products. Like so many developments it suffered several changes of name – a sure way to confuse clients – becoming a 'Record of Designers' and then 'Designer Selection Service'. Nevertheless, the Council steadfastly publicised this as a service to industry and it began to bear fruit.

Initially the number of requests was small, but soon grew from several dozen to several hundred per year. The range was immense, varying from the sublime to the outrageously silly. On the one hand commissions included engines and coaches for British Transport, on the other 'a lettered headstone for a grave'. Blakey's required designs for boot protectors, Ind Coope inn signs, Shanks sanitary ware, Thermos and Vacco vacuum flasks. Notre Dame High School required a new uniform and Shell required one for 'men who stoke bunkers'.

The designers involved included a who's who of talent. Amongst the very first names were Misha Black, Robert Gooden, Jacques Gloag and Bronek Katz recommended to Stirling Engineering Co. for electrical appliance work. Robin Day was suggested to the Ministry of Civil Aviation for airport furniture design and Basil Spence to Grahamston Iron Co. for factory colour schemes. When the Ford Motor Co. requested a young designer to select goods for a TV film, a certain Terence Conran was chosen.

All the outcomes of such recommendations were carefully recorded by Council officers and together they encapsulate the problems of industrial liaison. The following cryptic comments are selected from a few months' period in 1955:

> Were under the impression we gave free advice.
>
> Went to Royal Academy for their artist!
>
> Used one of their old designs instead of employing a designer.
>
> Worked out to be too costly – project dropped.
>
> Didn't take either designer – can't remember why.
>
> Decided against it as he is too experienced for the post.

4.32, 4.33 *Above and facing page.* The well-publicised re-design of Colchester lathes involved cooperation by staff engineer, design consultant and ergonomist. But, as we shall see in Chapter 8, even this could not stave off the pressure of fierce foreign competition in the sixties.

Of course, the new generation of designers still had their mistakes to make, as further comments indicate:

> B and C not used. Have a well-known designer going there next week.

> Did not commission D as they felt he had not an inventive mind, nor is he a good draughtsman.

> E's drill packs had no marketable value.

In the event, none of these comments proved too serious a setback, for B, C, D and E were destined to become the most successful designers of the post-war period! However, problems of liaison could not always be blamed on excessively critical manufacturers, as the following entry shows:

> F to design a floor polisher.

> F now designing them a washing machine.

> Abandoned due to disappearance of F.

However, until the CoID created a Design Centre of its own, the List of Designers did provide an essential means of industrial liaison. Over the years the attitudes of manufacturers towards design and designers was to remain one of the most intractable problems to be solved. Eventually new and more sophisticated 'Services to Industry' were evolved, although in the meantime another major exhibition was to absorb the energies of the Industrial Division.

5.1 Cover of Festival Exhibition Catalogue bearing Abram Games's Festival Star. This jaunty symbol of Britannia wearing a neoclassical helmet both captured the defiant mood of the organisers and epitomised the Festival Style.

—5—
FESTIVAL OF BRITAIN

INTRODUCTION

Like the Falklands War of the eighties, the Festival of Britain was for many people the significant event of the fifties. Politically it combined heroism and jingoism, aesthetically it combined boldness with an element of bad taste. But, in the words of Sir Gerald Barry, Director-General of the Festival, it provided 'A Tonic to the Nation'.

This second, larger, national exhibition decisively punctuated the history of the CoID. Responsibility was assumed for all industrial displays including much of London's South Bank, the Festival Ship *Campania*, Industrial Power in Glasgow and the largest Land Travelling exhibition ever. For many months Council staff, architects, artists and designers cooperated to create a success which owed as much to their own logistic and exhibition skills as to the design of British products.

CENTENARY COMMEMORATION

As far back as 1943 a centenary commemoration of the Great Exhibition was suggested privately to the government. Appropriately, this came from the Royal Society of Arts who envisaged that by 1951 Britain would be well enough on the way to recovery to hold an international exhibition on a grand scale. Towards the end of the war two letters publicly called for the same event. The first appeared in *The Times* from DIA stalwart John Gloag; the second in the *News Chronicle* from Editor Gerald Barry, addressed as an open letter to Sir Stafford Cripps.

Shortly afterwards the Secretary for Overseas Trade formed the Ramsden Committee to consider how exhibitions might promote exports. Prominent on the Committee was Sir Thomas Barlow, first Director of the CoID. Their report of March 1946 concluded:

> We are strongly of the opinion that a Universal International Exhibition should be held in London at the earliest practicable date to demonstrate to the world the recovery of the United Kingdom from the effects of war in the moral, cultural, spiritual and material fields . . . It should surpass the New York World's Fair of 1939 in scale and technical achievement, and the Paris Exhibition of 1937 in aesthetic excellence and personal appeal.[1]

5.2 A party of schoolchildren aboard Festival Ship *Campania* gazes at a relief map showing the main industrial centres of Britain, her chief products and their production sites.

Because the Victorians had organised their exhibition on a grand scale its centenary commemoration must be dealt with likewise. But international expositions such as the World Fairs in Chicago and New York demanded huge sites and resources. The only suitable site near London was Osterley Park, which at 1946 prices, with necessary transport links, would cost £70 million. This was unacceptable within the context of Britain's reconstruction programme, diverting scarce resources from new factories and homes. After six years of war Britain's overstrained economy could not cope with such a burden. Although industry was recovering, the country had an acute deficit. Finally, £12 million was allocated. Consequently, whereas the Victorians had expanded their exhibition from a national to an international one, the opposite was now necessary. To compensate, festivities would spread over Britain to include the moral, cultural and spiritual as well as 'material fields'.

Overall responsibility was placed in the hands of a Council having General Lord Ismay, Churchill's wartime Chief of Staff, as President. (A skilful choice by Herbert Morrison to cool Conservative criticism of a Labour Government project.) Planning lay with an Executive Committee with Gerald Barry as its Director-General and visual aspects were co-ordinated by a Presentation Panel. In turn, these were to rely on existing bodies such as the Arts Council and the CoID whenever possible. For the latter not to be totally involved with the industrial exhibits would have been, of course, unthinkable. Dr Edwards was placed on the Council, Russell on the Committee and Hartland Thomas on the Panel.

The task was immense. On being summoned to 10 Downing Street, the General had accepted the position, relieved that it was not something more distasteful, while Barry felt himself selected 'to make the punishment fit the crime'! At the first meeting of the Executive Committee the brief was set: to organise something called the Festival of Britain demonstrating 'the British contribution to civilisation, past, present and future, in the arts, in science and technology and in industrial design'.[2] For the remainder of the afternoon members brooded over their blotting pads, searching for some coherent themes!

One of the most important decisions, on Russell's initiative, was to link science and industry in a combined exhibition. On the one hand this sacrificed CoID rights to exclusive control over a single pavilion, but on the other it prevented elsewhere what Russell saw as 'the peculiar branch of chaos in which Britain tends to specialise'.[3] It soon became clear that this combined exhibition would be the centrepiece of the whole Festival, although exactly what form it would take and where it would be located had still to be decided. Eventually a narrative theme evolved, based on the Land of Britain, the People of Britain and the British Contribution to Discovery. This enabled a diversity of subject matter to be displayed within a meaningful context.

In addition the national programme included eleven further exhibitions with a Festival Ship, a Land Travelling Exhibition and an Exhibition of Industrial Power. The latter two were under the direct control of the CoID, and Industrial Power specifically under the Scottish Committee. Voluntary local activities were to be encouraged throughout the land and hopefully these might leave a legacy of well-designed facilities dedicated loosely to the 'Arts of Peace'.

Finding sites for such exhibitions offered minor problems, but the combined exhibition proved of a different order, demanding at least 500,000 square feet of covered space. Earl's Court and Olympia were ruled out because of that annual tribute to manufacturing industry, the British Industries Fair. South Kensington – the Science Museum, the

5.3–5.5 *Above.* The 30-acre South Bank Exhibition site, photographed in December 1949. From this dereliction a controversial group of buildings arose under the architectural leadership of Hugh Casson. The Hungerford railway bridge bisects the site. *Below.* A model of the South Bank site, showing display pavilions grouped around open fairways and piazzas. Downstream of the railway bridge lies the Royal Festival Hall with the Lion and Unicorn Pavilion directly behind. Upstream, the Dome of Discovery and Skylon dominate the site. *Opposite.* A model of the 37-acre Festival Pleasure Gardens in Battersea Park. The pier in the foreground receives visitors from the South Bank site. To the left can be seen the Big Dipper and in top centre the Dance Pavilion and Crescent Restaurant.

Victoria and Albert Museum and the Natural History Museum – were considered but given over to lesser displays. It was felt a demonstration of twentieth-century industrial skills could no more be held in such edifices to the past than the Great Exhibition in the British Museum. Hyde Park, Regent's Park and Battersea Park were all abandoned to cries of 'Hands off the People's Parks', although the latter was to become the Festival Pleasure Gardens, being miraculously transformed from wartime allotments and a cricket pitch.

Eventually the South Bank, suggested by the Ramsden Committee, then rejected and suggested again, was accepted by the government. It was central, amenable to river traffic and, above all, overdue for redevelopment. The L.C.C. had procured the site before the war but it was now a semi-derelict slum and a disgrace to the capital. However, before exhibition work could proceed a new river wall had to be constructed and the land levelled, drained and serviced. Even then the rats ate through electric cables causing further delays!

The 30 acres wedged between County Hall and Waterloo Bridge were still too small and certainly challenged architects wishing to create something imaginative yet practicable. Nevertheless, under the leadership of Hugh Casson a controversial group of buildings around open fairways and piazzas evolved. These included the egg-in-a-box Royal Festival Hall, the quite delicate Lion and Unicorn Pavilion, the not-quite-so delicate Dome of Discovery and, of course, the Skylon pointing, as it were, to the

5.6–5.8 *Above*. The spectacular 300-foot Skylon forming a night-time landmark for the city. Cynics joked that like Britain, it had no visible means of support. *Opposite, above.* The Dome of Discovery under construction in August 1950, prior to receiving its aluminium cladding. Designed by Ralph Tubbs, this was the largest dome ever constructed. *Opposite, below.* Night view of the Dome after completion. Under its glistening 'cranium' was told the story of British scientific achievement both in discovery and exploration.

future. At the last moment it was realised no reference to 1851 existed. So James Gardner, so successful with 'Britain Can Make It', designed a mini glasshouse Crystal Palace which delighted Gerald Barry.

Most buildings were only temporary although the extensive use of canvas-clad steel frames had to be abandoned because of unexpected snowfalls or of sparks from the Hungerford railway bridge. The latter inconveniently happened to split the site into two. Restrictions on materials, workmen's strikes and incessant rain all conspired to make completion a near-run thing. Steel and wood – the structural backbone of exhibitions – were in such short supply that many buildings, even including the Royal Festival Hall, had to be considerably replanned. Although less spectacular than the Dome or Skylon, many of the temporary buildings were impressive. These included the Power and Production, the Transport, and the Sea and Ship Pavilions.

5.9–5.11 *Above.* The CoID's Design Review display on the South Bank. In the bays over 20,000 photographs were housed in Roneodex cabinets. They represented the Stock List compiled between 1948 and 1951, and it was from this that all industrial exhibits were chosen. Prominent on the wall display is the Jaguar XK 100. *Centre.* Tractors mounted on adjustable pillars in the Country Pavilion. In the foreground is a Ferguson model equipped with Leverton rear tool bar. *Right.* Standing outside the Power and Production Pavilion was this massive 275,000-volt oil-brake circuit breaker by British Thomson Houston. Inverted it is reminiscent of the splayed legs and plastic feet that characterised Festival Style furniture.

THE 1951 STOCK LIST

The Festival Office was soon besieged with information relating to architecture and design:

> Models of every description, plans, maps, paintings, prototypes of chairs and litter-bins, women's uniforms, odd chunks of sculpture, lengths of luscious material, ship's cables, toy fountains – such assorted bric-a-brac became the accepted furniture and adornment of the place, spreading an irresistible mood of sharrawaggy† and slightly unhinged romance.[4]

For the CoID, working in close cooperation with, yet distinct from, the Festival Office, pressures were even more acute. As we have seen, the

---

† 'Appealing lack of obvious order or symmetry.'

Industrial Division processed some 10,000 exhibits from 3500 firms, then extended the operation to create a Stock List of over 20,000 products. Furthermore, unlike previous exhibitions on this scale, selling space to manufacturers to do more-or-less as they pleased was just not on. This was made clear in a no-nonsense guide to industry: '1951 will be entirely British and will show nothing that does not do this country and British industry the highest degree of credit.' In the words of the Director-General:

> There would be no Hall of Textiles or Pavilion of Confectionery or Palace of Gas; there would be no mammoth mounds of apples or effigies of Royalty moulded in edible fats.[5]

And it was on CoID shoulders that this 'invidious but crucial burden of choice and persuasion fell'.

The selection process was carried out in four stages. Firstly a detailed survey was made of current production. This involved fifty-eight discussion groups with representative bodies such as trade associations. Secondly an appeal to manufacturers requested photographs and details of their best products. It was from these that the 1951 Stock List emerged. Industry then made the primary selection, working to Council guidelines. Finally four specialist teams of officers under Hartland Thomas approved the selections. Russell himself, no doubt with 'Britain Can't Have It' ringing in his ears, emphasised 'these must be real goods to go into real shops for real people'.

5.12–5.14 *Above, left.* The Festival Ship *Campania* was transformed, under the direction of James Holland, from a rusting 16,000-ton escort carrier into a gaily floating exhibition hall to visit ports around Britain. Skeleton masts, white paint and a plentiful supply of bunting helped complete the transformation. *Above, right.* The Sea and Ships Pavilion, showing the open construction of latticed steel frames by Basil Spence. On display are three large models of a tanker, liner and whale factory ship by Bassett-Lowke and Bruntons. *Below.* Leading exhibit at the South Bank was this 2–8–2 W.G. class locomotive built by the North British Locomotive Company for Indian Government Railways. Obtaining her considerably taxed Gordon Russell's ingenuity, but she is seen here finally mounted outside the Transport and Communications Pavilion. Nearly 80 feet long, she contrasts strikingly with her forbear, the *Agenoria* (1829), standing shrouded on the right.

Not only were selections dispersed throughout the South Bank pavilions, but they supplied the Land Travelling Exhibition in Manchester, the Festival Ship in Southampton and the architectural interiors in Poplar. Controlling this logistical nightmare was retired General Jack Benoy whose experience of the North African invasion stood him in good stead. Another army officer, Colonel K. L. Beddington ran the Progress Section which efficiently kept things moving. The scope of the operation extended well beyond consumer goods, 'from locomotives to lipsticks and in value from many thousands of pounds to a few pennies'.[6] Russell described the problem of the locomotive. Earmarked for export to India and therefore of broad gauge, it had to be shipped from its Glasgow makers along with a special crane funded by donations:

> As I gazed at her – she was a beauty – I wondered how many people could possibly have guessed at the blood and sweat involved in getting her in place![7]

Considerably smaller but no less problematic was a casket for display in the Lion and Unicorn Pavilion. The casket, a gift from the Queen to George VI, had to be collected personally by Colonel Beddington from Buckingham Palace and protected behind armoured glass. Unfortunately, the glass was not available on time and he stored it at the bank. On 3 May, when their Majesties opened the Festival, the strongroom gates jammed shut. At the last moment the casket was placed in position for the King and Queen to visit the pavilion. Even then it was chipped by a cleaner, resulting in an extra private visit by the Queen after it had been repaired.

The Land Travelling Exhibition organised by the CoID remained the largest mobile exhibition ever produced. In all 1765 industrial products, with as their centrepiece a jet engine, were moved by a fleet of lorries from Manchester to Leeds, to Birmingham and Nottingham. On two of the sites it was housed in a prefabricated tented pavilion and once again expertise from the 'Arts of War' was applied successfully to the 'Arts of Peace'.

One widely publicised aspect of the Council's work, instigated by Hartland Thomas, was the Festival Pattern Group project whereby over twenty firms from many industries developed crystal structure diagrams into decorative patterns for textiles, floor coverings, pottery, glass and plastics. Additionally the Council was responsible for publicising at home and abroad all aspects relating to manufacture, supplying detailed entries for various exhibition catalogues, and publishing a fully illustrated handbook entitled *Design in the Festival* – all of which absorbed the energies of the Information as well as the Industrial Division.

5.15–5.17 A group of design-co-ordinated facilities on the South Bank. *Above.* Race chairs with splayed legs and ball feet are a lasting memory of the Festival Style, although his famous *Antelope* chair (centre rear with wingback) rapidly dated. Maria Shepherd's conical concrete plant-pots were to become fashionable in sixties city precincts. *Opposite, left.* One of the many signposts, the number of which was to increase, to direct thousands of visitors daily around the South Bank. It was questioned later whether condensed sans-serif capitals were the best choice of lettering. *Opposite, right.* The peculiar and ubiquitous South Bank litter bin, designed by Jack Howe, had to cope with large quantities of litter.

Through Hartland Thomas's membership of the Presentation Panel, the Council was able to influence many other matters of visual taste. These ranged from the architects' designs to the best breed of duck for the ornamental lake. In particular signposts, kiosks and even attendants' uniforms could be properly co-ordinated. Some proposals such as a model of the South Bank made from toilet rolls were easy to reject, others such as a Ministry of Pensions plea for 'A modest display of artificial limbs' were more difficult to refuse. Leading designers were commissioned and contributed to the overall effect of a Festival Style. Although more suited to outdoor than indoor application, this became surprisingly pervasive in the everyday interiors of the fifties.

THE SOUTH BANK AND OTHER EXHIBITIONS

In retrospect, May 1951 was hardly a festive month: Aneurin Bevan and Harold Wilson (President of the Board of Trade) resigned over NHS cuts, Burgess and Maclean defected to Russia and British casualties mounted in Korea. But King George VI's opening speech captured the defiant mood of optimism shared by Festival Organisers and the CoID:

> Two world wars have brought us grievous loss of life and treasure; and though the nation has made a splendid effort towards recovery new burdens have fallen upon it and dark clouds still overhang the whole world. Yet this is no time for despondency; for I see the Festival as a symbol of Britain's abiding courage and vitality...
>
> Many of these displays will be of lasting value. They will maintain the prestige of our arts and industries abroad by proof of our world-renowned skill in design and craftsmanship...

Initially dull weather was to cast its own shadow over the South Bank, sending visitors scuttling from pavilion to pavilion. But by the end of June the sun broke through and the many thousands of plants and trees

5.18–5.20 *Above, left.* Part of the 'abacus' screen along the South Bank perimeter, designed by Edward Mills. *Above right.* Detail from the Hobbies section of the Homes and Gardens Pavilion: plate glass held in place by rubber balls. *Below.* Detail from the Dome of Discovery: six pre-Buckminster Fuller polytopes representing the Earth's behaviour as a planet, executed by Hall and Maytum.

blossomed into full colour to generate a festival atmosphere. It was estimated that 60,000 people could visit the site daily, although critics felt this was an over-optimistic figure. In the event, during the final month the daily average was 76,000 and on 22 September 158,365 people passed through the gates.

On the whole the design-co-ordinated facilities coped well with this increase. For convenience the CoID had, of course, selected many items from the 1951 Stock List. As an example, 3000 seats of a new design were spread around the South Bank. These were praised for both appearance and comfort. But one miscalculation was the shortage of signposts – neat and tidy as they were, more (and more prominent) noticeboards had to be provided. Another was the shortage of litter bins. Despite the strategic placing of 1150 bins, within hours visitors found themselves wading ankle-deep in their own refuse. Only the prompt ordering of hundreds more, coupled with loudspeaker appeals, saved the South Bank from reverting to a slum. Perhaps this was a sad reflection on an environmentally insensitive people, or simply the first large-scale encounter with packaged refreshments.

As with 'Britain Can Make It' the national phenomenon of queuing, whether for buns or balloons, or in some odd cases nothing at all, made crowd control easier. However, although the designs of cafés and kiosks conformed to the highest standards, catering was restricted by ever-present rationing and a reluctance of firms to commit themselves for only one season. In the Commons, Major Legge-Bourke had perhaps not been facetious in asking Herbert Morrison, as Lord President of the Festival Council:

> To ensure a fair distribution of the crockery available for the catering, would the Right Hon. Gentleman give an assurance that the Dome of Discovery is not being reserved as a flying saucer by Lord Beaverbrook?[8]

Large queues formed for the Dome itself, the most striking building of the exhibition. With a diameter of 365 feet, the aluminium structure was claimed to be as revolutionary as the Crystal Palace of 1851. Inside, the story of man's exploration and discoveries was told. Most popular was a display of polar equipment convincingly set in an Arctic blizzard. Thousands waited patiently to see real explorers in action but characteristically it was a team of huskies which stole the show.

The Homes and Gardens section proved outstandingly popular because of the furnished rooms. These differed from 'Britain Can Make It' by showing smaller settings with a theme of 'limited space', thereby appealing to the majority of families facing the post-war housing

5.21 Entrance to the Grand Vista, Festival Pleasure Gardens, designed by Osbert Lancaster and John Piper. At night the chandeliers added to the fairy-tale atmosphere.

shortage. Groups of designers including Bronek Katz, Clive Latimer, Robin Day and Bianca Minns offered appealing solutions to six 'design problems' of the contemporary home. These centred around the child, the bed-sitting room, the kitchen, hobbies, entertainment and the parlour. This time goods were real and in the shops, no longer the pipe dream of five years before.

Out in the open, the Council found itself incongruously organising events in a small Sports Arena. However, this enabled it to demonstrate numerous sporting goods, in the design of which Britain still excelled. Nearby, model yachts and boats were sailed across a Boating Lake to illustrate another industry, toymaking, which was to feature increasingly in *Design Review*.

As yet, inclusion in the *Review* did not automatically endorse a product in the public's taste and consumption. 'By Appointment to His Majesty the King' was a far more famous seal of approval. Only one product in the illustrated handbook boasted 'Selected by the Council of Industrial design [sic] for the Festival of Britain 1951 Design Review', and that was a hospital bed. One firm also used the Council motto 'Good Design is Good Business' for promoting a range of fashion shoes. But these were early

5.22, 5.23 *Above.* Delightful miniature pavilion by James Gardner to commemorate the Great Exhibition – the only display specifically to do so. *Below.* The Pleasure Gardens Guinness Clock, designed by Hewitt and Him, being studied by a quizzical crowd.

5.24 Domestic interior strikingly displayed by Marcus, Latimer and Walters in the Homes and Gardens Pavilion. The aim is to demonstrate layouts for sitting, dining, cooking and cleaning.

times and *Design Review* itself was still being publicised under the seven arches of Waterloo Bridge. The 20,000 captioned photographs, 2000 samples and 4000 slides led to a reassuring number of inquiries.

Of the other exhibitions, as might be expected of a seafaring nation, the Festival Ship was a great success. In contrast the Land Travelling Exhibition, which was far more polished, being closely under Council control, was disappointing. Whereas the arrival in port of a gaily beflagged ship generated spontaneous publicity, an industrial display arriving in an industrial city needed more promoting than funds could provide. The exhibition of Industrial Power in Glasgow was also disappointing, attracting only one third of the expected crowds. Judged by many to be the most sophisticated of all displays, industrial power in another industrial city somehow lacked the cheerful appeal of the South Bank festivity.

Altogether 8½ million people visited the South Bank, despite the four-shilling entrance fee. Another 8 million continued to the Pleasure Gardens upstream which maintained the festival atmosphere. Of these 5

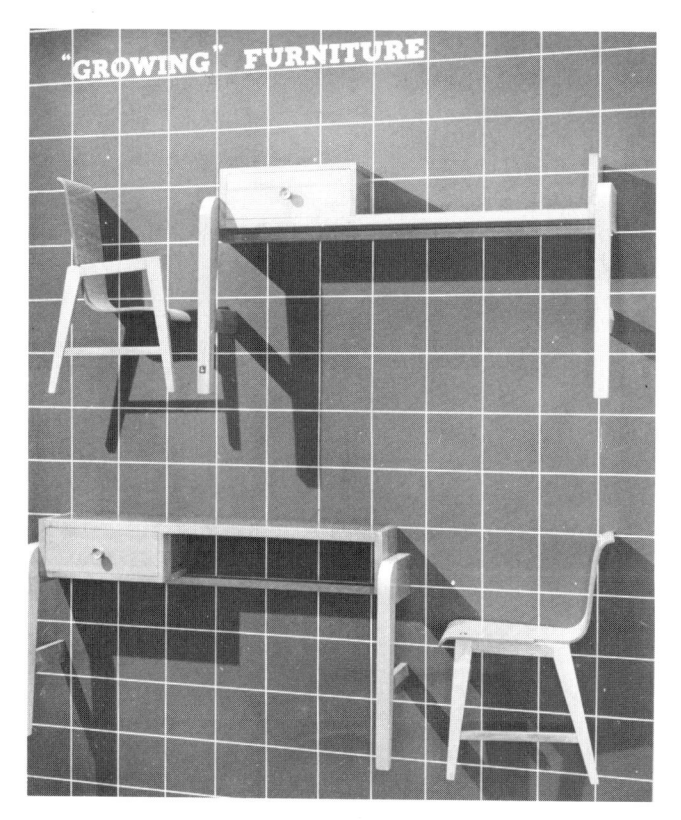

5.25 'Growing' Furniture display in the Homes and Gardens Pavilion. Chair seats and table tops are reversible to give greater height and width – relatively rare examples of designs which are both adjustable and attractive.

million travelled by water-bus routes, and overspill car parking facilities were pleasantly under-used. Foreign visitors to Britain rose by 15% in the Festival year bringing an estimated £74 million to the Exchequer. If fares paid to British shipping and airlines were included the figure became £104 million. This was in sharp contrast to the balance of payments and a rise in exports of only 3%. Such figures had to be taken seriously, for in terms of foreign currency one American travelling by British transport earned as much as the export of an average car.

Nevertheless, on the closing night of the Festival the Archbishop of Canterbury, deputising for the King who was sadly ill, was able to state:

> I am sure that the Festival has done a lot for our good name. It has brought a great number of visitors from overseas who have admired our spirit: it has won prestige outside our shores for the work of British manufacturers and designers and craftsmen, and the praise they have received has put them all into 'a good conceit' with themselves with the keenness to do even better which encouragement always brings.

5.26 Living room display of 'non-Utility' furniture by Eden Minns. The storage units by Hille and the bookcase by David Joel have a certain timeless quality. However the Race sofa and wingchairs have a distinct fifties look. The ugly trolley is, surprisingly, by Heal's.

PROGRESS REPORT

For the CoID, to be so intimately involved in the successful Festival clearly consolidated its position. But to what degree it had actually improved design standards was difficult to judge. Annual reports, while talking of 'quickening interest', fell short of claiming national improvement. At that time British design, in the transition from Austerity to Binge, was in a trough. In some fields such as school furniture and domestic equipment less influenced by fashion, simple functional designs had evolved. But in others a flimsiness and a fussiness were apparent. The Council, more than the designers themselves, could only work within the framework of the period, public taste and the products of others.

Since the Council's often repeated aim was 'to promote by all practicable means the improvement of design in the products of British industry' any discernible change, positive or negative, whatever the cause, would critically reflect on the Council itself. It was therefore of some concern when, towards the end of 1951, *Architectural Review* used the South Bank exhibition to provide the most comprehensive review of industrial design to date, with the title 'CoID: Progress Report'.[9] Furthermore, an attempt was made to judge 'absolute and relative merits

5.27–5.30 *Above, left.* Many of the souvenir designs of the Festival were criticised, but this tobacco tin by Metal Box uses Abram Games's symbol effectively. *Above, right.* Even this teapot stand which reverses into a food dish is enhanced by Games's design. Made by British Heat-Resistant Glass Co., it cost 2s. 6d. in 1951. *Below, left.* Glass ashtrays designed by E. Sykes – one of 26 manufacturers working in the Festival Pattern Group on CoID invitation. Crystal structure diagrams developed by Dr Helen Megaw of Cambridge were the source of inspiration. *Below, right.* Wallpaper designed by Robert Sevant of the Festival Pattern Group. A crystal structure diagram of Insulin provided the reference.

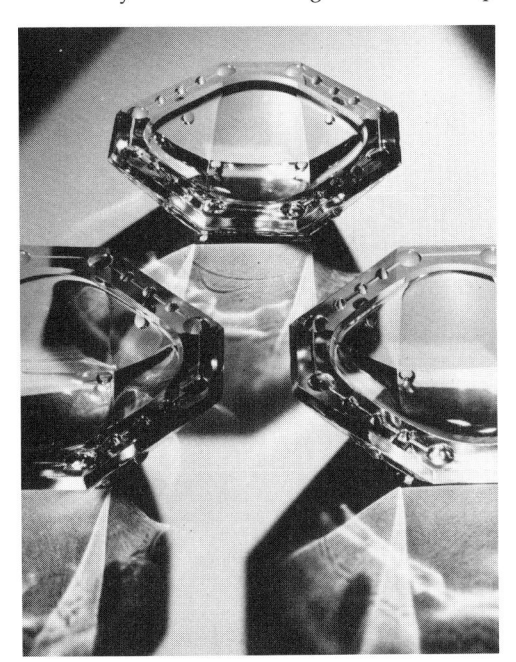

and demerits of what was shown and not shown' by referring back to a 1935 survey for the *Review* by Richard Dudley Ryder and to Nikolaus Pevsner's authoritative 'Enquiry into Industrial Art in England' of 1937. These were not figures to be dismissed lightly, for Dick Ryder was formerly the Council's Exhibitions Officer and Dr Pevsner, along with Michael Farr (then up-dating Pevsner's enquiry), were authors of the article.

It came as a relief to read that in no industry had standards gone down and that in quite a number it had gone up. But improvement was of quantity rather than quality. The most obvious case was furniture. Nothing in 1951 was superior to Gordon Russell's own pieces of 1935, but ten or more firms were now producing equally good work, including Heal's, Ernest Race and David Joel. Some industries registered design improvements, notably domestic appliances and plastics. In others such as jewellery, pottery and glass, 'The feeling of hopelessness one had fifteen years ago is exactly the same today'.

To what extent was improvement attributable to the CoID? *Architectural Review* conceded this was 'almost impossible to define'. However, since improvement was the result of a change of attitude, and since this was the result of propaganda, which was the 'chief job' of the Council, it followed that the CoID should be given its fair share of the credit for 'success or partial success'. But the real impossibility for *Architectural Review* was that of objectively defining improvement. This is illustrated by its comments on fashion changes. The disappearance of Jazz (Art Deco) 'so pernicious before the war' was welcomed, the appearance of Borax (streamlining) with its 'bogus' forms, deprecated with the fervour of DIA extremists.

On certain aspects of the South Bank exhibition *Architectural Review* was on safer ground – the poorly imitated period designs in textiles and porcelain, the hackneyed forms of jewellery and, above all, the kitsch of the souvenir kiosks. Admittedly the Council did not have exclusive right of veto over some of these, but as the *Review* was quick to point out:

> ... all manufactured exhibits were, if not chosen, at least sanctioned by the CoID. This has to be emphasised, for there were quite a number of real atrocities on show and a very large number of aesthetically indifferent products.[10]

None of them it felt should have been accepted into the Stock List or the Exhibition.

Clearly the decision to move from specific control to general involvement was reaping the consequences. What then of the one direct initia-

5.31 As with 'Britain Can Make It', display design matched or surpassed product design. The Power and Production Pavilion imaginatively mounted this range of goods on giant cogs.

tive on design, the Crystal Structure project? *Architectural Review* was not impressed. It did not deny the convenience of lichens, sparks in the fireplace or crystal structures as a source of inspiration. But there was a danger that they encouraged manufacturers to assume that 'science can take the place of the designer' and that money spent on the latter could be saved. Seemingly the Council could not win.

As to the future, how far should a government body go in controlling design? Here lay the paradox: control killed initiative, both for the purchaser and the manufacturer. They must be allowed to choose the multicoloured printed tie or the lamp with dancing lady in an iridescent turquoise frock. In turn, it was perfectly legitimate for government to demonstrate what it regarded as good design and explain why it regarded it as such. And here the CoID needed to take a bolder line.

Architectural Review suspected that the Council had been playing it safe and, indeed, sympathised with the problem it faced. No government agency could afford to be over-daring at that time. Nevertheless it needed to clarify its aims, particularly on such matters as whether to promote

5.32 Here an effective setting is provided in the Power and Production Pavilion for a pottery demonstration by A. E. Gray & Co.

good design in handicraft as well as industry, and in reproduction as well as contemporary products. Furthermore, there was the need for a third decision, namely what proportion of funds should be devoted to 'work addressed to the public, and work addressed to the manufacturers'. The two were complementary but manufacturers required 'perhaps more attention and a greater ingeniousness of propaganda than they have hitherto received by the CoID staff'.[11]

Publicly Russell had to defend his Council, and *Architectural Review* did give him the benefit of a substantial feature, 'The Director Replies'. In characteristic style he argued his cardinal principle:

> I cannot help feeling that when the *Architectural Review* says we have a lack of belief in a high aesthetic standard and have opened the flood gates, whilst the National Brass-foundry Association complains that selection was far too drastic we cannot be so far out.[12]

What neither the *Review* nor Russell could fully acknowledge was the extraordinary period in which the CoID was now operating. Such a long, detached view could be taken retrospectively some years ahead, or inter-

5.33 A sculptured background to 'The Living World' display in the Dome of Discovery. Based on organic cell formation, it was designed by Jacqueline Groag.

nationally by those who had already solved similar problems. A few leading American designers were in this position, but following the war maintained a 'rich neighbour' attitude reflected by Frank Lloyd Wright's comments on the Festival Hall: 'I don't think it's a particularly wonderful building, but I think it's wonderful that your country *has* a new building.' The self-deprecating British had already joked that the Skylon, like the country, had no visible means of support.

Perhaps the Swedes were best qualified to comment. In any event Arthur Hald's summary in *Form* magazine deserved special note:

> *Industrial Design.* In this field, progressive designers and producers in Britain have to contend not only with conservatism in general, and with class differences, but also with the heterogeneous demands of a world-wide market. The Council of Industrial Design, which struggles for good design in everything, propagates a consistent design policy applied to the products themselves, the advertising, the shop fitting, etc. This propaganda is almost wholly concerned with series and mass production – a situation considerably different to that obtaining in Scandinavia, where the interplay between machine techniques, handicraft and even homecraft is an everyday commonplace...

5.34 Mural in the Garden Café, Homes and Gardens Pavilion, painted by Marek Zulawski. A cheerful contrast is provided to the tea-urn, trays of buns and teacups.

> ... However, we concede that it is easier in Sweden than in Britain to be a radical propagandist, designer or producer. The present Battle of Britain is a hard one, and it is often difficult to gauge just how things are at any given moment. There are plenty of good designers and there is promising human material in the schools, but amid all the individual voices it is difficult to recognise a unifying and characteristically British note. Nevertheless, our final conclusion was that 1951 in Britain was something of a Victory Year for contemporary design.[13]

Within weeks a Conservative Government was elected, its sights firmly set on the forthcoming Coronation. David Eccles, the new Minister of Works, ordered immediate demolition on the South Bank. Apart from the Festival Hall and the Pleasure Gardens, the site was cleared for redevelopment. Appropriately James Gardner's miniature Crystal Palace was last to fall.

Twenty-five years later the long view was indeed taken in a compendium of comment compiled by Banham and Hillier. This ranged from fulsome praise to vehement criticism: 'to some, a glorious "monument to the future", to others, a tawdry carnival which set British design on the wrong course for years.'[14] As with 'Britain Can Make it', display design had equalled – if not surpassed – production design. Retrospectively, elements of 1951 did appear as suspect as those of 1851. Possibly 100 years was too short a time to eradicate entirely the excesses of British taste. But from the conflicting views of organisers, participants and visitors emerged a consensus that this giant cooperative effort of architects, designers, artists and sculptors was a considerable achievement in difficult times.

6.1 An early television broadcast *Plan for Your Lives*, 1947, focuses public attention on design. Frank Austin, furniture designer and teacher, shows a stool made by pupils of St Christopher's School, Letchworth. The stool legs are made of resin-bonded wood laminates, shaped by the mould lying on the table.

—6—
PUBLICITY AND PROPAGANDA

INTRODUCTION

Publicity and propaganda became a central feature of consumer society in the 'never-had-it-so-good fifties' and the 'swinging sixties'. Mass communication, as it were, followed on the heels of mass production, mass education and mass entertainment. Within this context the Council of Industrial Design's Information Division complemented the Industrial Division by raising levels of critical consumer demand. This was accomplished through publicity and propaganda aimed at schools, discriminating adults and the 'uninterested'. In the early years a lively programme of lectures, exhibitions and publications was evolved. Although this was curtailed in the fifties following cuts in the grant-in-aid, increasing attention was paid to the influential retail trade and government and local authorities.

REACHING THE PUBLIC

No matter how concerned the politicians and official organisations, how receptive the manufacturers and enthusiastic the retailers, how effective the art schools and imaginative their graduates, without a final ingredient of positive public support, industrial design lacks meaning. Therefore for a body such as the CoID to influence the attitudes and purchasing patterns of the public is of considerable importance. Hugh Dalton's original brief had not explicitly emphasised publicity and propaganda of this nature. It simply noted one function would be 'to provide a national display of well-designed goods by holding, or participating in, exhibitions and to conduct publicity for good designs in other appropriate forms'. This offered even looser terms of reference for the Information Division than for its Industrial counterpart. Beyond exhibitions no forms of publicity were stated, although lack of finance for direct advertising was an obvious limiting factor whatever the strategy.

Consequently the *First Annual Report*[1] had attempted to fill in guidelines for 'reaching the public'. Propaganda was aimed at 'rousing the public to a state of alert sensibility'. This should not be achieved

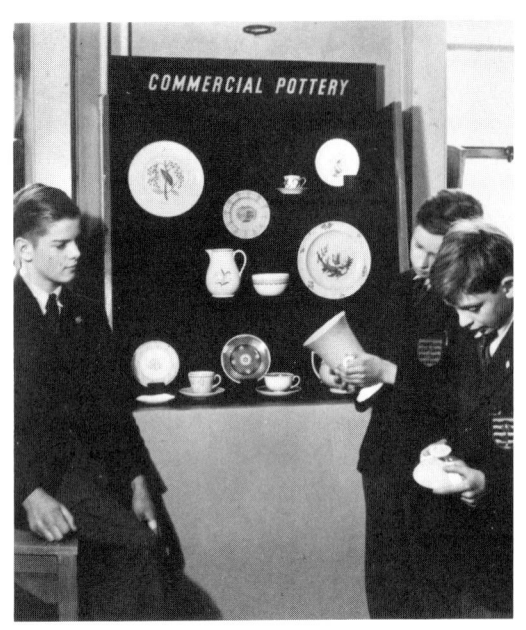

6.2, 6.3 *Left.* Paul Reilly became the CoID's Head of Information under the directorship of Gordon Russell in 1947. From 1960 until 1977 he was himself Director of the Council. *Right.* A small portable exhibition designed for the London County Council by the CoID. Such exhibitions were held in each school for a term at a time 'to give the children an opportunity of appreciating design in everyday objects'.

by 'pressing particular dogmas on it', but rather by explaining the principles of good design in the meaningful context of the consumer's own interests and needs. The Council would need to provide plenty of opportunity for the consumer to view 'all kinds of good things' in order that understanding be achieved.

The Report perceived the public as consisting of several groups. Firstly there were children of school age. These offered the 'soundest and surest, but also the slowest method'. To reach them, cooperation with the Ministry of Education, Local Education Authorities and Museums would be important. The Council's role would be that of preparing and circulating visual aids of various kinds, possibly including collections of objects.

Then there was the adult population, polarising at two extremes. One was the 'leadership group' whose members were 'alert and articulate' with a keen interest in design and anxious to learn more about it. For them the Council would produce a range of serious publications, exhibitions, documentary films and lecture materials. It also hoped to engage the cooperation of the BBC in broadcasting and television. But the second and larger group of adults were the real problem – the 'uninterested' who 'know what they like' and have no wish to change:

6.4 Early design exhibitions were attended by an interested cross-section of the public from stockbrokers to schoolchildren. Publications on sale included Herbert Read's classic *Art and Industry*, but the children's guide to 'Britain Can Make It' outsold all others with 138,000 copies at one penny each. Subsequently Reilly concentrated on extending CoID influence through films, broadcasting and a variety of teaching aids.

> There is no point in exaggerating the amount of interest they at present feel in design, or minimising the difficulty of raising their critical awareness. The way to do it is to find the points of common interest and work from them ... The normal arts of publicity can be used – entertaining films and broadcasts, popular booklets with a practical twist, 'home' exhibitions, and so on. The popular feminine magazines are very ready to help and the Council is grateful for their cooperation.[2]

Clearly, to lead such a programme an individual of diverse talents and experience was required. As might have been expected, Russell found such a person. While returning from America aboard the *Queen Mary* in 1946, he met a young man likewise interested in design. Paul Reilly had been sent to New York to carry out research for a plastics journal to be started in the UK. Unfortunately for his publishers the assignment could not be fulfilled because of a post-war shortage of paper. Fortunately for the CoID this released him to become their Chief Information Officer. Along with Richard Dudley Ryder in charge of Exhibitions and John Weyman in charge of Finance and Administration, Reilly completed Russell's senior team. For him the relationship was to be a long and fruitful one.

6.5 Teaching with the aid of CoID *Design Folios* in 1949. This series of pictorial essays proved extremely popular, covering fields as diverse as wallpaper and yacht design. The teacher's blackboard drawing shows a teapot with 'easy grip, cool handle, steady base' which 'strains and pours well'.

Whereas Russell was craftsman turned writer, Reilly was salesman turned designer. Son of Professor Sir Charles Reilly, Head of the Liverpool School of Architecture, after studying at Oxford he became, in turn, commercial traveller, journalist on the *News Chronicle*, Naval Lieutenant-Commander, Editor of British Plastics Encyclopaedia, eminent fabrics and textiles designer and, eventually, Director of the Council of Industrial Design. Over a period of twenty-nine years his ability to forge friendships in the cause of good design and of the Council itself, was to be of immense importance.

The task for Reilly and his team was daunting. The few Information Officers were as stretched as their Industrial colleagues, tackling parallel problems and prejudices, but on a broader front. As finance was limited, sensitive and time-consuming cooperation with other bodies was expedient. Russell's Policy Report of 1947 suggested: 'Much greater use should be made, where necessary, of existing outside bodies such as societies, publishers, teachers, designers, film producers etc.' To these he added in his 1949 Report 'Future Policy following the Festival' an emphasis on the role of the retailer. In effect, the majority of media was to be exploited through the majority of outside organisations. When the talented Dick Ryder left the Council in 1948 exhibitions work was also

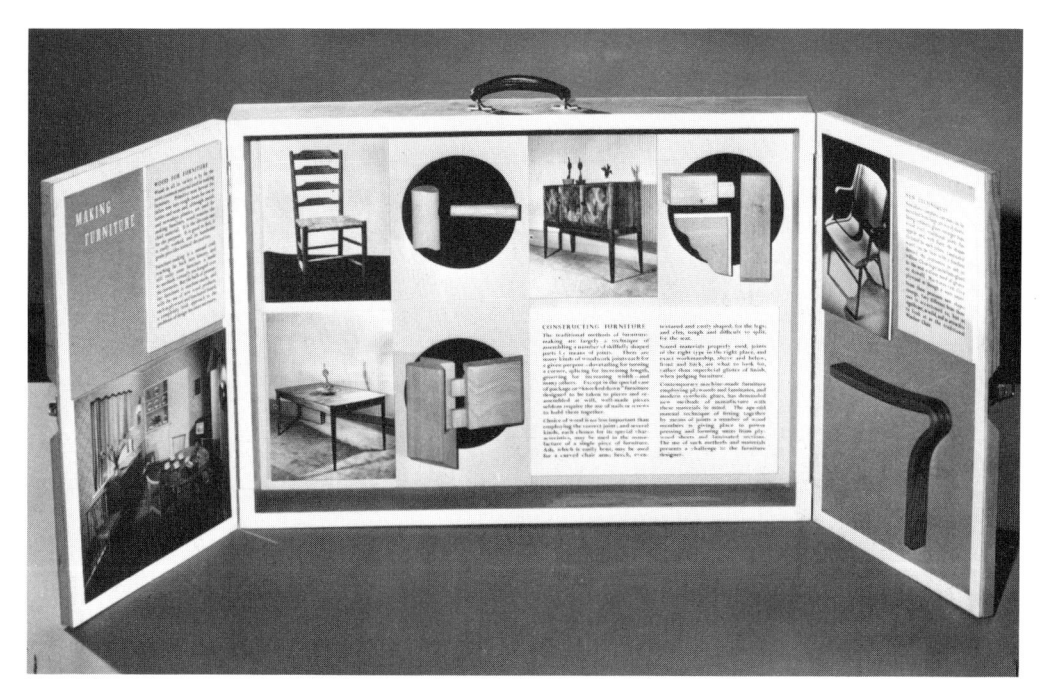

6.6 One of the portable box exhibitions which were in constant demand from museums, retail stores and colleges, as well as schools throughout the country. This example on furniture was prepared by the CoID Scottish Committee.

absorbed. Reilly took all this in his stride. He summarised the work of the Division as follows:

> The function of the Information Division is to stimulate the demand for better design. This is by and large a straightforward propaganda and publicity job and all the accepted media of publicity are open to us – such as publications, the press, films, film-strips, broadcasting, exhibitions and vartious teaching aids like wallcards and portable exhibitions.[3]

Notwithstanding the *First Annual Report*, in view of the size of the audience it was decided to concentrate on three main groups: the younger generation in schools and colleges, the distributive trades, and the voluntary organisations concerned with further and adult education. The work of the division was seen to fall logically into two parts, production and promotion. The former involved the preparation of display material, the latter publicising it. These were supported by the Education, Retail and Exhibitions Sections plus the Press Office, Photographic Library and Reference Library. In general the emphasis of the early years was very much on education, despite this being a long-term strategy carrying less kudos with the Board of Trade.

6.7, 6.8 *Above.* Launched in 1949 primarily for designers and manufacturers, *Design* magazine captured the interest of students and retailers, if not the general public. However, detailed analyses of consumer goods were a regular feature, including this one on food mixers in May 1959. Of the Kenwood *Chef* it said 'The full curves of the head and base, and the parallelism of the pillar make the Kenwood *Chef* look heavy. Mechanical details such as the louvre, the hinge lug, the locking button and the clamping screw, together with the old-fashioned trade mark, all conspire to suggest the *Chef* belongs to hotel kitchen rather than domestic interior.' But the machine was efficient, and in the same year the Consumers' Association magazine *Which?* voted it Best Buy. *Below.* The April 1961 issue of *Design* included a favourable in-depth report on the restyled and re-engineered *Chef*, as carried out by Kenneth Grange. The new design has remained virtually unchanged to this day and enjoys healthy exports.

PUBLICATIONS AND PROMOTIONS

Experimental production of a variety of teaching aids began almost immediately. Many of these were innovatory including film-strips with record commentaries and portable box exhibitions. More basic but extremely popular was the series of CoID Design Folios. The first set of twelve cards on Furniture Making appeared in 1947. Such was the demand for these as 'permanent' visual material that they were quickly followed by others on subjects as wide-ranging as wallpaper, street furniture and sports gear. By 1952 over 2000 schools had purchased sets and many former pupils will no doubt recall their use.

The first of the delightful series of travelling box exhibitions for schools was also begun in 1947. Each 'exhibition' consisted of six boxes travelling in two crates and contained notes, pictures and samples. Demand from colleges, museums, art galleries and even retail stores, in addition to schools, was considerable. Ironically, the post-war timber shortage prevented production of more than a few sets, and research into the use of alternative materials for the cases had to be carried out. However, it did not prevent the construction of some equally attractive scale models for 'demonstrating the planning of furniture to meet social needs'.

Publication of informative books, spurred on by the major exhibitions, also got off to a good start. Two Puffin Books and a leaflet on 'Britain Can Make It' were prepared for children, the leaflet selling an impressive 138,000 copies at one penny each! For the serious reader, a set of inexpensive Penguin Books entitled *The Things We See* was commenced. Additionally, the souvenir record of 'Britain Can Make It' contained twenty-seven weighty articles ranging from fashion to office equipment. To spice the mixture Bernard Shaw wrote a witty and intelligent conclusion on Aesthetic Science. In 1951 the Council's *Design in the Festival* was acknowledged to be one of the best souvenir books, selling almost 100,000 copies.

A reference library offering a specialised collection of books, magazines and press cuttings was rapidly accumulated for staff use. This was then generously made available to outside groups and individuals. A unique feature was the collection of classified photographs and 'lantern slides'. The Annual Report of 1946 had bemoaned the fact that 'Pictures and photographs for visual propaganda are at present scarce, except for well-worn pre-war material'. Within two years an independent Photographic Library had over 10,000 prints and expanded to become 'the most comprehensive in the country'. A slide collection was begun with just 350 black and white slides but new 'miniature' colour transparencies were soon included. Eventually these grew to 25,000 items with their own lending and sales service. Sets and accompanying notes came to be assembled upon subjects from Charles Rennie Mackintosh to the history of the slot machine.

Amongst the early duties of library staff was the compilation of *Design Calendar*, giving details of lectures and exhibitions throughout the country. There was even a weekly 'Intelligence Bulletin' containing short abstracts on design, made available by subscription. The contents were selected from other journals, but this was, in effect, the forerunner of the Council's own magazine, *Design*.

Proposals for a journal had been submitted to the Gorrell Committee in 1932 by Margaret Bully. Its propaganda message would be aimed at the public as well as industry:

> Might not such a journal be useful to all who know little or nothing about the principles of art, and therefore prove a powerful influence in that renaissance of industrial art which our committee believes no impossible dream? New ideas demand a new transmitter. A new journal taking long views of the future of British industry, might endeavour gradually to raise the public taste.[4]

The publication of *Design* in 1949 was seen therefore as 'the most notable venture of the year'. However, it was launched as a magazine aimed primarily at manufacturers and designers, but soon captured readers in art schools and the retail trade. Russell himself wrote the very first article 'Good Design is not a Luxury', in which he expounded the principles of good design with the determination of Walter Gropius's first Bauhaus manifesto:

> Good design always takes into account the technique of production, the material to be used, and the purpose for which the object is wanted.
>
> Good design is not precious, arty or high falutin'.
>
> Good design is not something that can be added to a product at a late stage in its planning or manufacture. It is fundamental.

Such principles, he argued, were the strong selling points for the future. But an informed public response was also required and, indeed, was being achieved in a two-way process:

> We cannot all become conductors but we can learn to appreciate music – and remember, no conductor could give his best to an audience of deaf mutes; there must be collaboration.[5]

6.9–6.12 The CoID produced several early films and filmstrips on design. These shots are from the filmstrip *Let's Look at Design*, 1947, which includes the production of a table lamp from drawing-board to display. Batch rather than mass production is the order of the day, but it offers viewers an insight into manufacturing which is more readily understood.

6.13, 6.14 The Design and Industries Association held the 'Register Your Choice' exhibition at Charing Cross Station in February 1953. Two identical living rooms were furnished for the same cost, one with popular selling lines, one with DIA-approved contemporary designs. The majority of the public was said to prefer the contemporary designs. *Left.* A 'popular' standard lamp. *Right.* A DIA-approved pendant light.

The magazine quickly established itself as a leading authority on industrial design, and sales grew steadily at home and abroad. Two thousand copies of the January 1952 issue, for example, were purchased by the Instituut Industrielle Vormgeving in Holland and issued with eight pages in Dutch. By 1954 subscription copies were being sent to fifty-eight countries and territories overseas. Features were devoted to different industries in turn and these included engineering and capital goods which, for the moment, were beyond the scope of the Council's usual activities. Claire Rayner wrote on the design of children's books and Bruce Archer's articles on Systematic Methods for Designers were reprinted as a single volume, quickly reaching a second edition. In-depth analyses of the development and performance of consumer products such as vacuum cleaners and food mixers were also possible. A reader inquiry service was introduced later which brought over 11,000 responses in the first year. The magazine attracted some knowledgeable writers including Michael Farr, author of *Design in British Industry* and John Blake, author of *The Practical Idealists*, both of whom were destined to become Heads of the Information Division.

A final service provided by the Council was its team of specialist lecturers. Initially the Design and Industries Association provided personnel – a positive example of cooperation between the two organisations – but as demand grew a list of Council Staff and outside speakers was drawn up. In 1950 the list contained an impressive 325 suitably qualified individuals and 237 lectures were given. Many famous names added colour and strength to the service by giving some esoteric yet entertaining analyses of the problems of design. A sense of preaching to the converted and of energetic optimism pervaded many of these lectures, very much reflecting the Council's own attitude. Gerald Barry, for example, addressed the Royal Philosophical Society, Glasgow, in the following terms:

> It is a curious anthropological fact that man by and large remains so obtuse to the meaning of design ... If we could teach people to use their eyes, really to take a look at what is around them for once, they would get such a shock they would insist on an improvement. It could be literally an eye-opener. We might then witness the most violent bloodless revolution in history.[6]

At a further lecture in Glasgow, Harold Hutchison, Chairman of the DIA, called for realism coupled with idealism and good hope: realism that public taste demands the *News of the World* and nude figure table lamps; idealism and good hope that the same readers might also choose the *News Chronicle* and 'well-designed contemporary furniture'.

All these many services catered well for the schools and leadership group, but what of the public at large? Here the emphasis was on the popular media including magazines, film and television. The Press Office played a vital role by feeding photographs and information to editors and reporters. It even provided free syndication of monthly features to house magazines. Particularly strong links were formed with the women's press which still bear fruit today. Among the early Council members were Mary Frieve of *Woman* and Alison Settle of *The Observer*.

The Council also produced its own popular booklets and films, which made a direct appeal to women. These demonstrated an attitude of realism not always shown by professional journals. For example, the first booklets *Buying for your Home* and *New Home* emphasised practicality as

6.15 A fifties furnished room arranged by the CoID in cooperation with retailers. All items appeared in the 1951 Stock List, but significantly the Primavera tables and lamp are handmade, emphasising the problem of obtaining suitable mass-produced goods. An element of Festival 'whimsy' is apparent in the splayed legs but is generally constrained.

well as beauty and the furnishing of old rooms as well as new. The first film, *Designing Women*, cast popular stars Joyce Grenfell and Joan Greenwood and went on general release in 1947. However, too flippant an approach was rejected when the comedy *Deadly Lampshade* failed to gain Council approval! From then on more responsible features such as *Home and Beautiful* were preferred.

Sadly, in the early fifties, reductions in the Council's grant-in-aid forced painful decisions. For the Labour Government the Korean War marked a turning point after which it even abandoned its all-embracing welfare

6.16 The set for the fortnightly television series *Joan Gilbert's Diary* in 1953 included furnishings chosen by Miss Gilbert from *Design Review*. This was the first time a contemporary setting had been used for a programme in which well-known personalities were interviewed.

state programme. The Council considered itself perhaps fortunate to sustain only a 25% cut. Rather than prune across the board it was decided to make one big cut. As is so often the case, because their benefits were long term, the educational services suffered. Publications were reduced, the library loan service stopped, the syndication of features ended, and so on. Exhibitions work was also curtailed, placing more dependence on outside groups such as the retailers who could bear the cost while the Council provided the 'know-how'.[7] Regrettably, recovery from such a cut could only be long term.

6.17, 6.18 *Left.* Poster designed by Judy Smith of Collett Dickenson Pearce & Partners for Pretty Polly. One of the 23 Design Council Poster Awards in 1973: 'What good fashion photography should look like. All-male jury were unanimous.' *Right.* Design by Bob Wright of Osborne Advertising for Elliott Leather. One of the 1974 Awards, described as 'Delicious'.

THE RETAIL TRADE

Russell had always considered it 'odd' that the retailer was not mentioned in Dalton's original letter. Consequently in 1949 he created a Retail Section within the Information Division. As Paul Reilly explained:

> The retail and the distributive trades hold a key position between manufacturer and consumer and it is our belief that they can very greatly influence for good or ill the standard of public taste and the design of manufactured goods.[8]

The enthusiasm of many retailers had been demonstrated at 'Design Weeks' in the provinces. Although the principal activity was to hold conferences for manufacturers, retailers and consumers, the Council's own small 'Design Fair' exhibitions were well supported by displays in local shops.

Another way in which retailers had cooperated was by exhibiting exemplar rooms from show houses. The original 'show house' was a furnished 'Prefab' in the 1946 Ideal Homes Exhibition. Such was its

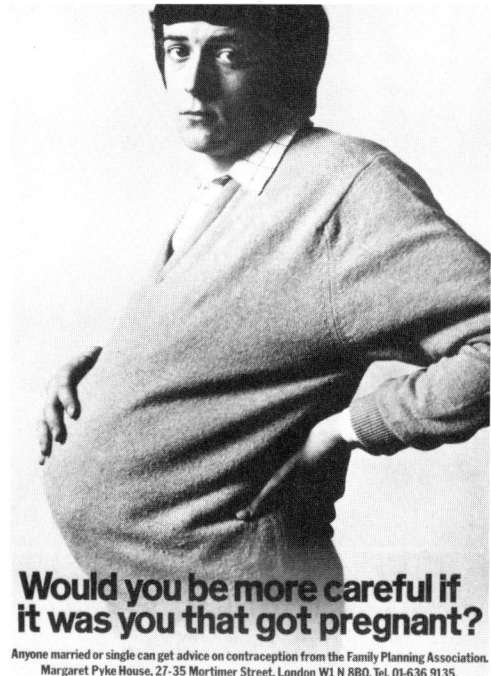

6.19, 6.20 *Left.* Poster design by William Hopkins of George Cuming for Bryant and May. Another of the 1973 Award winners: 'Extremely clever idea . . . house colours used to good advantage.' *Right.* Design by Atherton and Sinclair of Saatchi and Saatchi for the Family Planning Association. A 1971 Award winner, demonstrating 'effective technique – skilful and direct'.

popularity with the public that the Council furnished another twenty-two houses the same year! In 1949 the Council began to circulate the contents of selected show houses to stores in the provinces. Although the stores, in effect, financed the accommodation they were able to test demand before committing themselves to stock acquisitions.

The potential of the retailers for publicity was convincingly emphasised when the Council organised a shop window competition with the Regent Street Association. Thirty-five shops each offered a window to be dressed by art school students from London and the Home Counties. Their displays attracted massive crowds and were widely reported in the press and on radio and television.

Methods of utilising regional support varied, but the contribution of retailers steadily increased, particularly from progressive stores such as Brown's of Chester and Lewis's Ltd, whose directors were also Council Members. In 1952, for example, a show house in Birmingham was furnished by manufacturers and suppliers under Council direction and thirty-two local retailers held stocks of items and arranged their own displays. The *Birmingham Mail* produced the illustrated catalogue with all necessary details and sold 10,000 copies. Another approach was the touring exhibition such as 'Round the Table'. First shown at the Tea Centre, London, this display of pottery, glass, cutlery and flatware was circulated to stores such as Beal's of Bournemouth, Hammond's of Hull and Schofield's of Leeds.

Inevitably, the most consistent supporters were the few stores who combined quality goods with an interest in modern design. During the fifties these blossomed as rare provincial oases, yet were able to reach millions of consumers. Brave support also came from the Cooperative Movement which uniquely represented retailer, manufacturer and consumer. Yet sadly its products did not achieve a reputation for good design, emphasising the problem that good equates with expense. It was to take Terence Conran's Habitat stores to break this association in the sixties.

For a short time in 1955–56 exhibitions in the stores were curtailed while the Council prepared its own shop window, the Design Centre, Haymarket. But, if anything, this reinforced the need for national support, and in 1958 'The Design Centre Comes to Newcastle' heralded displays around Britain. Bainbridge's Store devoted 2000 square feet to a mini-Centre which attracted 50,000 visitors in three weeks. Subsequently, stores in every major city held Design Centre displays. Even so the Council's *Annual Report* of 1960 noted:

> ... a great deal needs to be done and it is still difficult in many towns to find a shop whose general level of merchandise makes it an obvious choice for a display of goods from the Design Centre.[9]

In contrast, the offices of high street stores and other commercial premises were often equipped to a high standard by contract suppliers, and the CoID's catalogue became a valuable reference guide.

A further extension of retail activities was to exploit stores overseas. Potentially this was one of the most effective means of penetrating foreign markets. The Council had already successfully cut its teeth by organising stands at international trade fairs and exhibitions. For example, 'Modern U.K.' in the 1953 British Pavilion at Toronto displayed 520 products suitable for contemporary homes. A special feature was the cooperation with retail buyers to stock Canadian stores. Now the Council was to exhibit directly in the stores themselves. In 1959, three exhibitions were staged in a chain of stores in the Hague, Amsterdam and Rotterdam. The opening ceremony was performed by the British Ambassador and such was the publicity that requests came from several other countries. By the following year the Overseas Promotion Section had arranged exhibitions

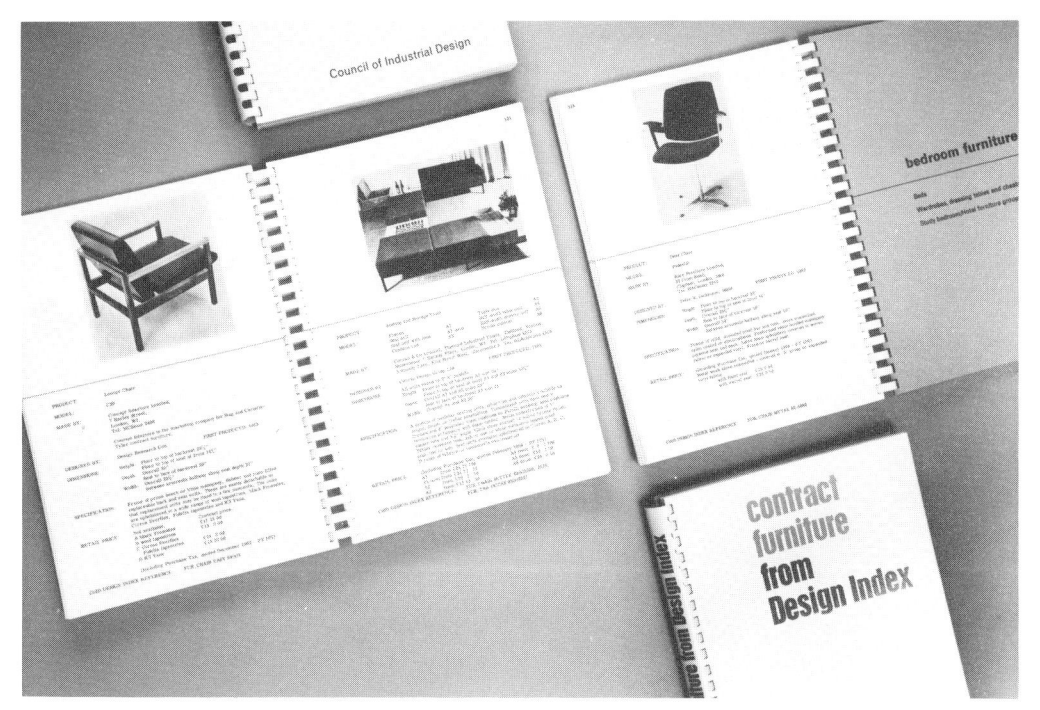

6.21 Pages from the illustrated catalogue of contract furniture which was presented to over 10,000 buyers to influence the furnishing of public and commercial premises. Ironically contract suppliers such as Hille International and Ryman were able to stock items more acceptable to the CoID than those in high street stores.

in stores in Berlin, Johannesburg, Helsinki, Milan and Tokyo, all of which gained extensive press and even peak television coverage.

The organisation of courses and conferences for the home retail community and, indeed, for all sections of industry, was a final means of extending publicity and propaganda. Courses for retailers began in 1949, initially for staff trainers and then for specialists in such fields as furniture and furnishing. As Russell pointed out to the latter group:

> *You* are in a position to influence public taste as no one else is. Public taste is always founded to a great extent on what people see in shop windows, since what they don't see they seldom ask for.[10]

Attractive and appropriate settings were carefully chosen for the venues. A popular choice was Attingham Park, Shrewsbury, which, after being bequeathed to the National Trust, housed both the Shropshire Adult College and well-furnished state rooms. It has since been suggested that such activities are hardly productive, being attended by individuals to escape the routine of work.[11] Yet an immediate response followed the original course by the formation of the influential Midland Retailers' Design Discussion Group.

Courses and conferences had the advantage of providing a two-way interaction, and the Council learnt from both audiences and guest speakers. On the first course the newly appointed Retail Officer demonstrated Council teaching materials for staff training. Rapid feedback came when it was pointed out that the slides were all 3¼ in. × 3¼ in. whereas modern projectors took 2 in. × 2 in. In the case of conferences for high level management and professional groups, some salutary lessons emerged. For example, at the Conference on Furniture Design in 1949 a paper by Dr Dennis Chapman offered a sociologist's perspective on public taste. The first basis of homemaking was a 'romantic illusion', followed by social considerations within the growing family and its relationship with the community. These factors were 'infinitely more complex' than the Council's 'somewhat naive appraisal'! Wives were primarily, even almost entirely, responsible for choosing furniture and women's magazines could be one of the few sources of education.[12]

The Council did in fact trouble to publish suggestions made by 'housewife designers' during a forum at Design Week Wales.[13] These included a well-designed kitchen stool ('The only comfortable stool I have seen is my dentist's'), square saucepans to save space, and longer sheets for single beds. Some ideas were already redundant ('Could our Welsh bake-stones be made with handles?') but others foretold national trends ('More food – especially bread – should be wrapped' and a suggestion for full-width cooker grills).

One important adjunct to retailing is, of course, advertising. A measure of the mushrooming expansion of this field is given by Society of Industrial Artists (SIA) membership figures, which rose from just thirty in 1930 to 3500 in the sixties, by far the largest group being the graphic artists. Of course mass advertising goes hand-in-hand with mass production, and well-designed products deserve the best publicity. Furthermore, advertisements, particularly posters, themselves affect the visual environment, whether on the underground or on city hoardings.

In order to 'stimulate interest in the use of posters as a form of publicity and to encourage a high standard of modern design' the CoID inaugurated in 1962 the British Poster Design Awards. Co-sponsors in the venture were fifteen organisations ranging from the Civic Trust to the SIA itself. During the sixties and seventies many of the winners became firmly imprinted in the public's memory. Pretty Polly Tights, for example, won several awards, offering a fresh and witty approach to advertising in this field. And some of the larger London agencies such as Saatchi and Saatchi were to gain reputations well beyond the confines of the profession.

6.22, 6.23 *Above.* The *Embassy* teapot by David Mellor, which was commissioned by the Ministry of Public Building and Works for use in British embassies in 1963, as part of a modernisation programme. *Below.* Prototype easy-chair designed by Roger Sale for the Ministry of Public Building and Works. Made in fibreglass on a swivel base, its upholstered stool has a removable top which serves as an occasional table. Shown at the 1970 CoID exhibition 'Supplies Supplies', which included products for government offices, residential accommodation, the armed services, museums and embassies.

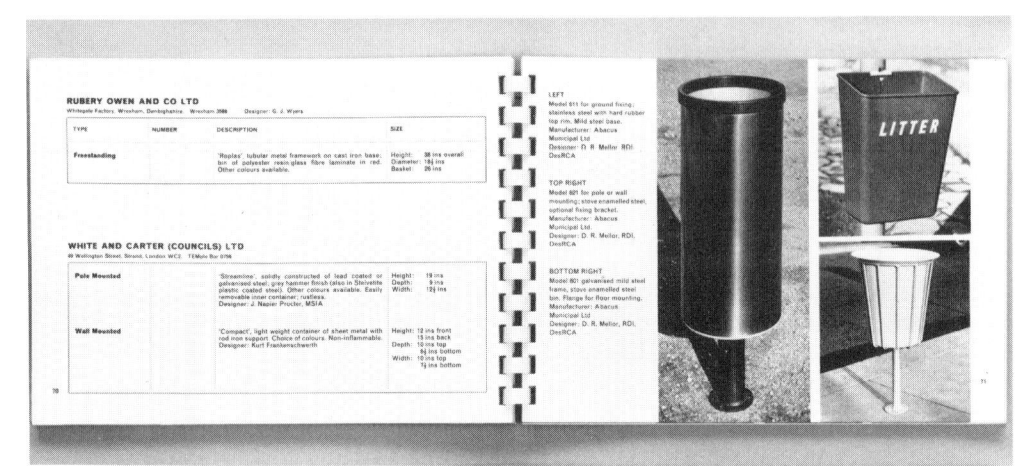

6.24 The CoID Street Furniture Committee first convened in 1952 to advise on concrete lamp posts. Scope soon widened to include bus shelters, litter bins and outdoor seating and the bi-annual catalogue *Street Furniture* became a valuable service to official bodies.

OFFICIAL BODIES

A final and fruitful field for propaganda was to be that of other official organisations. Dalton's letter had specifically recommended 'to advise, at the request of Government Departments and other public bodies, on the design of articles to be purchased by them . . .' However, ingrained conservatism along the corridors of power influenced decisions regarding the furnishing of their own buildings. Any propagada promoting new or untried products would have to be well conceived. If as a basic principle interiors are harmonised with exteriors then post-war designs would rest uneasily in gothic revival town halls and neoclassical ministries. Of course, certain products transcend such difficulties: for example, the

6.25 HRH The Duke of Edinburgh with Paul Reilly, inspecting the 1961 exhibition of street furniture on the South Bank.

range of civic and embassy plate commissioned from the elite group of graduate silversmiths. But here only craft or batch production was involved. It was in the requisitioning of furniture and fixtures of moulded plywood, veneered chipboard and tubular steel for new 'glasshouse' schools and offices that vast quantities were involved, and where the Contract Furniture Catalogue and *Design Index* played a valuable role.

Furthermore, the Council was soon to extend its brief beyond umbrella stands and school desks. In post-war Britain the control which central and local government came to exercise over the designed environment was

6.26 An attempt by the CoID to publicise well-designed products from *Design Index*. Four bright yellow showcases in Harlow Shopping Precinct display merchandise which is simultaneously on sale in local shops.

immense. Complete city centres were cleared and rebuilt, offering a unique opportunity to the planners. But it rapidly became clear that all was not well. Frank Pick had despaired many years before of unco-ordinated urban development. Now there was danger of even further confusion.

Although the CoID's terms of reference did not include architecture, outside furniture seemed quite appropriate. This is a field in which design requirements are surprisingly demanding. Considerable pressure falls on the responsible authorities regarding safety, lighting, information and traffic control, in addition to the duty to provide for the comfort and convenience of pedestrians. As with architecture, problems are as much to do with co-ordination as with individual designs. A Street Furniture

6.27 A seventies attempt to improve on the flat mounting of posters in an acceptable manner for the growing number of new shopping precincts.

Committee was therefore appointed in 1952 which initially had the restricted task of advising on lamp posts. Even these range from intricate sculptures in cast iron or bronze to utilitarian support apparatus in tubular steel or concrete. The former may be a unique feature of a road or concourse, the latter an unobtrusive cog in the machinery of urban survival. Work was soon expanded to include bus shelters, outdoor seats, bollards and litter bins, and the publication of a bi-annual catalogue became a valuable service to official bodies. The attractive book *Street Scene*, published in 1963, widened the appeal to heritage and local amenity groups with chapters as diverse as Conservation, Town Art, Playgrounds and Waterways.

In 1959 the Council was awarded the *Gran Premio Internazionale la*

6.28 By 1972 the CoID *Street Furniture* catalogue included advice about the mounting of road signs and planning of vehicle-free areas. This signpost is an example of the confusion which existed in Windsor before replanning.

Rinascente Compass d'Oro by a distinguished international jury. This award, sponsored by the great Italian store *La Rinascente*, is made annually for outstanding contributions to industrial design. The Council received the prize 'as the oldest and most efficient government organisation for the development and popularisation of good design'. The jury emphasised that a crisis existed in many countries which hinged on inadequate co-ordination between designers, producers and consumers. It hoped, therefore, that the Council would:

> ... serve as an example for all those governments which so far have ignored or ineffectively dealt with the need for a co-ordination of studies in the field of design.[14]

The Council's publicity and propaganda was sufficiently well established in the UK and abroad that, at least in this sense, it was honoured as leader of the field. As we shall see, particularly in one aspect of design promotion, namely the establishment of national design centres, the Council was to set a precedent for other industrial countries.

7.1 'The Design Centre for British Industries in Haymarket, London, is the most useful tool that the Council has devised for carrying out it task of promoting the improvement of design in the products of British Industry.' CoID *Twelfth Annual Report*, 1956–57.

−7−
DESIGN EXHIBITION CENTRES

INTRODUCTION

Provision of their own display centre has always been a concern of design propagandists, fulfilling a role somewhere between the spectacular exhibitionism of the Crystal Palace, the academic historicism of the Victoria and Albert Museum, and the entrepreneurial commercialism of Heal's or Habitat Stores. In 1956 the CoID finally opened its Design Centre in Haymarket, London. As a permanent shop window for British industry, this became a small but significant means of influence. *Design Index*, developed from the 1951 Stock List, was the basis of selection, encouraged by special promotions and awards. Royal patronage, ministerial support and media interest now focused on the Council's work. Mass Observation reported visitors full of praise, although they did tend to be from higher social and economic bands of the population. As an international accolade, countries throughout the world opened Design Centres in the following decade.

DESIGN CENTRE, HAYMARKET

On 30 November 1936, the Crystal Palace, after eighty-five years of service and by now resited on Sydenham Hill, provided a last great display by spectacularly burning down. However, there did remain in London a patchy provision of exhibition halls. The Alexandra Palace, renowned as the early BBC Television Centre, dates back to 1862. Originally erected in South Kensington for the 1862 International Exhibition and nicknamed the Brompton Boilers (being so ugly), it too burnt down after rebuilding and was rebuilt yet again. Olympia, opened in 1886 for entertainment spectacles such as Buffalo Bill, subsequently held Ideal Home and Building Exhibitions. Earl's Court was opened one year later to accommodate everything from circuses to trade fairs. Its present building, which dates from 1937, has popularly held the Boat Show and Motor Show. The British Industries Fair, established by the government in 1915, was held annually until 1957 in Earl's Court, Olympia and West Bromwich near Birmingham. Following the demise of the British Indus-

7.2 Haymarket House, acquired as premises for The Design Centre, October 1954.

tries Fair, the Board of Trade deliberated the need to build a brand new exhibition centre to promote British industry. Finally, in 1976 the National Exhibition Centre was opened in Birmingham for this task. But a centre solely for design under control of a body such as the CoID was something rather different.

Had the Victoria and Albert Museum been able to fulfil its original function, emphasising contemporary displays, arguably there would have been no need for such a centre to come into being. And had Terence Conran's three dozen or so Habitat Stores been free from commercial pressures they might well have usurped its function, at least with regard to consumer goods. But being smaller, non-commercial with constantly

7.3, 7.4 *Left.* Philip Fellows, the Council's Exhibitions Officer and Robert Nicholson, designer of the Centre's display fittings, examine a preliminary model. *Right.* One of the distinguished visitors to the newly opened Centre was Walter Gropius. He is seen here with Nicholson at the first exhibition in 1956.

changing displays of a highly selective nature, a design centre requires different premises, philosophy and organisation.

During the planning of the Festival of Britain, Gerald Barry, as always pressing for new ideas, had raised the matter of a permanent design centre. Gordon Russell, who liked the idea, replied '... we will bear it in mind'. But the concept was not entirely new: Gorell (1932) emphasised that a necessary provision would be an 'exhibitions building', preferably in the West End; Weir (1943) recommended a 'pavilion' to 'show the foreigner ... the best that British can produce'; Meynell–Hoskins (1944) noted that without a 'show house' the Council would 'lack public face and show an absence of official heart'; and the *First Annual Report* (1946) stressed that a 'central pavilion' would be of 'considerable importance to the Council's future exhibitions policy and to much of its other work'.

When Dr Walter Warboys became Council Chairman in January 1953, he decided momentum must be maintained following the Festival. Time was ripe for the Design Centre as the next major objective. Being a director of ICI he was a man of action and backed Russell to the hilt. After an intense search premises were found at 28 Haymarket, described by Russell as 'a new and ugly building but on an almost perfect site'. It was only 100 metres from Piccadilly, in the heart of London's West End and on the routes of thirteen buses! Whereas few people had ever heard of the original Council premises in Petty France, many came to know of the

The shopper's guide
to good design.
steel
appeal
selected for the
DESIGN
CENTRE
LONDON
selected for the
DESIGN
CENTRE
LONDON
The Design Centre 28 Haymarket London SW1Y 4SU
Open Monday to Saturday 09.30 to 17.30 hours
Wednesday and Thursday until 21.00 hours
Admission free

7.5–7.7 *Opposite, top.* Prince Philip opened the Design Centre on 26 April 1956 and annually selected a limited number of products for The Duke of Edinburgh's Prize. Spode *Appollo* ware, for example, designed by Neal French and David White, subsequently received a Prize for Elegant Design. The original models had been developed while both were students at the Royal College of Art. *Far left.* The Design Centre label was devised as a hall-mark of quality, primarily for consumer products, although eventually it encompassed engineering and capital goods. A grey and black version was specially designed for 'Steel Appeal'. *Left.* A group of visitors examines a Design Centre display of tableware and furnishings. Initially the emphasis was very much on domestic consumer goods. The displays attracted an average of over 2000 visitors per day.

Design Centre in the Haymarket and the offices so conveniently sited above.

Frank Austin and Neville Ward, both prominent in the Record of Designers, were asked to prepare a special treatment of the building's façade. Roger and Robert Nicholson, who had contributed to the Homes and Gardens Pavilion of the Festival, were appointed to design the exhibition fittings. The whole interior scheme was devised to be as flexible as possible so that the exhibits could be constantly changed. A range of display units was conceived which relied principally on materials and construction for effect and was illuminated from a ceiling grid of light points concealed by framed plastic panels. Overall, the square, neat theme represented a break from the delicate, though disproportionate, curvilinear Festival Style. For the Council a new era of Mainstream Modern had arrived.

It was to be two years before the premises were finally completed to the Council's satisfaction, during which time the successful opening became everybody's concern. The Industrial Division was encouraging manufacturers to produce and submit products worthy of selection. The Retail Section was persuading shops to stock and display the goods chosen. The Education Section was organising school visits. The Press Office was publicising the Centre. The Administration Division was organising staffing and financing. The reconstituted Exhibitions Division was planning the displays and the Reception Staff were answering inquiries.

While the building was being prepared, steps were taken to increase the number of goods submitted to the *Design Review* Committee, which now assumed considerable importance, having Russell himself as Chairman and Major-General Benoy as Deputy Chairman. Categories of goods, although still essentially domestic, were widened to include industries such as textiles and bicycles and, perhaps even then too late to stem the Japanese two-wheeled invasion, motorcycles.

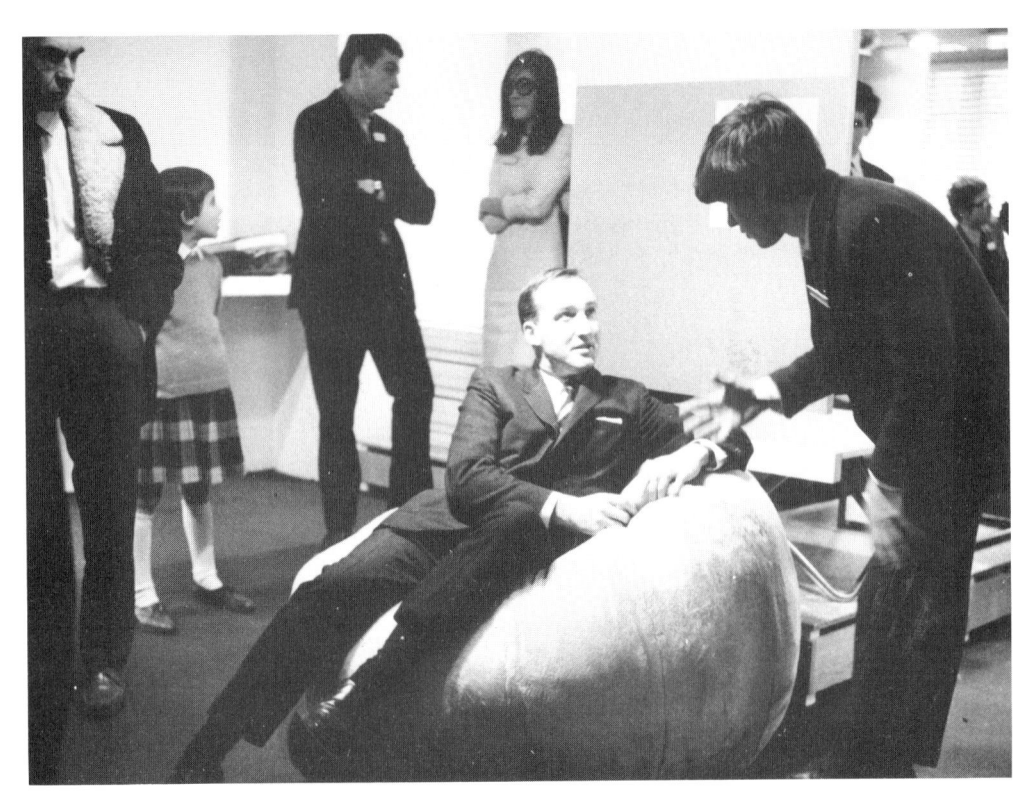

7.8 Furniture continued to be a major public attraction following the opening of the Design Centre. In January 1967 an exhibition of prototype furniture designed by students broke all previous attendance records. Illustrated above is the *Sea Urchin* dome chair, made up from twelve polyurethane foam sections by Roger Dean of the Royal College of Art.

The Centre even had its own symbol, registered under the Trade Marks Act, which manufacturers could link to any product chosen for display. Ideally suited to the fifties, being a combination of abstract eye on arrow on diamond, it was eventually superseded by the simpler, more rugged counterpoint design of today. However, this idea of a symbol to identify Council-approved goods was initially only adopted with reservation. At a furnishing salesmen's course in 1951 Russell had been questioned about such a scheme and replied guardedly, 'A hall-mark of this kind might be considered as an attempt by the Council to dictate, or as interference with private enterprise, and there is strong opposition in many quarters . . .'[1] Of course, as the Centre became famous its badge of esteem was to be conferred in ever-increasing numbers.

Another contentious issue was that of charges. Breaking a ten-year-old principle, the Council accepted with reluctance the government's view that manufacturers should be prepared to pay for the privilege of having goods on display. With an estimated running cost of £80,000 this was

7.9, 7.10 Another experimental design was this inflatable PVC chair by Quasar Khanh. *Below.* A range of children's furniture made in painted birch plywood by Susan Ekins of Newcastle College of Art and Design.

perhaps inevitable and the Board of Trade at least agreed to match half the receipts. For an average monthly period a wristwatch was therefore charged at £4 and a settee at £10. When the Finance and Executive Committee's accounts for the first year were submitted these showed that receipts of £40,000 had in fact accrued. To break even in the first year was quite an achievement. Additionally, industry had donated £27,000 towards the Centre with old friends such as the General Electric Company, Imperial Chemical Industries and Lewis's very much in support.

Despite temporary setbacks and delays, the whole complex operation of selecting, calling forward, invoicing and returning exhibits went remarkably smoothly. Appropriately the Nicholson Brothers were asked to carry out the first display which involved over a thousand items from 438 firms plus supporting window displays in over 100 shops and stores throughout the country. Great time and effort was directed towards interesting editors, radio and television producers and public bodies who fortunately realised that a pioneering project of national significance was about to commence. The effort achieved the desired result:

> No other country has anything like this. (*News Chronicle*)
>
> ... it is the sort of service that could revolutionise shopping ... (*Daily Telegraph*)
>
> ... should do much to mobilise public opinion behind the movement towards better standards ... (*Financial Times*)

To open the Centre on 26 April 1956 the Council was fortunate to obtain the services of HRH The Duke of Edinburgh who declared, 'I hope that the Design Centre will now enter upon an industrious, adventurous, controversial life, and I wish it the best of luck.' Its resultant success can be judged from the unexpectedly large attendances, averaging 2300 per day during the following year; by the time spent by visitors studying the exhibits; by the increasing submissions to *Design Review*; and by the vast amount of publicity accorded to this national shop window. The delight of the Council was reflected in its *Twelfth Annual Report* which commenced:

> The Design Centre for British Industries in Haymarket, London, is the most useful tool that the Council has devised for carrying out its task of promoting the improvement of design in the products of British Industry.[2]

Whatever reservations had existed about the Design Centre label, it was clearly here to stay. As a means of reaching manufacturers, retailers and consumers at one and the same time, the label was an obvious

7.11, 7.12 *Above.* Her Majesty the Queen visits the Cunard exhibition at the Design Centre on 28 February 1968. Weekly attendance records were broken when over 35,000 people came to the relatively small premises in one week. *Below.* James Gardner and Dennis Lennon, joint design co-ordinators of the QE2, were both recommended to Cunard through the CoID Designer Selection Service. Gardner was largely responsible for external styling while Lennon directed interior design. The construction, by John Brown's of Glasgow, brought a brief respite to ailing Scottish heavy industry, as had construction of the first liner *Queen Elizabeth* in the thirties.

7.13 Designed by Robert Heritage and manufactured by Race Furniture, the QE2 restaurant chair featured several important innovations. Its frame principles have since developed into a range of contract seating with minimum 'leg forest'.

success. Supplied in various sizes, in the first ten years over 60 million were bought by manufacturers. Subtle but significant changes were made to its appearance which came to be widely recognised as a mark of quality. Its scope was then extended to include capital and engineering goods and one version in grey and black was specially designed for 'Steel Appeal'.

Further projects and services relating to the Centre were developed: buyers' guides, special promotions for manufacturers, detailed information leaflets and inquiry cards. In 1965 a mezzanine office floor was converted to further exhibition space, enabling displays of industries such as printing, medical engineering and scientific instruments, ranging well beyond the domestic scene. A souvenir shop was also opened and, following successful experimentation with the sale of books, a permanent bookshop installed on an upper ground floor. This quickly established itself as a central source of books on all aspects of design and even offered its own mail order service.

The Centre was able to celebrate its tenth year by attracting nearly a million visitors, or an average of almost 3000 per day. Under the guidance of Philip Fellows who devoted himself to exhibitions work from 1947 to 1977, the Council won an international reputation for skilful, imaginative displays. In January 1967, an exhibition of student-designed prototype furniture broke all records for popularity. By the close of the sixties attendance figures had soared even higher, with new records being set repeatedly. The Council was particularly pleased that the joint design co-ordinators of the liner *Queen Elizabeth II*, James Gardner and Dennis Lennon, were both recommended to Cunard via the Designer Selection Service. The Cunard exhibition broke further records, only to be exceeded during the Victoria Line exhibition when the Centre reached saturation point.

DESIGN CENTRE AWARDS

Prince Philip himself was to be a regular attender at the Haymarket, for within a year of the opening he consolidated his support in a new and influential way. It was decided to select annually a limited number of products for special commendation. This offered prestige for both designers and manufacturers. It also offered publicity for the Council as well as enabling a re-examination of the many thousands of products shown each year. The Prince agreed to revisit the Centre to present certificates and through his own initiative established The Duke of Edinburgh's Prize for Elegant Design.

Each year a panel of eminent judges was drawn up and the selection procedure reviewed. Amongst the first were Professors Robert Gooden and Dick Russell who were gratified to find that former Royal College of Art students regularly won awards. The focus was initially upon domestic goods, but gradually the scope was widened, like the displays themselves, to include tools and instruments and eventually capital goods.

Initially the same designers appeared to be winning year after year: David Mellor gained one award in 1957 and two in 1959; Robin Day gained two in 1957; John and Sylvia Reid gained one award in 1957 and one in 1959. The same manufacturers' names also appeared regularly: Hille, Walker and Hall, Wilkinson Sword and Wedgwood. But these were the leaders of the day, encouraged by the Council to spearhead the gradual improvement which became noticeable in the sixties.

Both the Awards and the Prize were to provoke considerable interest and controversy. Paul Reilly, like Russell before him, found consolation in the fact that any extreme criticisms counterbalanced one another:

> In spite of the annual chorus of disappointment that the Design Centre Awards have been too austere, too frivolous, too banal, too expensive, too ordinary, too fashionable or too dull, there can be little doubt that these awards, and the even more controversial Duke of Edinburgh's Prize for Elegant Design, have well served the purpose for which they were intended, while incidentally producing some useful bonuses.[3]

7.14 Since their inception Design Centre Awards have aroused controversy, but there is no doubting the success of many chosen products. Alex Moulton's innovatory bicycle of 1964 has influenced competitors at home and abroad.

A criticism sometimes voiced was that Council approval spelt the 'Kiss of Death' to a product and that commercially an Award was a 'Fate Worse than Death'. Yet there are many examples to prove this untrue. The Rotaflex lampshade of 1957, designed by John and Sylvia Reid, helped establish modern light fittings at a time when no single retail store had a separate lighting department. Their spotlight of 1961 preceded a boom in this country as well as being manufactured immediately under licence in America and exported across Europe. In contrast, Old Hall's toast rack of 1958, designed by Robert Welch, was well ahead of public taste and although sales climbed slowly at first it became the company's best seller, eventually being copied by the Japanese.

Across a widening range of Award winners numerous successes could be recorded. The Brownie camera of 1960 sold so well that Kodak were unable to satisfy demand and had to extend production two years longer than anticipated. Alex Moulton's innovatory bicycle of 1964 received a considerable boost from the Awards poster before being copied by competitors at home and abroad. Yet one weakness to emerge was that of

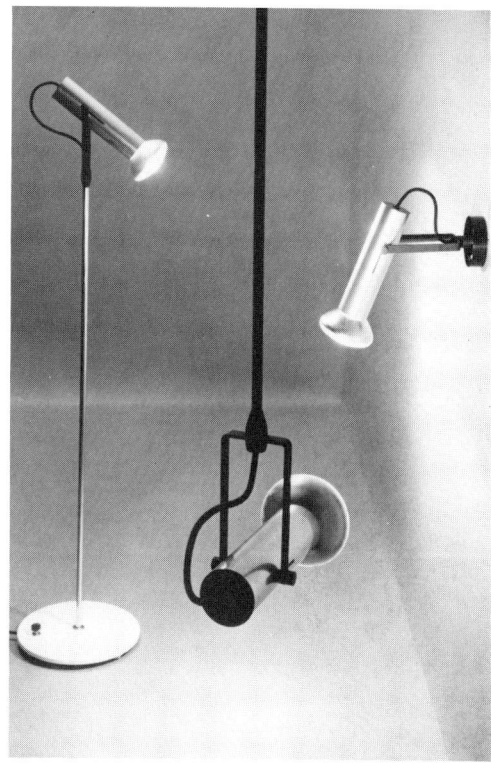

7.15, 7.16 *Left.* The Milward Courier cordless shaver, designed by Kenneth Grange, won the Duke of Edinburgh's Prize for Elegant Design in 1963. *Right.* John and Sylvia Reid won Prizes in 1957 and 1959, heralding a considerable improvement in modern light fittings. Shown here are their 1961 Lightplan Universal designs for Rotaflex.

certain retail outlets, justifying future Council attention. Twyfords, who won awards in 1963 and 1967 for their Solar and Barbican washbasins, felt that builders' merchants did not promote award-winning designs. A. G. Thornton, whose Pic slide rule won in 1963, found office equipment retailers lacked specialist knowledge, and the company began to sell direct to student shops, education authorities and public bodies.

Perhaps the most uncontentious claim by the Award winners was the effect on company morale. Joseph Gillott and Sons, whose Orbit castor won in 1961, stated:

> The castor had been in production for only about six months when it received an award, and the biggest thing it did for us was to boost internal morale. It was a tremendous shot in the arm, particularly as the castor was an entirely new venture in an entirely new field.[4]

7.17 The Design Centre endeavoured to reach the provinces through leading department stores. Their longest-running retail promotion was at Hammond's of Hull, where five consecutive displays were held in 1971, commencing with 'As selected for the Design Centre, London'. This included Arkana's futuristic GRP dining table and chairs, surmounted by Robert Welch cast-iron tableware.

PUBLIC OPINION

To gain objective information on reactions to the Design Centre, the Council commissioned Mass Observation to carry out a survey in spring 1957. This undertook to discover such facts as the type of person visiting the Centre, particularly trade buyers, how they heard of it, what they thought, suggested improvements, and so on. Most of the findings were encouraging, confirming the Council's faith in the new venture – those that were not, highlighted suspicions already felt. For example, Haymarket House scored both good and bad points; nearly one third of interviewees had discovered it in passing, but it was also criticised as overcrowded. Another third were paying at least their second visit. Of those on their first visit, less than half had planned to come at all!

An indication of the spread of design awareness amongst the British public lay in the fact that visitors were younger and of much higher social and economic status than in general. Of these many were on their second or third visits and had returned out of professional interest or because of a special concern with design and new ideas. Clearly, the 'leadership group' of the *First Annual Report* were dominant.

7.18, 7.19 *Left*. Hammond's Design Centre selection included the Lurashell blow-moulded acrylic chair suspended in nylon-coated steel frame, designed by Paul Alkin. *Right*. The 'Mainly for Men' display included the Moulton bicycle, the Bond Bug and, in macho manner, Norton's latest motor cycle. But pressures from foreign competition were already fierce in these fields.

Three-quarters of those interviewed had only favourable comments to make and only one in a hundred had nothing but unfavourable criticism. Many quite spontaneously praised the Centre before being asked. Typical of the trade buyers' comments was the following from a York shop owner:

> We think it essential for retailers like us to keep in touch with the Centre and with *Design Review* – it is the best way of finding out what well-designed goods are available and to see them all together. Of course, since the exhibition is changed every so often we have to come down fairly often, about five times in a year, perhaps. We often get in touch with new manufacturers through this. Of course we send our customers here too if we can. It is a great help to a small shop as we can't carry much stock. If we haven't got what the customer wants to see we can always say 'you can see it at the Design Centre in London'.[5]

On the question of special fields of interest the general public had changed little from 'Britain Can Make It' days – furniture, followed by glassware, china and pottery were still favourites. These were also the items which people most coveted for their own homes. Trade buyers had

7.20, 7.21 The designs on these pages typify the elegant, if up-market, consumer products with which the Design Centre has become associated. *Left.* Ferguson Formdesigns' slim acrylic stem vase suitable for a single bloom, displayed at the Centre's 'Shopping in Britain' exhibition, 1972. *Right.* Catherine Hough took a Royal Brierley Crystal decanter blank and applied this attractive 'V' pattern with silver neck fitting.

a more specific interest in furniture and soft furnishings but, surprisingly, very few were interested in domestic appliances of any kind.

Of the rare criticisms, there were naturally those from an elite group within the trade who demand only the best. One of these commented wryly, 'It would be a pity if it became a Council of *adequate* Design.' Another unequivocally stated:

> I don't think the products are good enough. I think the standards are too low. I know Russell said you should start at the bottom and work up, but I believe the opposite – start at the top and have only the best. Some of them are atrocious for a Design Centre. Look at this chair. It's a good wholesome English chair but you couldn't call it a success as a design. Although it might be very well made and a good fabric, design is the thing.[6]

As might be expected of design-conscious visitors, when asked if they had any suggestions for improvement, many interesting ideas emerged. These even included improving the toilet handle in the gents' cloakroom!

7.22, 7.23 *Above.* Hornsea Pottery's Concept tableware, designed by Martin Hunt with technical development by Colin Rawson, has layered, concentric circles, suggesting the ripples around a pebble dropped into water. The pond theme is enhanced by the humorous and elegant swan, which functions as a knob and indicates the locking position of the lid. *Below.* Rayner and Kraschai Design's acrylic chessmen bring a new permutation to a popular design exercise. Note the king and queen.

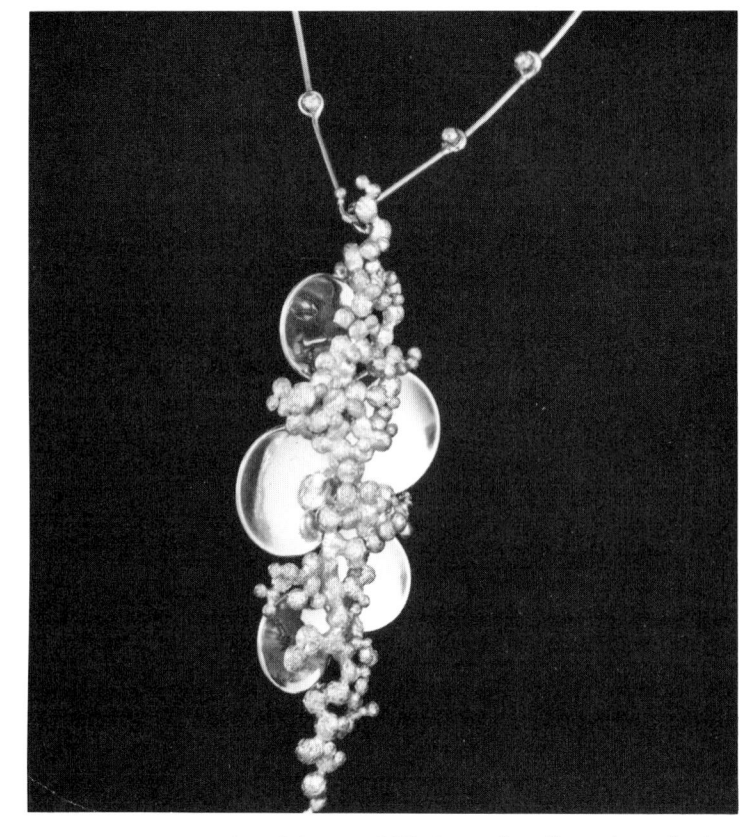

7.24 The Johnson Matthey Silver and Platinum Jewellery Award winners are exhibited annually at the Design Centre. David Robinson's platinum pendant of 1974 has the effect of a cluster of grapes, and was submitted in the category which permits the metal to be used without gems.

The most common were to enlarge the premises and show a wider range of goods, all fully priced. Two comments reminiscent of 'Britain Can Make It', the first from a trade buyer, the second from a housewife, were:

> I think your method of display of course is excellent. It's almost better than some of the pieces you're exhibiting. The kids annoyed me. The place is full of kids rushing round, working the gadgets and pulling out the patterns just for the fun of it – too many kids here.
>
> Nice if you could get a cup of tea – you'd stay much longer and plan to meet people here.[7]

The latter suggestion was eminently sensible, to be achieved some years later, along with a souvenir shop, retail shop and bookshop.

In 1960 Mass Observation was again called in to determine how adequate the Centre's services were for visitors connected with overseas trade.

7.25 An unusual industrial/craft link is the 'Wedgwood with Wendy Ramshaw' collection. Original prototypes by the jeweller were designed for multiple production using Black Basalt, carnelians, sapphires and gold by the jewellery division of Josiah Wedgwood and Sons.

As a follow-up to 1957, the survey also included a sample of the general public to discover any intervening changes. Regarding the latter, as might be expected, the majority of people were now on their second or more visit and encouragingly 40% were on their fifth or more. Even more encouraging was the increased number who listed an 'interest in design' as their reason for visiting – leading Mass Observation to suggest that the public were becoming more design conscious. Otherwise there were few changes, with highly favourable opinions all round.

Of the foreign visitors, the majority was on the first visit, and although a significant number had heard of the Centre through trade circles, even more had seen the building only in passing. Clearly the Haymarket site was permanently an important asset for publicity and propaganda. Products which visitors had particularly come to see were very similar to 1957, namely, glassware, china, ceramics, soft furnishings and furniture, with the latter featuring a little less prominently.

7.26 A Scottish Design Centre was opened in 1957, followed by a Welsh Centre in 1974. Local crafts including souvenirs, toys and jewellery were promoted alongside industrial design. The 1973 Souvenirs of Scotland competition included these delightful dolls of fabric and cardboard by Norma Fogge.

The role of the Centre's services was, of course, the main focus of the survey. On the whole the impression gained was an extremely favourable one: of providing a much appreciated trade function. The natural reluctance of a guest in a host country to make complaints may in some measure be responsible, but bearing in mind the type of person interviewed this would not seem to be of paramount importance. Any complaints were, in fact, similar to the British one, with perhaps more emphasis on clearer layouts and labelling. Lack of ventilation was a recurring theme, and the delight of one American that the Council should be so progressive as to have central heating was a somewhat doubtful compliment in view of the absence of any heating arrangements at all!

The main suggestion for improvement was for more information of a general nature on new designs – the kind of function already fulfilled by *Design* magazine which could therefore be publicised more abroad. Also follow-up services were suggested, again possible and later implemented through *Design* magazine. The fact that a high proportion of visitors to this country still discovered the Centre by casual means also suggested more publicity nearer home. A Canadian designer asked:

> Why doesn't the Design Centre advertise in places like Canada House – also at your airports, in aircraft, at the shipping agents? It could be a colour photo blown up to give an impact and put a large plaque there with 'ATTENTION OVERSEAS BUYERS'.[8]

7.27 The British Crafts Centre was opened in 1971. Justifiably it could promote handcrafts which fell outside the terms of reference of industrial design. In 1975 the Design Centre exhibited a wide selection of crafts from its new offspring, including this finely worked wooden doll's house by Jane Blythe.

FURTHER CENTRES

The Council was to extend its influence by the establishment of further centres, both in Scotland and Wales, each of which reflected the national culture and local industry. Because of the significance of rural crafts and tourism to their economies, the exhibition of souvenirs, toys and jewellery fell well within the terms of their brief. The Haymarket Centre did accommodate select displays of such products, but in 1971 a new body, the Crafts Advisory Committee – later to become the Crafts Council – was formed. This had its own British Crafts Centre, only a short walk from Haymarket. Finely wrought handcrafts, particularly those from a growing number of designer/craftsmen in wood, metal, glass and ceramics, could justifiably be exhibited without any conflict with the original terms of the Council of Industrial Design or the proposed Design Council, with its emphasis on engineering and capital goods. Nevertheless, domestic

7.28 Epitomising craft revival extremes is this immaculately carved ebony chair with woven seat and back in nickel silver. Designed by John Makepeace and carved by Andrew Whately, it contrasts with the bentwood chairs of Michael Thonet.

products were not neglected by the Council, and the Haymarket retail shop and magazine *Design Selection* had the consumer very much in mind. But publicity was very much to spread abroad during the sixties – a fact emphasised by the number of governments sponsoring their own design centres. For the Council, always a little apprehensive about its grant-in-aid, this was both compliment and assurance. Some centres were closely modelled on the Haymarket, others were radically different. Each in its own way laid a different emphasis and offered a basis of comparison. Additionally they provided reference points for the Council's own future development programme. As the *Nineteenth Annual Report* (1963–64) was to acknowledge, '... each new centre learns from the mistakes of earlier ones and the oldest of all must eventually be recast if it is to maintain its position'.[9]

7.29 This dining table was made by a former John Makepeace student, Robin Williams, to a special commission in the traditions of the designer craftsman. The laminated oak construction takes its theme of plant growth from a conservatory-like room. Burr oak veneers indicate eight place settings for guests of the client, who is confined to a wheel chair.

West Germany, advanced as ever in industrial matters, opened at least five centres representing different organisations. Of these the *Hans Industrieform Essen* was most like London, but stressed to consumers that design is more than superficial styling. Inevitably the Swedes were to open their own centre. This was situated in a converted four-storey warehouse in Malmö, with far more display space but fewer staff. Nevertheless exhibitions were imaginatively conceived, laying emphasis rather on the process of design by exploiting sketches, working drawings and models in addition to finished products.

Several centres emphasised consumer or student reference material. The Museum of Modern Art in New York had for many years included applied as well as fine art plus an index, but this was only available to scholars and professionals by appointment. The Philip L. Goodwin Galleries then opened in 1964 as the first permanent public gallery. Founded in the same year, the Belgium Design Centre saw itself rather as a product information centre emphasised by awarding a prize, the *Signe d'Or*, but on a three-year rather than an annual basis. In Japan the Industrial Design

7.30 Among consumer products, pottery and glass have continued to attract attention. The opening of a Design Centre Shop helped to publicise new designs and a magazine, *Design Selection*, was subsequently launched. Prime Minister Margaret Thatcher here examines the first issue with Design Council Director Keith Grant and Chairman Sir William Barlow.

Centre in Tokyo selected 'G mark' products in a similar manner to *Design Index*, but laid more emphasis on the country's regional industries.

Other centres developed their designer services. The Israel Design Centre in Tel-Aviv encouraged industry to exploit its professional consultancy service by awarding special grants. Additionally, it included an up-to-date library – something which the CoID had long since closed down. Perhaps most positive of all were the Kilkenny Design Workshops, established by the Irish Government in 1965. These opened up job opportunities for young designers, offering practical experience and overseas exchanges. A retail shop and exhibition centre were then opened in Dublin in 1976 to promote the work and generate income, a concern which increasingly was to occupy the CoID in its own activities.

On a cautionary note, the *Conseil Supérieur de la Création Esthétique* was charged by the French Government to alert manufacturers and consumers to the benefits of high standards of industrial design. But it found difficulty in defining a meaningful role and was closed down, particularly because industrialists resisted any proposals with interventionist implications. In contrast the *Centre de Création Industrielle* became firmly established in the *Centre National Georges Pompidou* occupying 4000 square metres of France's new architectural wonder. With its computer terminals providing information on 30,000 products plus slide, film and video tape libraries it laid emphasis on consumerism rather than criticism, thus avoiding some of the problems of selection faced by the CoID.

But by now the Council was so intimately linked with its own Design Centre that each could neither function nor survive without the other. Furthermore, powerful new demands arose in the sixties as British industry underwent major changes, placing further responsibility on the organisation charged with promoting 'improvement of design by all practicable means'.

8.1 Lord Snow, Parliamentary Secretary, Minister of Technology, examines a BMC *Mini* car at the Design Centre 'Design in Engineering' exhibition, which he opened on 20 October 1965.

—8—
ENGINEERING, INNOVATION AND EDUCATION

INTRODUCTION

Over the years British heavy engineering industries have relentlessly declined. Against a background of the looming economic crises of the late sixties, Director Paul Reilly extended the scope of the CoID to encompass engineering and capital goods. In April 1972, under the new name of The Design Council, a diversified but controversial range of activities was embarked upon to achieve pockets of success in otherwise declining fields. Whereas old strategies had involved promotion and persuasion, a much more interventionist approach was now adopted. By the mid-eighties, present-day Director Keith Grant had evolved a flexible role for the Council, including appropriate emphasis on engineering, innovation and education to meet the needs of an advanced technological society.

ENGINEERING AND THE DESIGN COUNCIL

For the country which sparked off the Industrial Revolution, the decline of engineering has been doubly damaging, both psychologically and economically. Britain once produced all the world's machinery for textiles, the industry which had so concerned Sir Robert Peel back in Victorian times. But by 1977 most of the plant, even for her own use, was made abroad. A survey of mill owners showed performance and quality to be key factors rather than price. It was Britain who pioneered the world's machine tool industry and once built the major proportion of its ships. Today she makes only 3% of the machine tools and little more than 3% of the ships. Even the latest Cunard flagship *Ocean Princess* was built in Finland. Following the Second World War Britain was still the third largest steel producer and almost every car on her roads was British. Today she ranks tenth in the league of steel producers and well over half her cars are foreign. Until relatively recently Britain exported motorcycles to 100 countries abroad. Today she has no indigenous industry and has to import machines from Japan and Germany.

Such imported engineering products are well designed, machined and finished. Spare parts with back-up services are readily available. Foreign capital goods have a reputation equal to ours – and are delivered more cheaply and quickly. Significantly, between 1967 and 1975 Japan doubled its research and development outlay to an estimated 20 billion yen and saw its share of world trade rise fourfold. West Germany increased its outlay by 50% and saw its share grow threefold. In contrast Britain's 6 billion outlay fell 10% in real terms and its share of world trade declined 75%. Recession followed and unemployment soared, not least amongst designers.

Since the late forties Gordon Russell had, of course, been warning against the dangers of complacency. Although the attention of the CoID was in those days directed towards domestic consumer goods there is ample evidence of concern for the design of engineering products. Indeed the very first *Annual Report* saw the industrial designer working essentially within the context of production engineering to achieve a 'synthesis of visual imagination, machine technique and public service'.[1] In turn its Training Report emphasised the need to include aesthetic instruction in all technical courses and append design endorsements to National Certificates in engineering.[2] In pursuit of this general aim a Joint Design Committee was set up with the British Engineering Association and short courses for junior draughtsmen and designers from engineering, metal and electrical firms were organised by the Council.

At the time of the Festival of Britain Survey, 'machinery, electrical engineering, road vehicles, railways, ships and boats and aircraft' constituted six of the fifteen sub-groups. Regrettably, when the permanent Stock List (later *Design Review*) was compiled these could no longer feature prominently, for the grant-in-aid was reduced by 25% in 1952–53. Nevertheless Industrial Officers had made valuable contact with each group – contact which was maintained throughout the fifties via Design Advice Service which both supplied expertise and recommended appropriate designers. In fact, the very first illustration of the service was of a Rapier fork-lift truck, followed by Schweppes Sparkling Lemon labels, fountain pens and a hearing aid! *Annual Reports* subsequently illustrated spot welders, switchgear and crude oil burners which, although not necessarily visually stimulating, demonstrated Council involvement. Analysis of requests to the Service (later renamed Record of Designers) shows a steady increase in engineering emphasis until the opening of the Design Centre when the figure actually doubled in one year. Many smaller engineering products were displayed in the Centre, although the *Twelfth Annual Report* (1956–57) delineates the 'limits' as essentially ... 'cycles, motorcycles, lamp posts, hand and gardening tools, cameras

8.2 Anthony Wedgwood Benn, Minister of Technology, addresses the 1966 International Design Congress on the theme of combining technology, management and design to ensure economic success. To his right sits Lord Snowdon, an active member of the Council of Industrial Design.

and field glasses'.[3]

By the early sixties there was at last sufficient government disquiet over Britain's declining share of international trade in engineering for a small but high-powered Committee on Engineering Design to be appointed by the Department of Scientific and Industrial Research. G. B. R. Fielden, Group Technical Director of Davy–Ashmore, was chairman and S. H. Grylls, Chief Engineer of Rolls Royce, M. C. de Malherbe of Imperial College and Professor D. A. Saunders, Past President of the Institution of Mechanical Engineers, were members. Most significantly they received written or oral evidence from key individuals and organisations throughout the country, from Alec Issigonis to Hugh Conway, from the War Office to the Council of Industrial Design. Their exhaustive and highly critical findings were published in June 1963 and, in the words of Paul Reilly, 'Nothing could ever be quite the same again in Britain in the field of engineering design after that report, for Fielden made mincemeat of the self-satisfied traditions of British engineering'.[4]

The Fielden Report emphasised that design was not sufficiently appreciated by managements of engineering businesses. The engineering profession had a lower social and economic status in Britain than in any other highly industrialised country and technology attracted fewer able school-leavers than science. Of graduates entering the engineering industry, most were attracted by research and management and very few took up design appointments. The effects of this shortage were shown by the inadequate application of new knowledge to the design of traditional British engineering. For example, when the North British Locomotive Company belatedly changed to diesel, it found its staff were totally 'steam-minded' and was forced into liquidation. In addition, the Committee discovered 'failures resulting from a lack of attention to detail in almost all fields of mechanical engineering design'.[5] As future technological progress made the task of the designer more complex it was feared that these weaknesses could become even more critical.

To remedy the situation Fielden recommended fourteen main points of action, the first five of which were:

(1) to impress upon the managements of engineering businesses the vital importance of the design function in engineering activity and the need to encourage more talented engineers to make their careers in design;

(2) to use all available means, especially television, to draw attention to the great importance of engineering in the national economy and to the urgent need for more able people to train as professional engineers and to make their careers as designers;

(3) to increase the prestige of design and the status of designers within the engineering profession and, where necessary, to amend the membership requirements of the professional Institutions to give more prominence to design qualifications;

(4) to encourage and co-ordinate experiments in methods of teaching design at undergraduate levels in universities and colleges and in industry;

(5) to reorganise the practical training of professional engineers to include more emphasis on modern production methods, works organisation, costs and the influence of design; and to bring about a closer integration of the practical and academic elements of education.[6]

Had such recommendations been made and implemented a century before, the face of British industry might have been altogether different. Indeed, had they been seized upon just two decades ago their impact still could have been considerable.

Government and industry, perhaps surprisingly, were slow to react. The Council of Industrial Design on the other hand endeavoured to lay increasing emphasis upon engineering through its Industrial Division. Despite its original terms of reference and long-standing bias towards consumer goods it well knew that the principal contribution to exports

8.3, 8.4 From the late sixties the concept of design was more broadly extended to include engineering and technology. Two present-day employees of British Telecom demonstrate the range of 'design' work. *Above.* Dick Thornborrow works on a *'System X* prototype digital subscriber switching sub-system'. *System X* is the family of digital switching systems that will carry Britain's telephone system into the 21st century. *Below.* John Williams hand-carves and paints wooden mock-ups of handsets for the future.

8.5, 8.6 Car design has long been the subject of interest and concern, used by many as a barometer of British industrial health. *Above.* The first car to be shown at the Design Centre was in 1962, the Ausper Formula Junior Racing Car, in co-operation with the Aluminium Development Association. *Below.* Manufacture of British sports cars, including Triumph and MG, had faded by the eighties, although foreign designs such as the exquisitely engineered Porsche continued. Jaguar was to survive after a purge on quality control.

8.7 By 1980 considerable hopes rested on the successor to the *Mini*. On the eve of the Motor Show the Secretary of State for Industry unveiled the new Austin *Mini Metro* at the 'Miles Ahead – British Car Design' exhibition. The *Metro*, shown here in cut-away version, won a Design Council Award for efficient use of space.

came from heavy engineering. Against the problematic industrial and economic climate of the late sixties this change of direction was to assume considerable importance.

At the beginning of this period the Division employed just one Industrial officer for Capital Goods and its total scope could not extend far beyond parking meters, street furniture and farm buildings. With limited resources it now attempted to encompass such fields as industrial machinery, electrical and electronic equipment, scientific instruments, and industrial and commercial road and rail transport in a more active manner. The Record of Designers and the Annual Awards were further enlarged to include these categories and a series of conferences, debates and factory visits commenced. The Design Centre began to include within its programme exhibitions to publicise the change of emphasis, commencing with the first ever car to be shown, the Ausper Racing Car of 1962, through to the Design in Engineering exhibition of 1965 which gave pride of place to the BMC Mini.

By 1967 proposals were emerging in the engineering world, with its powerful institutions, for a Council of Engineering Design to assume separate responsibility for such activities. Paul Reilly saw the warning light and argued forcefully for a single Design Council based on the

CoID's structure. At the Council there was a certain self-interest in this advocacy, but clearly it would have been bureaucratic and wasteful to have two publicly financed bodies working in such closely allied fields.

The Council of Engineering Institutions assembled a working party to submit recommendations to the Ministry of Technology in 1968. Chairman of the working party was Hugh Conway and amongst the distinguished membership were Robert Fielden, Robert Lickley and, fortunately, Paul Reilly himself. In a convincing paper he presented the theoretical and practical arguments for a single body.

Firstly the theoretical. The profession of industrial design had grown in the United States during the Depression to stimulate a sluggish economy. Being concerned with the market, the emphasis was on sales appeal and superficial appearance. These self-confessed 'stylists' differed from engineering designers, much more important numerically, who were concerned with function, economy and efficiency. But the differences between the two factions were now out of date. The industrial designer rejected styling for its own sake. He respected function and efficiency. His goals were economy of means and simplification rather than embellishment and addition. He was concerned with both ergonomics and aesthetics to achieve fitness of purpose, finish and appearance that might otherwise be overlooked. A product on which a designer worked alongside his engineering colleagues should therefore have a clarity and directness that expressed its function and efficiency without recourse to styling. Indeed, it was the engineer, untrained in present industrial design concepts, who was likely to introduce old-fashioned stylistic details remembered from earlier days. The fact that the industrial designer was still accused by the engineer of the faults he most abhorred was an argument for much closer collaboration and understanding. To set up a separate Council of Engineering Design would perpetuate a false dichotomy and undo much of the good work already undertaken by the CoID.

From a practical point of view the Council already had the basic framework required for design promotion in engineering. It had more than twenty years' experience of influencing management in industrial design and for the previous four years had been turning its attention increasingly to the field of capital goods. Though understaffed and under-financed on the engineering front, it had evolved prototype activities that would be equally applicable to an organisation specifically addressed to engineering design. Any new body would have to start from scratch and would be some time before becoming effective. The CoID was ready-made for expansion and could quickly adapt to meet any new requirements.

8.8, 8.9 An engineering product which succeeded for many years with surprisingly few styling changes was the Land Rover. *Above.* The first production model, and the one millionth vehicle nearly thirty years later. For a number of years the Range Rover managed to extend the success of the Land Rover, despite intense foreign competition. *Below.* This four-door version won a Design Council Award in 1982.

8.10, 8.11 *Above.* British motorcycles, like cars, faced increasing competition in the seventies, particularly from Japan and Germany. Shown here is the Triumph *Trident T150* which along with the three-cylinder BSA *Rocket 3* featured in *Design Index* in 1969. *Below.* The six-cylinder Honda *Sport CBX* makes an interesting contrast with the earlier British machines. Note the pressed-steel wheels and disc brakes.

8.12, 8.13 The BMW, like the Porsche, remains in demand, despite a price above that of many saloon cars. Design improvements include disc brakes and light alloy wheels.

The Conway Report consequently came out strongly in favour of one Council to promote both engineering and industrial design. It recommended that:

> ... a national Design Council be set up, taking over the present activity of the Council of Industrial Design, and building on its organisation; that it be given an adequate budget; that the new Council include a strong Engineering Design Activity led by an engineer of national standing; and that early action be taken to implement these recommendations.[7]

Many of the functions of the new Council were to be similar to those of the old, including the training of designers, creating a better management climate and stimulating public awareness. But others were altogether of a different order. For example it was proposed that:

> ... the Design Council might act as a stimulant to innovation replacing in some degree the benefits of technological fall-out from ambitious space and similar programmes carried out in the USA and the USSR which have no direct counterpart in Britain.[8]

217

To implement such a programme an extra £250,000 was suggested to supplement the CoID budget of £800,000 (of which rather more than £500,000 was by government grant). This figure was considered 'relatively modest' when compared with other public bodies such as the Arts Council with its grant of £7.2 million.

Despite the call for 'early action' the government prevaricated and decided to invite consultants John Hoskyns and Co. to review the management and activities of the Council. It was something of a rare experience for an educational, non-profit-making body to find itself now being reviewed by outside consultants with a focus on cost-effectiveness. Happily their report was complimentary:

> The organisation was efficient and well run. The enthusiasm of the staff at all levels is outstanding. In most of the Council's activities the benefits are measurably greater than the cost. Beyond the measurable benefits, the impact of the Council's work on the life of the nation is felt to be remarkable, especially when contrasted with cost.[9]

Further prevarications ensued until finally, after five years of advocacy, four years of alternating expectation and disappointment, and nearly ten years after the Fielden Report, it was announced in the House of Commons that the CoID was to become the Design Council. On 13 March 1972, in answer to a Parliamentary Question, the Under Secretary of State for Industry replied:

> The Council's present plans for expansion include new design advisory and information services for engineering management, an enlarged programme of courses and conferences, an increased engineering content in its exhibitions and new publications on engineering design . . . In view of the changing balance of its activities, my Rt Hon. Friend has agreed that the Council of Industrial Design should change its title to the 'Design Council' as from 1 April 1972.

Paul Reilly communicated this victory to his staff with the rider: 'I hope you will agree with me that the new name makes good sense . . . and it is less of a mouthful!'

The very factors which stimulated the Conway Report, namely declining economic and industrial activity, now prevented implementation of the crucial clause – that of granting an adequate budget. Nevertheless, the Council's Engineering Design Advisory Committee under the chairmanship of none other than G. B. R. Fielden did enable it to explore ways of stimulating progress within limited means. As a further boost Hugh Conway himself was appointed Deputy Chairman and a new senior post,

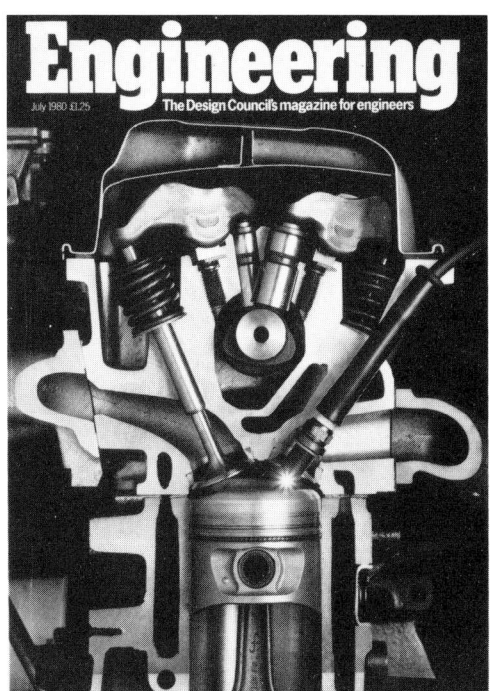

8.14, 8.15 *Left.* In 1972 the CoID became The Design Council and a new senior post, Head of Engineering Design, was created. This was filled by Geoffrey Constable, formerly a chief engineer and executive of Smith's Industries. *Right.* The old-established journal *Engineering* was absorbed by the new Council and soon ranked first amid the engineering press.

Head of Engineering Design, was created within the Industrial Division. This was promisingly filled by Geoffrey Constable, formerly a chief engineer and executive of Smith's Industries.

After some 'preliminary canters'[10] the sudden provision of extra funds made possible real progress under the new leadership. No fewer than thirty-one extra members of staff were recruited for engineering activities. These included a dozen Engineering Field Officers for the Design Advisory Service, briefed to visit manufacturers and diagnose problems and opportunities for improvement in their products. To support them, Information Research staff built up the Record of Engineering Design Expertise (a parallel to the Designer Selection Service). Of 400 or so contacts in the pilot survey, approximately one third led to immediate action and a further third promised future cooperation.

These developments heralded a significant change in the Council's modus operandi following the adoption of its new name. The emphasis of the old CoID had been very much on promotion and persuasion. However, an interventionalist approach developed once officers came actively to diagnose problems in companies they visited and recommend

8.16 Design Centre exhibitions are frequently on specific engineering themes such as Tribology. Illustrated is the Award winning Pegasus engine at the 'Rolls Royce Design in Action' exhibition, 1982. This engine made vertical take-off jets a reality.

sources of design and technical expertise. In the words of Geoffrey Constable, it was a process of persuading companies to 'look beyond their own factory gates' for expertise they did not have within. This was essentially the process which later came to be adopted for the successful Funded Consultancy Scheme.

Even within 'engineering', as distinct from 'industrial' design, the range of problems was extremely wide. Such matters included the reduction of high noise levels in pneumatic tools, foundry techniques for large iron castings, the redesign of a power transmission system for a railway traction unit, pneumatic valves for vehicle application and new designs for optical measuring instruments. However, from 1976 DAS integrated the two fields of industry and engineering to cover the whole spectrum of design and began to charge for its services. In return for an annual subscription, member companies could call on the field officers whenever their assistance was required. Today there are some 450 member companies served by twenty-four officers. Prominence is given to their success as a tangible record of progress in British industrial design in the face of industrial decline.

Whilst for the engineers emphasis was on direct action, the purchase of

8.17 The 1974 'Tomorrow's World' exhibition attracted a record number of visitors to the Design Centre. Huw Weldon and Raymond Baxter here examine the Puch Electric Moped, one of a selection of innovations chosen from the BBC television programme.

the old established journal *Engineering* was something of a coup for publicity and propaganda. Existing editorial and advertising personnel joined the Council in 1973, and it soon ranked first amongst the engineering press. A businessman readership survey found that penetration of the journal in engineering management was second only to the *Sunday Express* amongst the eighty-eight most widely read newspapers and magazines in that sector.

The Design Centre, *Design Index* and the Awards scheme further adjusted to accommodate the new emphasis. However, the deepening economic recession of the seventies was to cause serious problems. The energy crisis, three-day week, value added tax, bankruptcies, mergers and take-overs all restricted company design and development programmes. New ranges were rationalised, old products given a face-lift or nostalgic rather than bold innovative concepts recreated. Consequently, the choice of goods for Council activities was restricted. Furthermore, hard-pressed manufacturers were no longer prepared to pay for the privilege of having their products on display.

For a time, in 1973–74, attendance figures at the Design Centre dipped. Thanks, however, to a brilliantly successful exhibition based on BBC

Television's *Tomorrow's World*, the year ended with record figures. Opened by Raymond Baxter and introduced by Huw Weldon (Managing Director of BBC TV and a Council Member), queues of people formed to see 'frontiers of technology' exhibits the Council now wished to promote. A second exhibition the following year, opened by Anthony Wedgwood Benn, Minister of Technology, was financed by an experimental 20p entrance fee.

The twenty-first anniversary of the Design Centre in 1977 happily coincided with the year of the Queen's Silver Jubilee. The occasion was marked by the largest exhibition ever, occupying the whole of the ground and mezzanine floors. Called 'Enterprise and Innovation', the exhibition illustrated the products and design policies of eighty companies manufacturing goods ranging from cranes and earth-moving equipment to pottery and textiles, and chosen for their design leadership in their respective fields. A record number of journalists attended the press conference, as much to pay tribute to Paul Reilly on the last occasion of its kind before his retirement, as to report on the exhibition.

Paul Reilly, like Gordon Russell before him, had already received a knighthood in recognition of his achievements. As a further accolade he was now made Lord Reilly. A man who conceived the Design Council essentially as a catalyst, he himself had been exactly that. In the words of Lady Reilly, 'He is King Catalyst. He loves introducing A to B and seeing a result.' For the Council he brought together engineering and industrial design to form a secure base from which his successor could work.

The new director, Keith Grant, inherited the post at the commencement of further upheavals in industry and the British economy. Nevertheless, he had broad commercial as well as arts experience, having worked for his father's wholesale food distribution business and a leading advertising agency before becoming General Manager of the Royal Opera and Secretary of the Royal Society of Arts. The latter post has been likened to *being* the RSA, which still exercises considerable powers in the arts and crafts whether organising lectures or disseminating bursaries. Keith Grant's commercial and administrative experience was soon to be put to the test.

In 1977, as North Sea oil swung the country's current account back into balance for the first time since 1972, the strong pound eroded price advantages which exporters had enjoyed during its decline. At the same time industrial officers became preoccupied with finding suitable products to promote – and persuading manufacturers to meet the rising costs of display. Although successive governments increasingly acknowledged the Council's importance they urged more financial independence, and grants-in-aid were reduced in real terms.

8.18–8.20 Today Design Council Awards cover a diversified range of activities. *Above.* The Duke of Edinburgh, with Director Keith Grant, examines the Moore and Wright digital electronics micrometer. *Below, left.* A model of the *Sealion* marine crane by Priestman Bros. at the Awards presentation ceremony of 1981. *Below, right.* The award-winning ORLAU Swivel Walker is demonstrated to Prince Philip at the 'Design and Disability' exhibition, 1981. A patient can get in and out of the walker alone. He or she then rocks from side to side, leaning forward slightly, and 'walks' on swivel bearings.

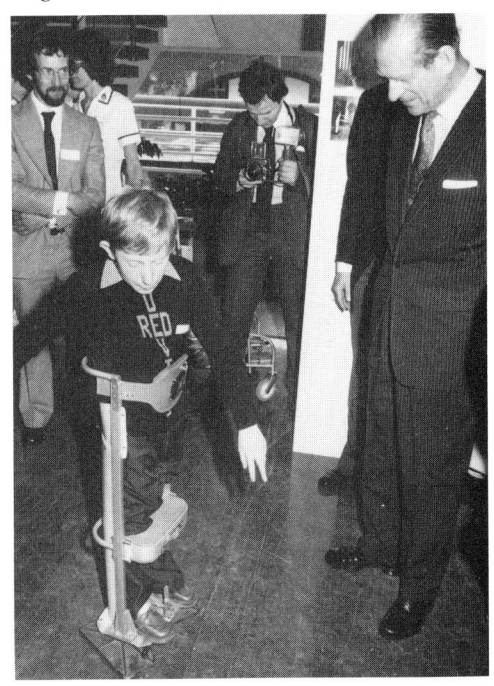

However, on its twenty-first anniversary the Department of Industry did agree that the Council might at last abolish display charges in order to raise the standard of design amongst exhibits. But the agreement was not achieved without one important condition – there would be no additional grant to compensate for lost revenue! A profitable Souvenir Shop had existed from 1971 but, if expansion had taken place in this direction, there would have been a danger of trivialisation of the Design Centre. It was therefore decided to turn the mezzanine floor into a shop to sell portable household goods which had been accepted by *Design Index*. This meant both a new source of income and marketing assistance to manufacturers. Subsequent exhibitions clearly demonstrated the improvement which abolition of charges made possible. Coincidentally a major review of *Design Index* was carried out to raise standards and devise more rigorous selection procedures, particularly regarding technical content. Some 2000 products were thus removed from the 9000 previous total.

Detailed attention to the performance of products was a necessary step to allay two suspicions of the public; firstly that good design is expensive and secondly that aesthetics and efficiency are somehow mutually exclusive. Such doubts had been reinforced by certain products, including the infamous plastic nut crackers which could not crack anything bigger than a peanut. Attempts to sponsor innovatory designs, the Council found, are inevitably fraught with problems. However, under Keith Grant's leadership closer links with test laboratories, the Consumers' Association and the British Standards Institution (BSI) were developed.

For 1980 an ambitious scheme for an eye-catching Design Centre front and layout was planned. But the money set aside was used to make good shortfalls in general funding during the year. Instead a simpler and cheaper scheme prepared by Conran Associates was implemented. This made it possible to integrate the three trading areas of the Design Centre Shop, with gifts and souvenirs on the ground floor, household goods on the mezzanine floor, and books on the upper ground floor. Space was also found for the coffee shop at mezzanine level as an added attraction to visitors. Today these commercial ventures help finance the broader spread of activity.

A final rationalisation to take place was to integrate the work of engineering and industrial officers. Such separate divisional interests were naturally a matter of concern in an organisation preaching the indivisibility of design. Elements of engineering and industrial design were present in the majority of products, and the subtlety of distinction beyond most outsiders. The difficulty was resolved by appointing a single Head of Industrial Division to co-ordinate activities, whether advisory services, product selection or design education. Geoffrey Constable, formerly Head of Engineering, now took charge. In addition, following the retirement of Philip Fellows, it was decided to merge the Exhibitions and Information Divisions under the experienced hand of John Blake. Keith Grant, as Director, had this to say:

> The biggest step for which I am solely responsible, and which has caused the biggest flutter in the dovecote, has been the appointment of an overall head of the industrial division. Where before the industrial division had two separate cells – and I mean cells, and I mean separate – I soon decided that I couldn't bear it. It was so obviously an inefficient way of working, a divisive way of working (the Design Council clearly not practising what itself preaches about the unity of design) that something had to be done.[11]

EVALUATION

Such changes have not taken place without a background of critical evaluation. Criticism, of course, is nothing new to the Council, as the experience of Gordon Russell had demonstrated. From Bernat Klein, the innovative textile designer, who served on the Scottish Committee of the Council for seven years, came scathing criticism for the earlier period of change to engineering, prior to 1976. Scotland's industry has undergone even more dramatic changes than the rest of the United Kingdom, and the Committee has had to wrestle with extremes from small souvenirs to gigantic oil-rigs. In those years Klein attended numerous meetings, his participation coloured by the frustrations of a practical man used to more direct forms of action. As an overview he stated:

> The Design Council is not a Civil Service department or a privately subsidised foundation; and it is not a business enterprise. It is a compromise of compromises, and it shows. Resembling the British Broadcasting Corporation in some ways (officially independent but indirectly government controlled), staunchly presenting only the British point of view instead of comparing British products with what other people are offering to the world, it is obviously a very different kind of animal: controversy and a critical approach are inimical to it. Officially conceived to increase to healthy proportions the aesthetic appetite of the British public and correspondingly to strengthen the aesthetic muscle of British industry, it has, over the years, evolved an esoteric game of musical chairs/spot the trend/ a thousand and one exhibitions and conferences, which are marvels in their own spheres but seem to me irrelevant to our industrial and economic problems.[12]

Specifically, Klein questioned the following features: diversified activities, preaching to the converted, unproductive conferences, unnecessary services to industry, too many staff, not enough designers, awards being

8.21, 8.22 *Above*. Although criticised for concentrating on 'sludge-extractors, earth-diggers and cranes', some elegant and well-engineered products were recognised by The Design Council. This truck-mounted telescopic boom crane by Cosmos was seen to combine 'aesthetic appeal, safe and efficient operation, and versatile performance to meet the most exacting requirements'. *Below*. The JCB excavator loader, as a result of constant research and development, offers improved digging and loading, outstanding fuel economy, unrivalled standards of comfort and low in-cab noise levels. Not only has the company staved off American and Japanese competition, it has considerably expanded its share of the market.

a 'Fate Worse than Death', the swing to engineering away from consumer goods, and the lack of emphasis on education. Above all, he felt that rather than concentrating its attack on the appearance and design of 'sludge-extractors, earth-diggers and cranes', the Council should aim to educate an aesthetically badly housed, badly furnished and badly clothed nation. This, he claimed, should be tackled at school level by 'a down-to-earth approach to aesthetic awareness particularly in regard to our living and working environment and to objects in everyday use'.

Despite his critical stance, Klein conceded that:

> The concept of the Design Council is important; its existence essential, perhaps more today than ever before; but its ends and means should be re-examined and if relevant, brought up to date, clarified and reaffirmed in so far as they still apply to today's conditions: or dropped if they do not apply.[13]

Had the Council been funded by the Department of Education and Science rather than the Department of Industry, it might well have evolved along the lines he envisaged. However, in the period since 1976 there have been many changes as we have seen, such as a renewed consumer and educational emphasis, no doubt to Klein's approval. At the same time worthy engineering products such as the JCB excavator with its impeccable design logic have received unreserved support. The Design Council, more than most organisations, has demonstrated a continuing capacity for self-appraisal and meaningful evolution while still pursuing its original goal.

Architectural Review, having made the comprehensive 'Progress Report' back in Gordon Russell's time, was to carry out subsequent critical forays. Russell himself, on the tenth anniversary of *Design* magazine referred to the seven stages of design policy for manufacturing companies. The final one was a comprehensive policy and a 'source of pride'.[14] In 1982, Alastair Best briefly used the same analogy for the Council. But the seventh scene was less than complimentary. Indeed although *Architectural Review* was by then an elderly institution in its own right, Best was critical of 'benign institutions ostensibly dedicated to the common weal'. Like Orwell's ministries of Peace, Truth, Love and Plenty – purveyor's respectively of War, Lies, Hate and Austerity – he felt many had come to be associated with the precise opposite of declared aims:

> Thus the name of the National Building Agency will be for ever linked with the greatest period of jerry building in British history; the Arts Council with the decline into obscurantism and triviality of the arts; and the Design Council with the tasteful whimsicality of the souvenir oven-mitt.[15]

Ironically, the humble oven glove is a product where safety is of the utmost importance. At that time many failed because of poor insulating material and the Council happened to be working with the BSI to establish standards. Meanwhile, at least those carrying Design Centre labels had undergone stringent safety checks!

Taking a seemingly more detached view than Klein or Best, Beryl McAlhone has recently carried out a survey of opinions of one hundred leading design consultants for *Campaign* magazine.[16] The replies hold some useful evaluations and are peppered with some selectively biased quotations (which at least act as an antidote to the usual fulsome praise any organisation is apt to promote about itself). For example, her questionnaire listed current activities of the Council and asked respondents to grade importance and performance. (Seventy-nine consultants responded.)

Although little credit was given to the finding, the Council's principal activities were regarded as 'very important' or 'important'. But one activity, the Souvenir Shop, was dismissed as 'inappropriate' – clearly anathema to professional designers. More worrying was the rating on performance. Only the bookshop got an enthusiastic response as 'above average', followed by exhibitions and awards. In contrast to Klein, the consultants favoured a more industrial and professional, rather than educational role although like him they opposed the engineering bias. One commented '. . . at the moment the Design Council is an Engineering and Souvenirs Council, used only by tourists, designers, kids on obligatory school trips and design-conscious companies'. Being design consultants, not unnaturally they felt particular weaknesses were 'the way it relates to the design profession', 'its understanding of business' and 'the way it puts its message across'.

McAlhone did concede that only a minority of respondents had been directly involved with the Council, and the most positive responses came from those who had. Furthermore, although the sample was claimed to represent 'every manifestation of professional excellence', only a minority were product designers (the Council's field of obligation under its charter) and not one was an engineering designer. Nevertheless the question persisted of whether the Council had swung too far, because of the political and economic climate, towards engineering and retailing.

In the words of another consultant, 'The strength of the Design Council lies in the relationship which it currently enjoys with government. This gives it a position of power, privilege and patronage.' What critics must acknowledge is that such a position has been hard earned under careful management. The Council has a grant of several million pounds from the Department of Trade and Industry, but its successful revenue-earning

8.23 It is difficult to equal the romance of the steam locomotive and British Rail have often been criticised for new designs. Nevertheless Kenneth Grange, in consultation with the British Rail design team, achieved a successful solution to the power cab of the High Speed Diesel train of 1975.

activities, such as publishing and retailing, make a total budget of double the figure. This provides a more secure base for reflection and re-orientation. No doubt the most senior appointment, to Head of Industrial Design, will be to the approval of McAlhone: June Frazer was a former director of Design Research Unit, Head of Graphic Design in the John Lewis Partnership and President of the Society of Industrial Artists and Designers.

INNOVATION AND THE GRADUATE DESIGNER

No matter how prestigious and efficient the Council becomes, fundamental problems remain to be solved. The 'vicious circle' described by Owen Jones in 1852, survives almost complete. British manufacturers and retailers still propagate mediocrity for a large section of a visually illiterate community, while discriminating purchasers look to foreign designs for elegance at a price. Expensive furniture is imported from Scandinavia, sophisticated electrical goods from Japan and luxury cars from Germany. Of most concern is the apparent lack of the innovative, entrepreneurial spirit possessed by the Victorians.

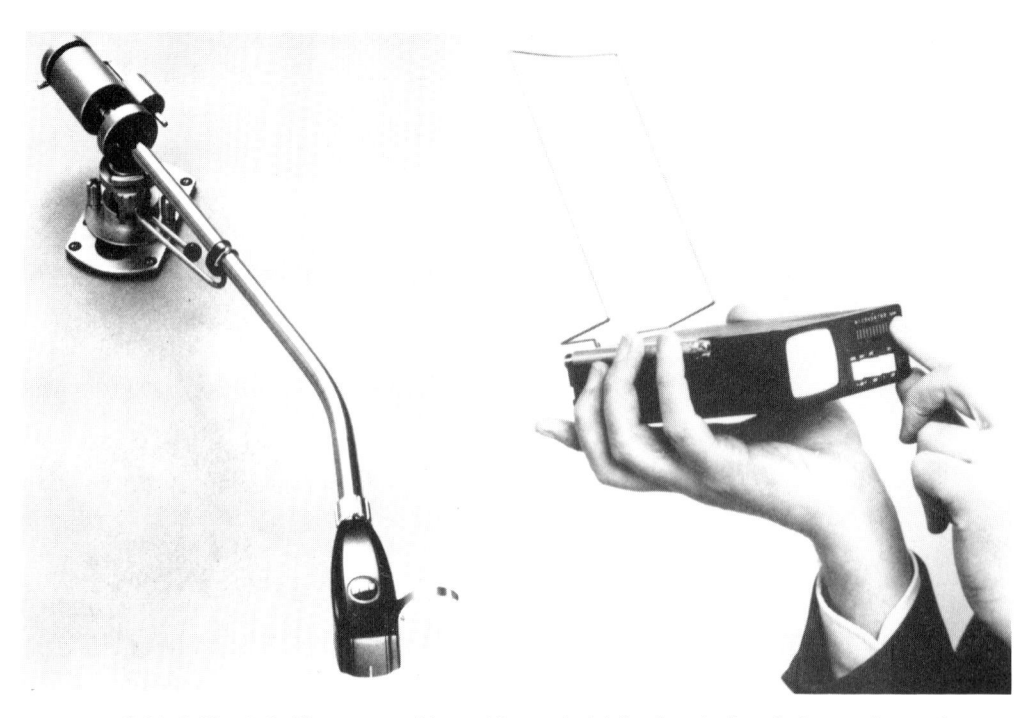

8.24, 8.25 *Left.* The competition of Japan in hi-fi, electrical and electronic goods has given increasing cause for concern. Yet British designers have produced many innovations. The SME tone arm of 1959 was the first of its kind in the world, introducing knife-edge bearings and precision balances. *Right.* Clive Sinclair's *Microvision* television of January 1977, was the first pocket TV, and the only set able to receive transmissions anywhere in the world.

If these facts are hard to admit, they are nevertheless endorsed by recent events at the V. and A. In 1982, the Museum at last fulfilled its original function by exhibiting contemporary consumer goods – in the old boilerhouse converted with a £1 million gift from Terence Conran. Of the first exhibits only one was British made, a Gestetner copier, and that was designed by an American! In the ensuing exhibitions (consumer electronics, small domestic appliances and private cars) few British products were included. A Clark's plastic-soled shoe and a Land Rover vehicle from some years ago were notable exceptions. Brand names like Sony, Braun and Volvo reigned supreme. There was little evidence of Britain's creative talent.

This was perhaps surprising, for ostensibly one of the traditional problems of industrial design, namely the supply of well-qualified graduates, had by now been solved. Furthermore, commencing with reorganisation at the Royal College, plus change of emphasis at schools of art such as Birmingham, Manchester and Central, due recognition had been given to engineering and technology. Many of these changes were consolidated with the granting of degree status.

The RCA always had been a post-graduate institution skimming the cream from regional schools of art. The improved image of the latter followed the Coldstream Report of 1960 and Summerson Report of 1970. The lowly National Diploma in Design became a transitional Diploma in Art and Design and then a fully fledged Bachelor of Arts. A two-tier system (three with the RCA) evolved when selected schools were absorbed into a national polytechnic grid. Syllabuses were suitably upgraded, although not without some reservations. Central control by the Council for National Academic Awards led to suspicions that the straightjacket of academia was for many students less conducive to creativity than the freedom of the old schools. To counter this argument was a consciousness of the gulf between education and industry, exacerbated by the radical student ideology of the sixties and the craft revivalism of the seventies. One clear advantage of a large polytechnic was opportunity for forging links with subjects outside the field of art and design. Coldstream had seen fine art as a necessary component of any form of specialisation. The new degrees were able to offer a different emphasis. Computer-aided design, electrical engineering, basic physics, statistical sciences and a foreign language were seen as more relevant to the needs of industry.

The problem now to be faced was not one of supply, but of residual mismatch between education and industry. As long ago as 1937 the Gorrell Report had forewarned the problem of 'mismatch' between the supply of design talent and demands of industry:

> History shows that the artistic resources of Great Britain are very considerable and in some directions pre-eminent; but partly owing to a mutual distrust between manufacturers and artists, we have not used these resources for industrial purposes as fully as we have our technical resources. Similar courses have operated abroad, but in many foreign countries steps have been taken to secure active measures for improving industrial design by the full cooperation of industry with art.[17]

The result has been, as one recent headline bluntly indicated, 'Design talent faces future on the dole'. Between 1976 and 1982 the proportion of polytechnic design graduates finding permanent employment was only slightly more than half. Even graduates of high-powered courses have been unable to obtain work. By 1982, only one fifth of a leading polytechnic's students obtained posts and another claimed its best students were going abroad. This is no exaggeration, for when the Design Council held an exhibition as a tribute to British designers it embarrassingly found most no longer worked in this country. The 1981 exhibition 'Designed in Britain – Made Abroad' emphasised the point that our

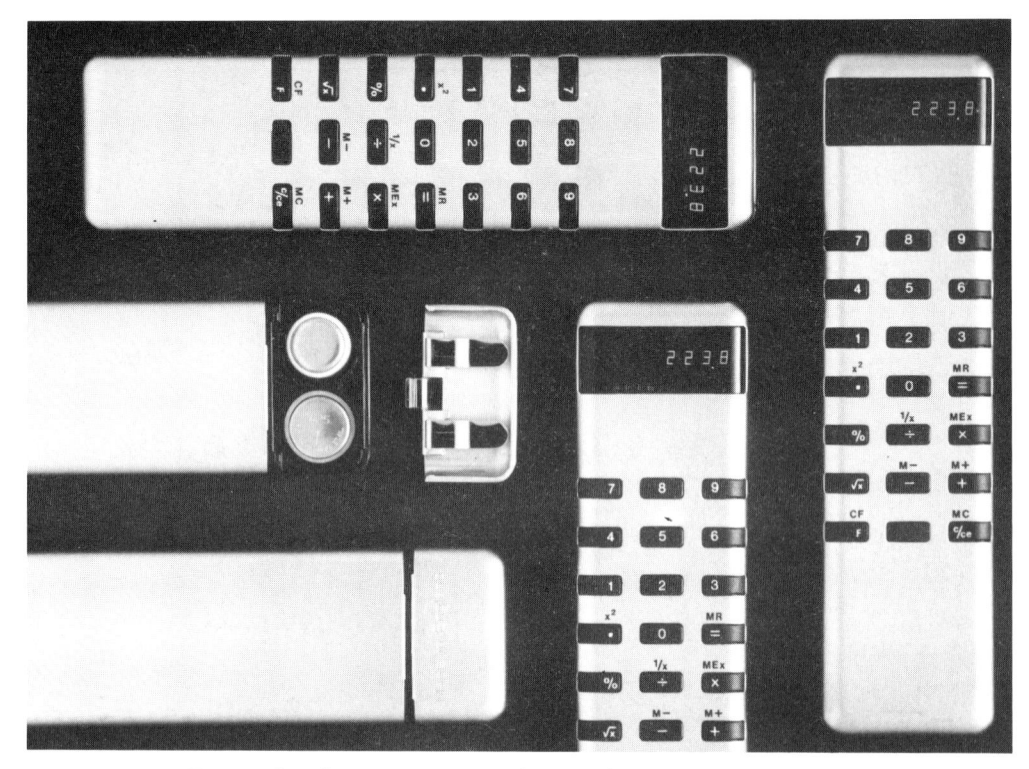

8.26 Despite headlong progress in design of pocket calculators, the *Sovereign* model of 1977 has a visually timeless quality. Like the *Microvision* it won a Design Council Award for Sinclair Radionics.

design studios are earning foreign profits which might otherwise have been ours.

Meanwhile the prestigious Royal College of Art continued its troubled history. It was training many fine designers, but was criticised for having a bogus university structure with five faculties, innumerable professors and only 600 students. Sir Terence Conran resigned from the governing council and stated, 'There is a crying need for a really first-rate industrial design school in this country, which the RCA could be.' Perhaps a total commitment will come with a change of name to Royal College of Design. In contrast, certain departments of Cranfield Institute of Technology, for example, with highly specialised courses, can advertise 'Last year all our U.K. graduates obtained posts'. Holding some hope for the future is a new shared higher degree between the two institutions, suggested by Lord Reilly, who received an Honorary Doctorate from Cranfield in January 1983.

The suggestion that graduates in Art and Design were unable to meet fully the exacting demands of British industry was raised in the Design Council's 1977 Carter Report 'Industrial Design Education in the United

8.27 First prize in the ICSID (International Council of Societies of Industrial Design) Philips Award 1983 went to this Integrated Electronic Workstation by Gustavo Rodriguez.

Kingdom'. To test the truth of the alleged mismatch, in 1979 the Department of Education and Science in association with the Council commissioned Chris Hayes Associates to research 'The Industrial Design Requirements of Industry'. Their subsequent report, however, found that the problem lay as much with industry as with the designers. Certainly graduates did not properly understand the demands of the business world or the relationship between design and profitability. But foreign competitors were no better in these respects. Indeed, European companies regard British design education as superior to theirs and think well of their British employees. Furthermore,

> As a generalisation it appears that continental European firms value the contribution made by design more highly, spend more money on design, give designers more authority and, as a result, attract and motivate highly competent and creative designers.[18]

A later Design Council report, the Mellor Report of 1983, expressed concern not only over the attitudes and aptitudes of manufacturers, but also of retailers, towards design and designers. The Committee, under David Mellor's Chairmanship, inquired into 'Standards of Design of Consumer Goods in Britain'. By then, even non-technological mainstream industries such as textiles, cutlery, and ceramics were suffering serious competition from abroad. And yet the new design talent was not being fully exploited:

> Our national system of design training has for many years been the envy of the world. Our government-supported organisation for the improvement of design standards in industry has been the model for similar organisations in many other countries. Our professional designers have a high international reputation, as evidenced by their recent record of employment by foreign manufacturers. A high level of national investment has, most particularly in the past two decades, been directed towards design education and design promotion. British design quality, and the added value it can give to British products, could and should be an important national asset. But why is it on almost every side so undervalued?[19]

The Mellor Report also offers a useful update on those areas of design with which the Council has been traditionally concerned. Feedback was provided by working parties looking into ceramics, domestic appliances, furniture and textiles. For example, the ceramics tableware industry relies very much on the excellence of its traditional designs such as Josiah Wedgwood's Black Basalt teapot. For British manufacturers, the best of their designs tend to be traditional whereas with competitors a healthy proportion of the best will be new. Whilst most sizeable companies employ designers, annual recruitment is only a fraction of the graduates produced and even then the industry feels it is difficult to recruit designers to suit its needs.

Although the situation was not as acute in other areas, problems including retail, technological and international pressures were found. For example, in the domestic appliance industry, television is one healthy growth area, but there has been a dramatic reduction of man-hours per set manufactured. Furthermore, an increasing number of companies are foreign-owned, carrying out design work in their parent country and offering few openings for design graduates. Within the furniture industry, the Council's original focus of interest, production of domestic articles, has shown a steady decline. Whereas it is possible to obtain backing for investment in hardware or plant, it is very much harder to obtain backing for design, research and development. There also exists a 'deep misunderstanding' between manufacturers who expect the graduate to be trained and ready to perform and students who expect free rein after having received an education, but not necessarily a training. Finally, the textile industry has been subject to severe contraction, and although it has design and production capability in plenty, once more the two elements do not necessarily come together. Since the demise of the Textile Council there has been no one place for manufacturers, buyers and designers to come together.

Much of the Mellor Report's criticism (and, indeed, the manufacturers' self-defence) turned on the retailer. High Street discounting of appliances reduces manufacturers' margins for investment in design. 'Own-branding' by giant retailing organisations, who are governed by short-term marketing concerns, inhibits innovation. The power of large furniture retailers has squeezed manufacturers to the point of bankruptcy. There is also a resistance amongst retailers to accept a degree in art and design as a qualification for any job other than as a designer.

One recent move by over fifty independent designers, principally from the furniture and textile industries, has been the formation of the Independent Designers Federation (IDF). Most members operate small prototype/production facilities and experience difficulties with batch production by which product unit costs are lowered. In generating links with retailers and larger manufacturers the IDF aims to provide means for successful designs to be produced at costs which are more competitive. The Federation proposes to operate from premises which will house exhibition space for trade visitors plus an information exchange and data base in the manner conceived for the original design centres for industry.

Against this general background, the role of the Design Council would seem to be more vital than ever. During the eighties the Council did, in fact, suffer under a grant aid reduction when the new government came to office. However, strong support then came from the Prime Minister Margaret Thatcher. The third of her famous Downing Street soirées on pressing industrial problems was a ninety-minute teach-in on design. Well-rehearsed arguments were presented by leading gurus that, from the schoolroom to the boardroom, design needed stimulus from government. Subsequently a programme of '42 Action Points' was drawn up, including appointment of a minister with responsibility for design and designers. A campaign involving the Design Council and the Department of Industry in tandem publicised a new consultancy scheme. Full-page newspaper advertisements showed products such as the Sinclair ZX81 Computer and Harrier Jump Jet under the slogan:

>IT'S NOT THE BEST OF BRITISH LUCK
>IT'S THE BEST OF BRITISH DESIGN THAT
>MAKES THEM SO SUCCESSFUL.

8.28, 8.29 In recent years, encouraged by awards and scholarships, a new generation of graduate designers has emerged from higher education. Carole Ingham of the Central School of Art and Design won a 1973 Leverhume Travelling Scholarship with this set of three-dimensional numbers, designed as an educational toy. All the pieces are interchangeable, so that not only numbers, but a wide variety of other shapes can be built as well. *Right.* First prize in the 1981 DIA Melchett Memorial Award went to Gary Ross, shown here with a scale model of his redesigned ambulance. The Melchett Award is for socially responsible design.

(The ZX81 had, of course, already soothed the nation's technological ego and the Harrier saved its political pride.)

Design Advisory Service was considerably extended to include the Funded Consultancy Scheme. Without this kind of support many firms had not previously employed designers to improve existing products. And many more had not kept pace with rapid technological progress to create new ones. The scheme provided manufacturers with fifteen days free consultancy followed by a further fifteen at half cost. Launched in June 1982 with an allocation of £3 million, the take-up by industry exceeded all expectations and a further £7 million was allocated within a year. Essential to the Service were the records of engineering and industrial design expertise compiled by the Council. These contained extensive, continuously updated sources of help available from research organisations, specialist companies, universities, polytechnics, consultancies and individuals.

By matching the right technology or skill to the problem, many companies have been able to improve their products and achieve important savings in development time and money. In May 1984 Sir William Barlow, Chairman of The Design Council, reported that 1707 companies

8.30 Following the RCA Hospital Bed project, some impressive medical equipment has been created by students. This operating table by Kevin Thompson was exhibited in the Central School's 1976 Degree Show. Hydraulics raise and lower the table and individual sections are adjusted by screw drive.

had applied for assistance under the scheme, of which 1026 were using design consultants for the first time ever. Ninety-four per cent considered that the work completed to date was 'worthwhile' or better. Of particular relevance to the graduate designer was the following statement:

> Inevitably some of the FCS projects will not be successful in the market place. Design and product development is a process which is beset with risk and uncertainty. However, when the history comes to be written, I am sure that the failures will be a small minority. What is more, I am already certain that the FCS will have succeeded in its broader intention, which is to persuade companies to keep on using design consultants.[20]

One group of graduates who suffered far less than industrial designers during the recent recession were the engineers. In fact, demand soon began to exceed supply, particularly in electrical and electronic industries. For the engineers, design primarily involves the use of scientific principles in the creation of products, and traditionally their education has concentrated on engineering science. It is therefore gratifying to perceive in recent years, not complacency, but active moves to implement the far-reaching recommendations of the Fielden Report. These follow a number of subsequent reports by the Design Council, the prestigious Science and Engineering Research Council, and the recently formed Engineering Council. In future students will be required to demonstrate an awareness and understanding of the crucial factor of *application*.

One of the first activities of the CoID Engineering Design Advisory Committee, under the chairmanship of Robert Fielden himself, had been to organise a series of fact-finding visits to selected universities and polytechnics. EDAC then formed an Education Sub-Committee to investigate the education of engineering designers and recommend future policy and action. Their subsequent Moulton Report (for Alex Moulton who designed the Moulton cycle was Chairman) emphasised that design should be a thread running through all normal engineering degree courses, and that 15 to 20% of content should be given over to its study. Furthermore, the Committee recommended that the Design Council should encourage and help co-ordinate postgraduate courses in engineering design.[21]

These recommendations were strongly endorsed in 1983 by the Engineering Board of the Science and Engineering Research Council in the Lickley Report. Serious moves were now under way to heal the historical breach between design and engineering for the report stressed:

> ... we have been impressed by the weight of opinion deploring the present schism between engineering design, with its tradition growing out of Mechanics Institutes, and industrial design, wholly rooted in art colleges. While it may be argued that the complexities of modern life prevent any but the most gifted of individuals to be expert in both fields, it surely cannot be right for the products of Colleges of Art and Design to be so lacking in training related to the disciplines and analytical strengths of engineering and for engineers to neglect the value to them of the aesthetic and innovative strengths of the industrial designer.[22]

Finally in 1984 the Engineering Council produced its 'Standards and Routes to Registration' which gave a new coherence to professional qualifications and stressed the importance of design expertise. Regarding the status of Chartered Engineer (CEng) it had this to say:

> Chartered Engineers are concerned with the progress of technology through innovation, creativity and change. They should be able to develop and apply new technologies, promote advanced designs and design methods, introduce new and more efficient production techniques, marketing and construction concepts and pioneer new engineering services and management methods.[23]

The Engineering Council and Dr Lickley, himself a past President of the Institution of Mechanical Engineers, were echoing sentiments close to those of another past President, Sir Joseph Whitworth, expressed one hundred and thirty years previously.

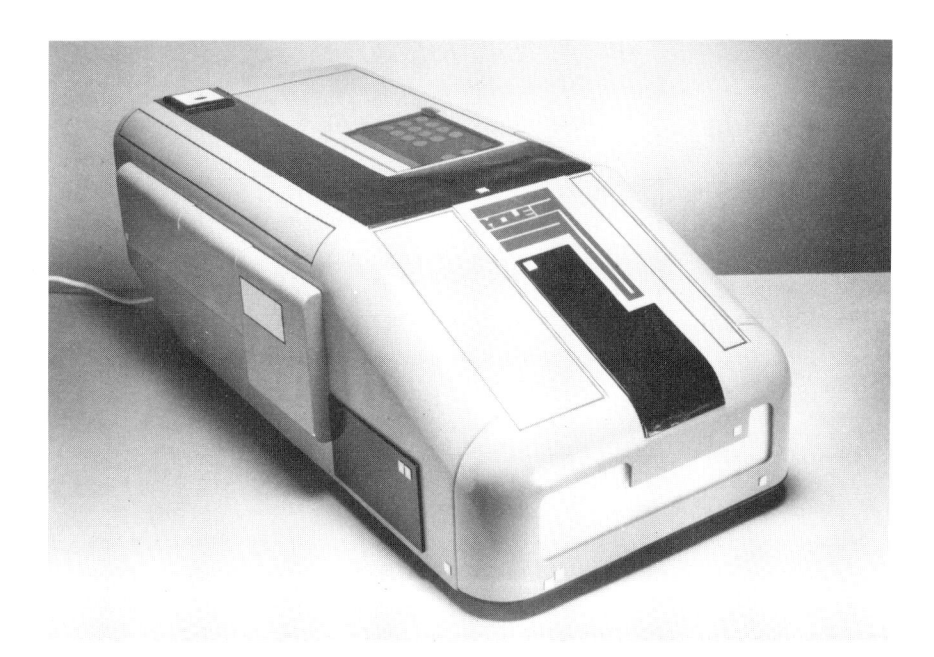

8.31, 8.32 *Above.* The *Mole* prototype vacuum-cleaning robot was designed by John McCormick of North Staffordshire Polytechnic. It contains a microprocessor and memory chip so that it can remember the dimensions and furniture of a room. *Mole* appeared at the Design Centre 'Microelectronics Come Home' exhibition in March 1981. *Below.* RCA Student Philip Davies won the Philips Award Bursary and Master's Medal of the Faculty of Royal Designers for Industry with this electronic 'baton'. The portable device incorporates a radio, cassette recorder and small TV.

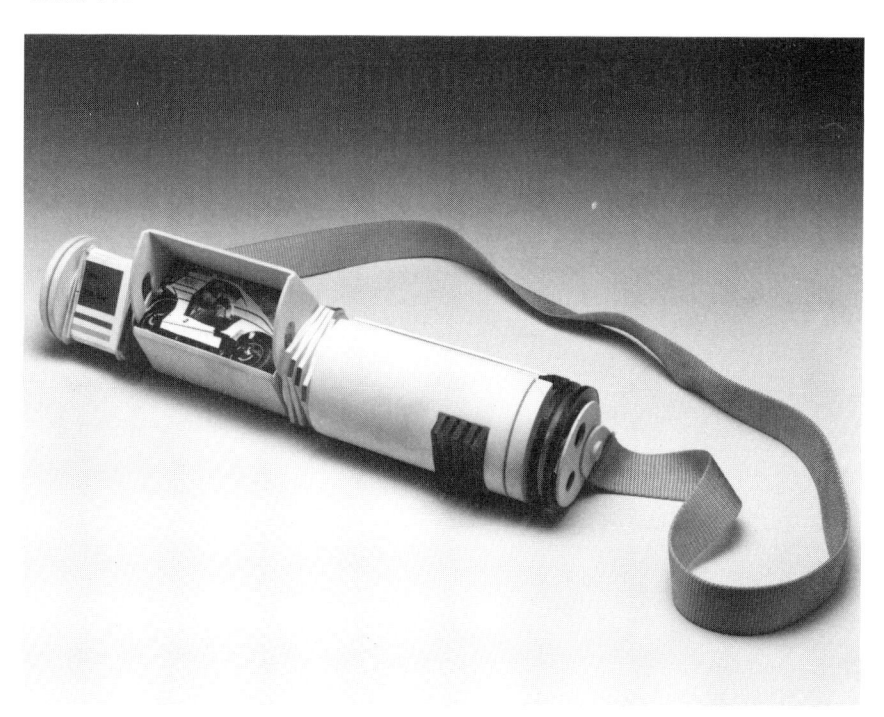

8.33 Future generations of designers are being encouraged by new courses and awards for secondary schools. Prime Minister Margaret Thatcher here inspects a play-structure for young children, by Amanda Grace of Manshead Upper School, Luton, an award winner in the 1981 Schools' Design Prize. Coloured squares are assembled using plumbers' piping joints and children soon learn how to construct tunnels, tents, shops and puppet theatres.

DESIGN IN GENERAL EDUCATION

Most specialist reports tend at one point or another to extend their recommendations beyond the confines of industry and tertiary education. The root cause of so many problems is seen to be in general education. Perhaps in the long term it is only primary and secondary education which can reach all sectors of Owen Jones's vicious circle. Within the schools are future graduate designers, manufacturers, retailers and consumers of society. The subject which most nearly provides a vehicle for design education is 'Craft, Design and Technology'. For a period in the seventies, the integration of art and handicrafts offered possibilities for visual education, but also posed dificulties. Mrs Thatcher herself had this to say at the Downing Street seminar:

> Design is too often taught in secondary schools as an art subject. It is rarely taught as it should be – as a practical, problem-solving discipline that is ideal for preparing young people for work within the constraints of user needs and the market. Its status as an O or A level subject is dismal. Many employers and higher education establishments do not recognise it as a qualification. Teachers themselves are often not fully aware of the real scope of the subject. Syllabuses are arranged to give greater merit to 'pure' art than the practical application of design.

Some valuable research work had been carried out by the Schools Council followed by the RCA's own 'Design in General Education' project. These firmly emphasised the problem-solving approach. However, by the eighties the subject rested uneasily at the interface of science and craft, with deep suspicion on both sides. Rather than all these activities being meaningfully subsumed under the concept of 'design', the official title 'CDT' had emerged from Her Majesty's Inspectorate, battling bravely with the elusive activities and semantics of 'craft, design and technology'.

Until recently no coherent image or lobby existed. CDT is emerging from being the lowest status, most confused and understaffed element of the curriculum. Few courses and examinations, particularly at a follow-up tertiary level, employed such a broad concept literally. A minority of pupils, parents, headmasters and employers value it. At best professions and universities reluctantly accepted design qualifications, at worse they contemptuously rejected them. Until recently the Civil Service remained aloof and the engineering professors remained cynical. This was disastrous, for such groups in turn affect the schools.

Here the Design Council, which sees itself first and foremost as an educational body, is beginning to build up pressure. 'Education' is now second in priority only to 'Advice to Industry'. Special working parties and reports establish and promote policy. Prizes and teaching materials offer practical help. A definitive document 'Design Education at Secondary Level' has been produced which both clarifies the concept and offers valuable guidelines on examinations:

> To design is always to prescribe some form, structure, pattern or arrangement for a proposed thing, system or event. A design is always an integrated whole, a balanced prescription – a product of judgement and invention as well as knowledge and skill. We consider that design should be an essential part of the education of all children at all stages of secondary education up to the age of 16, and that it should be taught and examined in that light. It should encourage creativity and develop the skills of problem solving, decision taking and evaluation, all of which are valuable in adult life, while generating an awareness of the qualities of the man-made world. Design education should also provide an introduction for those who may wish to pursue the subject further with a view to making their careers in or allied to design.[24]

The first success came in March 1982, when the Engineering Professors Conference agreed to accept a limited number of specified syllabuses as possible qualifications. But art teachers saw the document as too craft-orientated, craft teachers saw it as too art-orientated, and technology teachers saw it as too art and craft-orientated. Perhaps as the Design

8.34 David Chorley of Ifield Comprehensive School, Crawley, demonstrates his aquarium breeding tank which won a 1981 Schools' Design Prize. The tank clips over the edge of an aquarium and has water-circulating and cleaning facilities. The pregnant fish is placed in the small trap which has slits in its base. The young fish fall through into the breeding tank so that the parent fish cannot eat them.

Council manages to solve the problems of design at secondary level, the problems of design at other levels will begin to solve themselves.

To further the cause a new magazine *Designing* has been introduced jointly with the Crafts Council. This A3 tabloid has colour throughout and its large format double-page spreads are particularly useful for displaying in schools. Practical, vocational and entertaining aspects of design are included with topics as varied as the design of the Ford Sierra car, cheap jewellery, fast food, the home of the future and the BMX bicycle. Most important, ideas and products of young people are well represented from engineering and technology to fashion and illustration.

Further publicity for this creative talent is offered through the annual Schools' Design Prize. This operates with sponsorship from leading manufacturers such as Rolls Royce. Pupils with ideas for new or improved products suitable for manufacture are invited, through their teachers, to enter the scheme. Although only a small proportion of secondary schools as yet participate, some remarkable results have been

8.35 Adrian Davies, 15, a farmer's son from Dyfed, and his friend Dewi Jones, designed this simple portable heater, powered by a standard car battery, to rescusitate new-born lambs likely to die of exposure. Because the ewe can stay with her lamb there is less chance of it being rejected. The boys were among twelve winners of the 1982 Schools' Design prize.

achieved. Many are from pupils, both boys and girls, following the new design examination syllabuses. Entries demonstrate a strong social awareness, to some extent negating Victor Papanek's criticism in *Design for the Real World* that designers are a 'dangerous breed' whose skills are being 'taught carefully to young people'.[25]

At tertiary level scholarships are awarded by the Leverhume Trust in cooperation with the Design Council and SIAD, ensuring encouragement to the new generation of polytechnic graduates. Similarly the Molins Design Prize is awarded to engineering students at university or polytechnic. In many cases prize-winners have isolated and solved problems neglected by their professional counterparts, ranging from pain detectors to lamb resuscitators. The Prime Minister has shown considerable interest and herself has made the presentations.

Design Centre exhibitions of students' work are well attended and perform a valuable publicity function. 'The Young Creators' exhibition,

8.36 Jonathan Cameron of Edlington Comprehensive School designed this cheap, easy-to-use paper counter for a local printing works. When run down the edge of a pile of fanned-out paper, a record player pick-up receives pulses which register on a liquid crystal display. The counter won a 1981 Schools' Design Prize.

sponsored by Lloyds Bank, sets out to illustrate the role of good design in everyday life and provide information about careers. In addition companies are encouraged to exploit the wealth of talent to improve competitiveness in world markets. More specifically, the annual trade show 'Texprint' presents the textile designs of fifty or so leading graduates. The standard is high and graduates do well in terms of sales and commissions and, indeed, of permanent employment with British and foreign manufacturers. The increasing interest and competence of students in electronics has been demonstrated in several exhibitions with products ranging from portable television sets to remote-controlled vacuum cleaners.

In future, particularly welcome will be the opening of the Innovation Centre on a newly acquired floor within the Design Centre. The project has several objectives: to assist the promotion and marketing of innovative British products, particularly those from small businesses; to encourage industry to take up for commercial exploitation the development work carried out by universities and other research organisations; to show the work of design students and inventors; and in general to demonstrate to the public at large the significance of creative design to economic success and the quality of life.

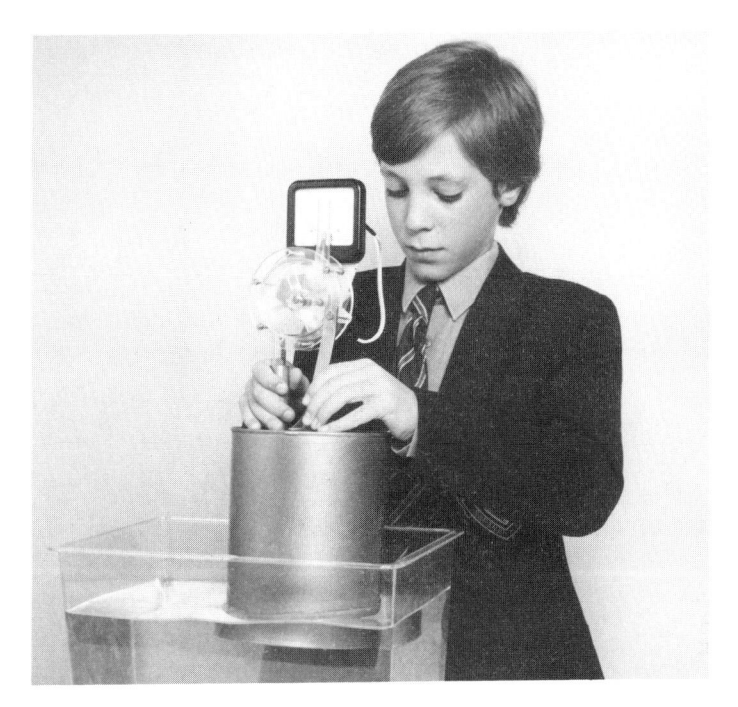

8.37 Richard Marsh of Durham Johnston Comprehensive School demonstrates his winning entry in the 1983 Schools' Design Prize, a turbine to convert wave power to electricity.

POSTSCRIPT

In late 1984 the Strategy Group established by John Butcher, Parliamentary Under Secretary of State for Industry, issued its report 'Policies and Priorities for Design'.[26] While acknowledging the argument that industry should be capable of putting its house in order, it noted that this clearly had not happened. Therefore, the report stressed, government must fund design on an ever-increasing scale while attempting to hold down other public expenditure. The rich rewards to be won were likened to the gains from North Sea oil.

As an accolade to The Design Council, many of the report's detailed proposals were extensions of already existing schemes. Six priorities were listed to bring about the improvement of design in products ranging from those which depend primarily on visual appeal to those with an advanced technological content. The priorities included improving design education and training, supporting and stimulating product innovation, influencing management attitudes, developing the Funded Consultancy Scheme, and stimulating the purchase of well-designed British products.

Most significantly, the final priority was to reinforce and extend the role of the Council such that it should be the main source of advice to the government on its future policies for design, the main instrument through which government-supported design promotion is carried out and, in addition, the focal and co-ordinating agency for design-related initiatives not falling directly within its remit.

Moves to implement these recommendations led to an unprecedented award in the summer of 1985 by the International Council of Societies of Industrial Design (ICSID). The citation stated:

> Mrs Thatcher's initiative has given birth to a wide range of new activities in Britain. Her government has established a new programme to include design education in the school system. It has financially supported the introduction of design awareness modules in business schools. And, last but most significantly, it has provided incentives for manufacturers to use design consultants. In short, the Government of Great Britain has made design a central force in its industrial policy.

Mr Butcher, receiving the award on behalf of the government, said:

> We could not, of course, have achieved what we have without a good base. We have a first-class design education system which has given us the designers we need. And they and their representative bodies have given us wholehearted support. We have relied heavily on the experience and depth of knowledge of the Design Council.
>
> But we still have a long way to go in increasing the awareness – in many sectors of society – of the national benefits which flow from good design.

Thus, while the Council has put design on the map with some success, its job is far from finished and much remains to be done. Time and time again it is shown that design improvement can make current products very much more profitable by increasing market demand, decreasing manufacturing costs or reducing investment in factory stocks and work in progress. Gaining commercial advantage by improved product design is not just scraping the barrel; there is considerable scope for improving our international competitiveness by this means. Furthermore, there is equal scope for other nations to use design improvement to compete even more effectively against us, so the Council's objective 'to promote by all practicable means the improvement of design in the products of British industry' is as valid now as when it was drafted in 1944.

Although its objective is clear enough the Council continues to face several difficulties. For reasons of history the Council is still strongly associated with 'art and design' even though its activities are now aimed squarely at all aspects of product design including the appropriate elements of engineering design. Adopting this even-handed approach to the full range of design disciplines inevitably causes distress to some specialist practitioners. The art and design lobby fears that engineering is taking the major share of the Council's attention while, at the same time, engineers suspect that the Council is only giving token attention to their interests, while retaining its traditional affinity with 'art'. These fears and prejudices are deep-rooted and will, at best, subside slowly over many years. Considerable forbearance and understanding will be required by all (not least the Council's own management) in the meanwhile.

Difficulties of a different nature may arise should there be a change in the currently supportive attitudes of government. One source of anxiety may emerge from such questions as 'If good design is good business why must public money be used for promoting it?' or 'Are not normal commercial pressures sufficient?' The fact is that normal commercial pressures are not sufficient for promoting good design, largely because of the long lead times that exist between expenditure on design and payback from the market. The need for government to intervene in this process seems now to be accepted for manufacturing companies of all kinds.

But such intervention may pose a different threat to the Council in that the government may wish to work on a contract basis using the Council, and other bodies, as sub-contractors. The operation of the Funded Consultancy Scheme is an example of this practice. If this trend were to continue the sub-contracting role of the Council would predominate and it would no longer function as a principal agent, independently devising and pursuing its own policies.

Notwithstanding these factors there are many encouraging signs for the future. The commitment of the government to the cause seems secure and there is a minister for design in fact, if not in name. The design message is being taken up by schools and colleges with enthusiasm and the Council's education policies, as stated in the Moulton, Carter and Keith–Lucas Reports, are currently in the course of implementation. The recent initiatives in the field of primary education and post-experience education and training are likely to be equally fruitful. The Funded Consultancy Scheme is yielding an impressive portfolio of case histories demonstrating that good design is indeed good business and the Council is currently embarking on other lively ventures, including the Innovation Centre and the consumers' magazine *Design Selection*.

Clearly the design message has got through to government and is getting through to education, the institutions and, to a lesser extent, industry and consumers. It would be ironic if, having been copied by so many other nations, the Council itself were to fade away, but there seems currently little prospect of this. On balance it seems likely that the Council will continue and thrive in one form or another for many years to come.

REFERENCES

Chapter 1

1. Smith, A., *Inquiry into the Nature and Causes of the Wealth of Nations* (Penguin, 1970), p. 113.
2. ffrench, Y., *The Great Exhibition* (Harvill Press, 1951).
3. Hudson D. and Luckhurst, K., *The Royal Society of Arts 1754–1954* (John Murray, 1954), p. 187.
4. ibid., p. 193.
5. Ruskin, J., *The Nature of Gothic* (George Allen & Unwin, 1935), p. 16.
6. Mayall, W., *Principles in Design* (Design Council, 1979), pp. 26–7.
7. ibid., p. 26.

Chapter 2

1. Clutton Brock, A., *A Modern Creed of Work* (Design and Industries Asociation, 1916).
2. Carrington, N., *Industrial Design in Britain* (George Allen & Unwin, 1976), p. 74.
3. Board of Education & Board of Trade, *Report on Art Training and Industrial Art* (Meynell-Hoskin Report, Unpublished, 1944), p. 2.
4. Mortan Shand, P., 'Type forms in Great Britain', *Die Form*, Jahrgang 5 (1930), p. 312.
5. Board of Trade, *Report on the Production and Exhibition of Articles of Good Design and Every-Day Use* (Gorell Report) (HMSO 1932), p. 30.
6. Bayley, S., *In Good Shape* (Design Council, 1979), p. 17.
7. Mortimer, R., 'Decorative Art', *The New Statesman and Nation* IX (19 Jan, 1935), pp. 41–2.
8. Carrington, N., op. cit., p. 158.
9. Russell, G., 'National Furniture Production' (Unpublished paper, 1947, later included in *Designers' Trade*).
10. Board of Trade, *Report on Industrial Design and Art in Industry* (Weir Report, Unpublished, 1943).
11. ibid., p. 3.
12. ibid., p. 4.
13. Board of Education, *Advanced Art Education in London* (Hambledon Report) (1936).
14. Meynell, F., *My Lives* (Bodley Head, 1971), p. 272.
15. Council of Industrial Design, *First Annual Report*, 1945–46 (HMSO), p. 5.

Chapter 3

1. Casson, H., '1946: Knockout for tired eyes', *Design*, 253 (January 1970), p. 52.
2. Architectural Review, 'Industrial design', *Architectural Review*, Vol. C, 598 (October 1946), p. 92.
3. Board of Trade, 'Britain Can Make It', supplement to *Board of Trade Journal* (28 September 1946), p. 4.
4. CoID, *First Annual Report, 1945–46* (HMSO, 1946), p. 11.

5. CoID, *A Pictorial View of Enterprise Scotland*, CoID Scottish Committee (Oliver & Boyd, 1947) p. 173.
6. Carrington, N., *Industrial Design in Britain* (George Allen & Unwin, 1976), p. 173.

Chapter 4

1. Farr, M., *Design in British Industry* (Cambridge University Press, 1955) p. 224.
2. CoID, *First Annual Report, 1945–46* (HMSO, 1946), p. 13.
3. CoID, *Second Annual Report, 1946–47* (HMSO, 1947), p. 3.
4. ibid.
5. CoID, *First Annual Report, 1945–46* (HMSO, 1946), p. 14.
6. Russell, G., *Designer's Trade* (George Allen & Unwin, 1968), p. 226.
7. Hartland Thomas, M., Internal Memorandum, 'The Industrial Division in 1952', 4 July 1950.
8. ibid.
9. Russell, G., op. cit., p. 238.
10. CoID, *Fourth Annual Report, 1948–49* (HMSO, 1949), p. 11.
11. Russell, G., op. cit., p. 236.
12. CoID, *Report on the Training of the Industrial Designer in England and Wales* (HMSO, 1946).
13. Russell, G., op. cit., p. 234.
14. Russell, G., op. cit., p. 235.

Chapter 5

1. Board of Trade, *Report to consider the part which Exhibitions and Fairs should play in the promotion of Export Trade in the Post War Era* (Ramsden Report, HMSO, 1946), p. 15.
2. Barry, G., *The Festival of Britain, 1951*, Cantor Lecture, Royal Society of Arts, 22 August 1952.
3. Russell, G., *Designer's Trade* (George Allen & Unwin, 1968), p. 249.
4. Barry, G., op. cit.
5. Barry, G., op. cit.
6. CoID, *Sixth Annual Report, 1950–51* (HMSO, 1951), p. 3.
7. Russell, G., op. cit., p. 253.
8. Legge-Bourke, Mjr., House of Commons Hansard, 6 November 1950.
9. Farr, M. & Pevsner, P., 'CoID Progress Report', December *Architectural Review* (December 1951), pp. 349–59.
10. ibid., p. 349.
11. ibid., p. 352.
12. Russell, G., 'The Director Replies', *Architectural Review*.
13. Hald, A., 'The Festival of Britain', *Form*, no. 7, (1951).
14. Banham, M. & Hillier, B. (eds.), *A Tonic to the Nation* (Thames and Hudson, 1976).

Chapter 6

1. CoID, *First Annual Report, 1945–46* (HMSO, 1946), p. 20.
2. ibid., p. 20.

3. Reilly, P., *The aims and organisation of the Council of Industrial Design*, Report on Design Conference for Retailers (CoID, 1949), p. 8.
4. Board of Trade, *Report on the Production and Exhibition of Articles of Good Design and Every-Day Use* (Gorell Report) (HMSO, 1932), p. 50.
5. Russell, G., 'Good design is not a luxury', *Design* (January 1949), pp. 2–6.
6. Barry, G., 'The importance of design today', *Five Lectures on Design* (CoID, winter 1952–53), pp. 1–2.
7. Russell, G., *Designer's Trade* (George Allen & Unwin, 1968), p. 258.
8. Reilly, P., op. cit., p. 9.
9. CoID, *Fifteenth Annual Report, 1959–60* (HMSO, 1960), p. 27.
10. Russell, G., *The retailer's responsibility* (Report on Design Course for Furnishing Salesmen) (CoID, 1951), p. 42.
11. Klein, B., *Design Matters* (Secker & Warburg, 1976), p. 157.
12. Chapman, D., *Families, their needs and preferences in the home*, Report on Conferences on Furniture Design (CoID, 1949), pp. 17–38.
13. CoID, *Design Report: Ideas for Industry from Design Week Wales* (CoID, 1948), pp. 4–6.
14. CoID, *Fifteenth Annual Report, 1959–60* (HMSO, 1960), p. 4.

Chapter 7

1. Russell, G., *Open Forum* (Report on Design Course for Furnishing Salesmen) (CoID, 1951), p. 46.
2. CoID, *Twelfth Annual Report, 1956–57* (HMSO, 1957), p. 7.
3. Reilly, P., 'Ten Years of Design Centre Awards', *Design*, 208 (May 1966), p. 58.
4. Carr, R., 'The award winners speak out', *Design*, 208 (May 1966), p. 73.
5. Mass Observation, *Report on the Design Centre* (Mass Observation, 1957), p. 12.
6. ibid., p. 15.
7. ibid., pp. 18–19.
8. Mass Observation, *Report on the Design Centre Overseas Buyers* (Mass Observation, 1960), p. 8.
9. CoID, *Nineteenth Annual Report, 1963–64* (HMSO, 1964), p. 4.

Chapter 8

1. CoID, *First Annual Report, 1945–46* (HMSO, 1946), p. 11.
2. CoID, *Second Annual Report, 1946–47* (HMSO, 1947), pp. 9–10.
3. CoID, *Twelfth Annual Report, 1956–57* (HMSO, 1957), p. 7.
4. Reilly, P., 'The evolution of The Design Council', *Management and Engineering Design* (1972), p. 23.
5. Department of Scientific and Industrial Research, *Engineering Design* (Fielden Report) (HMSO, 1963), p. 1.
6. ibid., pp. 1–2.
7. C.E.I., *A National Design Council* (Conway Report) (Council of Engineering Institutions, 1968), p. 9.
8. ibid., p. 4.
9. CoID, *Twenty-fifth Annual Report, 1969–70* (HMSO, 1970), p. 3.
10. Design Council, *Twenty-eighth Annual Report, 1972–73* (Design Council, 1973), p. 1.

11. McAlhone, B., 'A year at the top', *Designer* (July/August 1978).
12. Klein, B., *Design Matters* (Secker and Warburg, 1976), p. 152.
13. ibid., p. 167.
14. McAlhone, B., 'Consultants call for shake-up at the Design Council', *Campaign* (13 May 1983), pp. 12–20.
15. Board of Trade, *Report on the Production and Exhibition of Articles of Good Design and Every-day Use* (Gorell Report) (HMSO, 1932).
16. Chris Hayes, *The Industrial Design Requirements of Industry* (DES and Design Council: not published until 1983), p. 12.
17. Design Council, *Report to The Design Council on the Design of British Consumer Goods* (Mellor Report, 1983), p. 5.
18. Barlow, W., Speech delivered at the presentation of the Design Policy Statement of the Under Secretary of State, Department of Trade and Industry, at the Painters' Hall, 10 May 1984.
19. Design Council, op. cit., p. 31.
20. ibid., p. 25.
21. Design Council, *Engineering Design Education* (Moulton Report) (Design Council, 1976).
22. Engineering Board, *Report of the Engineering Design Working Party* (Lickley Report) (Science and Engineering Research Council, 1983), p. 16.
23. Engineering Council, *Standards and Routes to Registration* (Engineering Council, 1984), p. 10.
24. Design Council, *Design Education at Secondary Level* (Keith-Lucas Report) (Design Council, 1980), pp. 4–5.
25. Papanek, V., *Design for the Real World. Making to Measure* (Granada, 1982 Edn), p. 9.
26. Barry, G., *The importance of design today* (Five Lectures on Design) (CoID, winter 1952–53), pp. 1–2.
27. Strategy Group, *Policies and Priorities for Design* (Design Council/Department of Trade and Industry, 1984).

BIBLIOGRAPHY

The following list includes both general references on the history of design and further specific publications to supplement the chapter references.

Ames, W., *Prince Albert and Victorian Taste* (Chapman-Hall, 1967)
Archer, B., *Systematic Method for Designers* (CoID, 1965)
Ashford, F., *Designing for Industry* (Pitman, 1955)
Banham, R., *Theory and Design in the First Machine Age* (Architectural Press, 1961)
Barty, E., *Management and Engineering Design* (Design Council, 1972)
Baynes, K., *Industrial Design and the Community* (Lund Humphries, 1967)
Baynes, K. & K., *Gordon Russell* (Design Council, 1980)
Benton, C. & T., *Form and Function. A Source book for the History of Architecture and Design 1890–1939* (Crosby, Lockwood, Staples for Open University, 1975)
Bertram A., *Design in Daily Life* (Penguin, 1938)
Bishop, T. (Ed.), *Design History: Fact or Function?* (Design Council, 1978)
——, *Design History: Past, Process, Product* (Design Council, 1979)

Blake, A. (Ed.), *The Black Papers on Design. Selected writings of the late Sir Misha Black* (Pergamon Press for Faculty of Royal Designers for Industry, 1983)
Blake, J. & A., *The Practical Idealists: A History of Design Research Unit* (Lund Humphries, 1969)
British Institute of Industrial Art, Catalogue: *Industrial Art for the Slender Purse* (Victoria and Albert Museum, 1929)
Coulson, A. J., *A Bibliography of Design in Britain, 1851–1970* (Design Council, 1979)
Council for Art and Industry, *Design and the Designer in Industry* (HMSO, 1937)
CoID, *Announcing the Design Centre for British Industries* (CoID, 1956)
——, *Britain Can Make It* Exhibition Guide (HMSO, 1946)
——, *Design Conference for Scottish Co-operative Retail Societies* (CoID Scottish Committee, 1955)
——, *Design '46: A survey of British Industrial Design as Displayed in the 'Britain Can Make It' Exhibition* (HMSO, 1946)
——, *Design in the Festival* (HMSO, 1951)
——, *Design Report: Ideas for Industry from Design Week Wales* (CoID, 1948)
——, *Design: Reports on Three Lectures, Royal Philosophical Society, Glasgow* (CoID Scottish Committee, 1954)
——, *Five Lectures on Design, Royal Philosophical Society, Glasgow* (CoID Scottish Committee, 1953)
——, *Notes for Industry on the 1951 Exhibitions* (FOB Office and CoID, 1949)
——, *Report on Conference on Furniture Design* (CoID, 1949)
——, *Report on Design Conference for Retailers* (CoID, 1949)
——, *Report on Design Conference for Retail Staff Trainers* (CoID, 1949)
——, *Reports on Design Courses for Furniture Salesmen* (CoID, 1950, 1951)
——, *Street Furniture: List of Approved Designs* (CoID, 1961)
——, *The Design Centre Book* (CoID, 1961)
——, *The Design Centre Awards* (CoID, 1959)
——, *What is a Design Centre?* (HMSO, 1947)
Cox, I., *The South Bank Exhibition: a Guide to the Story it Tells* (HMSO, 1951)
Crawford, A., *Robert Welch, Design in a Cotswold Workshop* (Lund Humphries, 1973)
Design Council, *Street Scene* (Design Council, 1976)
Dover Publications, *The Crystal Palace Exhibition Illustrated Catalogue* (Republished by Dover Publications, 1970)
Farr, M., *The Council of Industrial Design* (re Gran Premio Internazionale Award) (CoID, 1959)
Festival Council, *The Story of the Festival of Britain 1951* (HMSO, 1952)
Gloag, J., *Victorian Taste* (George Allen & Unwin, 1962)
Heskett, J., *Industrial Design* (Thames & Hudson, 1980)
Hillier, B., *Austerity Binge: the Decorative Arts of the Forties and Fifties* (Studio Vista, 1975)
Jervis, S., *The Penguin Dictionary of Design and Designers* (Penguin, 1984)
Lethaby, W., *Form in Civilization* (Oxford University Press, 1922)
MacCarthy, F., *A History of British Design, 1830–1970* (George Allen & Unwin, 1979)
——, *British Design Since 1880, a Visual History* (Lund Humphries, 1982)
Mills, E., *The National Exhibition Centre* (Cosby Lockwood Staples, 1976)
Naylor, G., *The Arts and Crafts Movement* (Studio Vista, 1971)

Pevsner, N., *An Enquiry into Industrial Art in England* (Cambridge University Press, 1937)
——, *High Victorian Design: a Study of the Exhibits of 1851* (Architectural Press, 1951)
——, *Pioneers of Modern Design* (Pelican, 1970)
Read, H. *Art and Industry* (Faber & Faber, 1971)
Russell, G., *How to Buy Furniture* (HMSO, 1951)
Sparke, P., *Consultant Design: the History and Practice of the Designer in Industry* (Pembridge Press, 1983)
White, J. (Ed.), *Profit by Design* (*Financial Times* and CoID, 1965)
Woodham, J., *The Industrial Designer and the Public* (Pembridge Press, 1983)

INDEX

Numerals in **bold type** refer to illustrations.

Aalto, Alvar **52**, **53**
Adam, Robert **15**, 18–19
Aesthetic Movement 27
Albert, Prince Consort 8, 20
'American System of Manufacture' 36
Anglepoise Lamp **38**
Architectural Review 146–50, 227
Art and Manufactures, Select Committee on, 1836 22–3
Art Furniture Manufacturers 28
Art Nouveau 28–**30**, 30–1, 42
Arts and Crafts Movement 26–7, 39
Ashbee, Charles Robert 27
Ausper Racing Car **212**, 213
Austin, Frank **154**

Barlow, Sir William **204**, 236
Barr and Stroud Binoculars **98**
Barry, Sir Gerald 127, 129, 135, 165
Behrens, Peter 42
Belling electric fire 41
Bertoia, Harry **110**
Blake, John 225
Blythe, Jane 201
BMW motorcycle **217**
Board of Trade 21, 23, 25, 39, 47, 64, 104, 184
Breuer, Marcel **54**, **55**
'Britain Can Make It' exhibition 74–95
British Coal Utilisation Research Association **107**, 108
British Institute of Industrial Art 39, 47
British Rail, **229**
Brunel, Isambard Kingdom 36
Bryant and May 169
Burlington House exhibition 59–60
Butcher, The Rt. Hon. John 245, 247

Campania, Festival Ship 128, **136**
Carrington, Noel 47, 99
Carter Report 232
Central School of Art and Design 230, **236**–7

Chippendale, Thomas 18–19
Chorley, David **242**
Clutton Brock, A. 44–5
Coates, Wells **85**, 87
Colchester Lathe **124**–5
Cole, Sir Henry 20
Conran, Sir Terence 123, 182
Constable, Geoffrey 219, **219**, 220, 224
Contract Furniture **171**, 175
Conway Committee 217
Cosmos Crane **226**
Council for Art and Industry 39, 52–62
Council of Industrial Design (CoID) 46, 47, 64–73, 75–99, 101–15, 122–5, 134–43, 146–51
Crafts Advisory Committee (later Crafts Council) 201
Crane, Walter 14
Crystal Palace **8**–**11**

Dalton, Dr Hugh 70–1, 72–3, 76, 155
Darwin, Robin 116–18, **117**
Davis, Adrian **243**
Davis, Phillip **239**
Day, Robin **117**, 191
Dean, Roger **186**
Design Advisory Service 191, 220, 236
Design and Industries Association (DIA) 18, 39, 42–7, 58, 59, 164
Design Centre, Haymarket 170, **180**–9, 181–91, 221, 224, 244
Design Centre label **184**, 186, 189–91
Design Centres for Industry 101–8, **103**, **106**, 112–13
Design Council 213–48
design education 240–4
Design Folios, CoID **158**, 161
Design Index 187, 224
Designing Magazine 242
Design Magazine **160**, 162–5
Design Research Unit 86, 94, **95**, 229
Design Selection Magazine **204**, 247
Design Selection Service 123
Design Strategy Group 245
Deutscher Werkbund 37, 42

254

Dome of Discovery, Festival of
  Britain **133**, **140**, 141
Dorland Hall exhibition 51, 58–9
Dresser, Christopher 29, **33**
Dreyfuss, Henry **112**
Dudley Ryder, Richard 148

Eakins, Susan **187**
Eames, Charles **110**
Elizabeth II, H.M. Queen **189**
Elliott Boots **168**
Engineering Council 238
Engineering Magazine **219**
Enterprise Scotland exhibition 95–9

Festival of Britain exhibition 126–53
Festival Pattern Group 137, **147**
Festival Pleasure Gardens,
  Battersea **131**, **142–3**
ffrench, Yvonne 11
Fielden Committee 209–10
Films and Filmstrips, CoID **163**, 166
Folkstone express locomotive 11, 35
Fogge, Norma 200
Frazer, June 229

Gardner, James 77, 79, 96, 133, **143**, **189**
Genalex washing machine 41
George VI, H.M. King 80, 89, 139
Gillott, Joseph and Sons 103
Godwin, Edward 28, **28**
Gooden, Robert 63, 64, 81, 83, 191
Gorell Committee 52–6, 231
Grace, Amanda 240
Grange, Kenneth 193, **229**
Grant, Keith **204**, 207, 222, **223**, 225
Gray, Eileen **57**
Gray, Milner **84**
Great Exhibition (1851) 7–17
Groag, Jacqueline **151**
Gropius, Walter 43, **183**

Hald, Arthur 151
Hammond's Store, Hull **194–5**
Hartland Thomas, Mark **112**, 112–14, 137, 138
Hayes Report 233
Heritage, Robert **190**
Honda motorcycle **216**
Hoover vacuum cleaner **40**

Hornsea Pottery *Concept* ware 197
Hough, Catherine **196**
Howe, Jack **139**

Independent Designers'
  Federation 235
Industrial Division, CoID 101–25
Information Division, CoID 155–79
Ingham, Carol **236**

JCB excavator **226**, 227
Jones, Dewi **243**
Jones, Owen 13, 28, 25

Kenwood *Chef* **160**
Khahn, Quasar 187
Klein, Bernat 225–7

Lethaby, William Richard 27, 43
Lickley Report 238
London Underground 47, **48**

McAlhome, Beryl 228–9
McCormick, John **239**
Mackmurdo, Arthur Heygate 27
Makepeace, John **202**
Mass Observation Report 89–93, 194–200
Maudslay, Henry 35
Mayall, Bill 32–3
Mellor, David **120–1**, 121, 122, **173**, 191
Mellor Report 233–5
Meynell-Hoskins Committee 49, 69–70
Meynell, Sir Francis 93, 98
Mini Metro motorcar **213**
Morphy-Richards electric iron 109
Morris, William **6**, 9–11, **24–6**, 26
Morton Shand, Phillip 50
Moulton, Alex **192**, 192
Moulton Report 238
Murphy Radio **60**, 61

National Register of Industrial Art
  Designers 122
Nicholson, Roger and Robert 185, **183**
Norton motorcycle **44**

Omega Workshops **50**

Peach, Harry 43, 44
Peel, Sir Robert 22

255

Philip, H.R.H. Prince   **175**, 189, **223**
Pick, Frank   43, 45, 47
Porsche motorcar   **212**
Portable Box exhibitions, CoID   **156**, **159**, 161
Poster Awards, Design Council   **168–70**, 172
Pretty Polly Tights   **168**, 172
Priestman Bros.   **223**
Pugin, Augustus   14
Pyrex glass   **58**

Race, Ernest   **82**, **90**, **138**
Ramshaw, Wendy   **199**
Reid, John and Sylvia   192, **193**
Reilly, Paul (later Lord)   **136**, 157–9, 168, **175**, 191, 209, 213, 218, 222
retail trade   168–72
Rietveld, Gerrit   51, **58**
Robinson, David   **198**
Rodriguez, Gustavo   **233**
Rolls Royce motorcar   **45**, **46**
Rolls Royce *Pegasus* engine   **220**
Ross Ensign camera   **96**
Ross, Gary   **236**
Royal College of Art   23, 39, 69, 116–22, **117**, **122**, 231
Royal Society of Arts   18–21
Ruskin, John   26
Russell, Dick   61, **63**, 116, **117**, 191
Russell, Sir Gordon   43, 62–4, **63**, 71, **100**, 109–13, 116, 118, 150, 157
Ryder, Richard Dudley   59, 157

Saatchi and Saatchi   **169**, 172
Sale, Roger   **173**
Schools' Design Prize   **240–5**, 242–3
Scottish Design Centre   **200**, 201
Semper, Gottfried   37
Shipley, William   18–19

Sinclair Radionics   **230**, **232**, 235
Skylon, Festival of Britain   **132**
Slide Library, CoID   161
SME tone arm   230
Smith, Adam   7–8
Snow, Lord   **206**
Spence, Sir Basil   79, 96
Spode *Apollo* ware   **184**
Stephenson, George   33–4
Stephenson, Robert   34
Stock List (later *Design Review* and later *Design Index*)   114–15, 134–8, **166–7**
street furniture   **174–8**, 176–9
Sumlock Adding Calculator   **94**

Thatcher, The Rt. Hon. Margaret   **204**, 235, **240**, 246
Thompson, Kevin   **237**
Thonet, Michael   13, 29, **31**
'Tomorrow's World' exhibition   **221**
Triumph motorcycle   **216**
Tubbs, Ralph   **89**, 133

Utility Furniture   39, 62–4, **63**, **65**, **66**, **67**

Victoria, H.M. Queen   9
Victoria and Albert Museum   23, 47, 183

Wedgewood Benn, Anthony   **209**
Wedgwood, Josiah   28, **32**
Weir Committee   64–8
Welch, Robert   **118–19**, 121–2, 192
Whitworth, Joseph   35–6
Williams, Robin   **203**
Windsor chair   **105**
Worshipful Company of Goldsmiths   106

Zulawski, Marek   152